Viral Performance

Viral Performance

Contagious Theaters from Modernism to the Digital Age

✦

Miriam Felton-Dansky

NORTHWESTERN UNIVERSITY PRESS
EVANSTON, ILLINOIS

Northwestern University Press
www.nupress.northwestern.edu

Printed in the United States of America

10 9 8 7 6 5 4 3 2 1

Library of Congress Cataloging-in-Publication Data

Names: Felton-Dansky, Miriam, author.
Title: Viral performance : contagious theaters from modernism to the digital age / Miriam Felton-Dansky.
Description: Evanston, Illinois : Northwestern University Press, 2018. | Includes bibliographical references and index.
Identifiers: LCCN 2017057481| ISBN 9780810137165 (cloth : alk. paper) | ISBN 9780810137158 (pbk. : alk. paper) | ISBN 9780810137172 (ebook)
Subjects: LCSH: Experimental theater—20th century. | Experimental theater—21st century. | Theater and society. | Theater and social media.
Classification: LCC PN2193.E86 F45 2018 | DDC 792.022—dc23 LC record available at https://lccn.loc.gov/2017057481

CONTENTS

ACKNOWLEDGMENTS

This book would not be—and I would not be where I am—without the generosity and guidance of Tom Sellar. He championed the idea of this book from its earliest stages and provided trenchant, challenging editorial suggestions as it grew. In "Crit" classes at the Yale School of Drama, he taught clarity of thought and expression, and in the offices at *Theater* magazine, he taught editing as well as editorial vision. It was because of him that I attended my first scholarly conference, published my first scholarly essay, began reviewing theater professionally, and gained exposure to more pathbreaking contemporary performances than I can name. I will always be grateful.

Having Elinor Fuchs as a mentor, professor, and role model has likewise been nothing short of transformative. She taught me to search for the deep structures underpinning drama and performance—to always look, and look again—and provided critical feedback as I researched and wrote this book. Her influence is on every page, as well as in every critical review I write and in every classroom where I teach. I am also deeply grateful to the entire faculty of Dramaturgy & Dramatic Criticism at Yale—James Leverett, Gordon Rogoff, Catherine Sheehy, and James Magruder—who have shaped my writing and teaching since my first year of graduate school, and particularly to Marc Robinson, who taught me (again) how to read plays.

Much of this book was written while I was teaching at Bard College under the inspiring leadership of Gideon Lester, who created the ideal setting for thinking—and rethinking—contemporary performance. I am also grateful to my colleagues in the Theater & Performance Program—Jorge Cortiñas, Jack Ferver, Chiori Miyagawa, Jonathan Rosenberg, and Jean Wagner—and to Jennifer Lown, our program administrator, without whom nothing could happen.

Upon arriving at Bard, I was lucky to join a cohort of welcoming, highly collaborative junior faculty. I am grateful to Marisa Libbon, Christian Crouch, Erika Switzer, Lauren Curtis, Maria Cecire, Ben Coonley, and everyone involved with the Experimental Humanities concentration, which has supported my research in numerous ways. I am also grateful to my students at Bard, whose intelligence and inquisitiveness has inspired me to think harder about my own work, and who have proven among the best companions for viewing contemporary performance.

My critical prose has benefited from the work of many rigorous editors during my years at the *Village Voice*. I'm particularly grateful to Brian Parks, my first editor there; as well as to Jane Kim, Angela Ashman, Zoe Beery, and Danny King.

This book has benefited from the work of excellent editors at Northwestern University Press. Thanks to Mike Levine for encouraging the project, and for perceptive edits; and to Gianna Mosser for her sensitive and insightful guidance, as well as to Maggie Grossman, Anne Gendler, and the entire production team. My peer reviewers—whose insights and suggestions challenged me to push my ideas, research, and writing in new directions—also deserve deep thanks.

Many archivists, librarians, and artists have provided invaluable support to me as I researched this book. I'm particularly grateful to the Beinecke Rare Books and Manuscript Library at Yale, which provided a summer research fellowship in 2010, so that I could begin my research on the Living Theatre. Susan Brady of the Beinecke, and Tom Walker, the Living Theatre's archivist, provided knowledgeable assistance as I continued this research. Nancy Goldman and Mona Nagai of the Pacific Film Archive arranged for the reproduction of an image of the Dilexi Broadcast, and Jim Newman granted permission to publish it. I am grateful to Philip Dombowski at Canada's National Gallery, who provided assistance as I researched General Idea, and to AA Bronson of General Idea for generous permission to quote and to publish images. Library staff at the New York Library for the Performing Arts and at New York University's Fales Library & Special Collections were immensely helpful, as was Bronwen Bitetti at Bard's Center for Curatorial Studies library. I am grateful to Steve Kurtz of Critical Art Ensemble, Marc Estrin, Franco Mattes, Kathryn Blume, Joanna Warsza, Joanne Pottlitzer, Sheila Cohen Tissot, Robert Neblett, and Iman Aoun for their generosity in speaking with me about their work and for allowing me to publish images of it. I'm grateful to Matthew Cornish, Ryan Davis, and Lauren Dubowski for assistance with translation.

Early research for this book developed with the support and insight of numerous editors. I'm grateful to Tom Sellar at *Theater* magazine, which published an early version of portions of chapter 3; Nadine George-Graves, editor of *The Oxford Handbook of Dance and Theater*, which published my previous research about the Living Theatre; T. Nikki Cesare-Schotzko and Mariellen Sanford at *TDR*, which published an early version of my discussion of Caryl Churchill's *Seven Jewish Children*; Bonnie Marranca and Joseph Cermatori at *PAJ*, which published a book review of Gregg Bordowitz's *Imagevirus*; and Anna Gallagher-Ross at *aCCeSsions*, who commissioned a short essay about General Idea's *Going Thru the Motions*, and who provided insightful copy-edits to many sections of this manuscript.

This project has benefited from the insights of colleagues in many working conference working sessions and panels. These included many American Society for Theatre Research groups—those dedicated to Theater & Transmedia; Sustainable Tools for Precarious Subjects; Afterlives of the Sixties;

Contaminating Bodies, Infectious Displays; and Massed Subjects, Massed Power—as well as the Theatre History Focus Group at the Association for Theatre in Higher Education, the Mapping Theaters of Exile seminar at the American Comparative Literature Association, the writing workshop at the Mellon Summer School for Theater and Performance Research at Harvard, and Yale's Performance Studies Working Group.

This project, and my development as a scholar, have been strengthened by the examples and the generous mentorship of many senior colleagues, including Cindy Rosenthal, whose work on the Living Theatre has deeply influenced my own, and Paige McGinley. I also count myself lucky to be part of a cohort of young scholars—classmates, then colleagues—whose adventurousness, insight, and dedication to mutual support have been invaluable to me: John Muse, Julia Fawcett, Christopher Grobe, Matthew Cornish, Joseph Cermatori, Ryan Hatch, Julia Jarcho, Alex Ripp, and Jennifer Buckley.

Shonni Enelow provided moral and editorial encouragement when I needed it most. And Kate Bredeson has been the most stalwart of supporters, in challenges professional and beyond, from our earliest conversations at Harvard's Mellon School. She offered editorial insight about several sections of this book, particularly its Living Theatre chapter.

More than ten years ago, Jacob Gallagher-Ross edited a class assignment about Strindberg's *To Damascus*. He has read—and offered intelligent, insightful, and necessary editorial suggestions about—nearly everything I have written since. That includes every section of this book, many times over; I could not have completed this work without him. A person could not ask for a better strategic ally, editor, collaborator, or friend.

This book is dedicated to my family. To my parents, Nancy Felton and Joel Dansky. Their constant belief that the world can be better is undoubtedly one of the reasons I write about artists who believe that, too. To my chosen family—Katya Schapiro, Catherine Wallach, Stacey McMath, Avi Glickstein, and Simon Glickstein—for making a home. And to Pete: the newest and best arrival, who entered the world just as I was finishing this book.

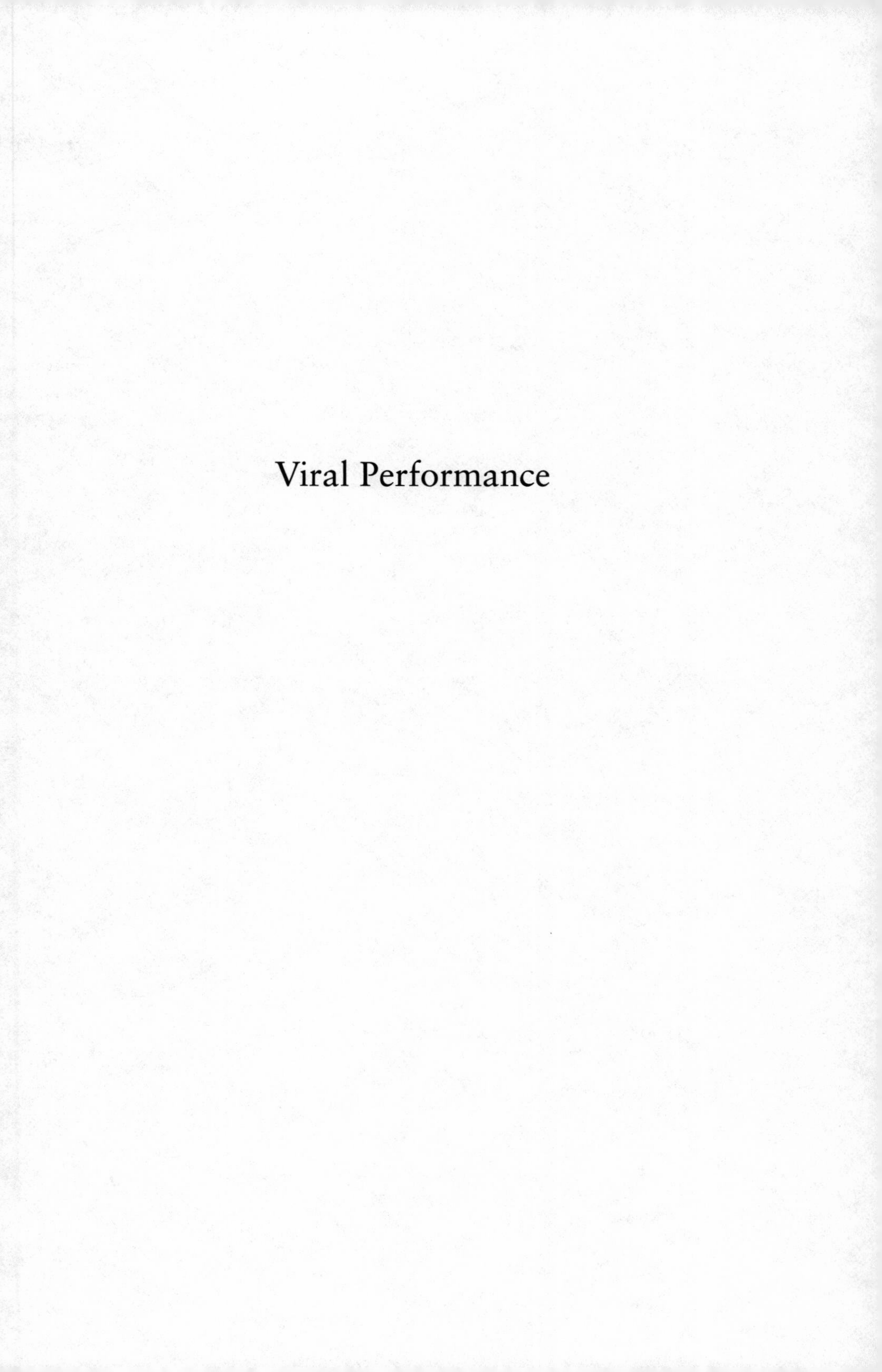

Viral Performance

Introduction

✦

A History of Contagion

In February 2009, Caryl Churchill premiered a short play called *Seven Jewish Children* at London's Royal Court Theatre. This pointed, poetic meditation on contentious Jewish, Israeli, and Palestinian histories is both compact—its printed text running a scant six pages—and oblique, containing neither named characters nor specified settings. Each of the brief, elliptical scenes features adult voices arguing over how to explain fraught historical events to an unseen, voiceless child. They debate how to talk about the Holocaust, and later the Israeli war of independence and the Israeli occupation of Palestinian territories. By the time *Seven Jewish Children* had its American premiere at the New York Theatre Workshop, the text had sparked local, and then international controversy. Viewers were outraged by what they perceived as biased depictions of Jewish and Israeli actions and rhetoric. But not only viewers. Equally angry responses came from those who had not seen or read the play but had instead heard of its subject matter secondhand.

As the debate surrounding *Seven Jewish Children* circulated through international media, the play began to proliferate too. Activists performed it at political rallies and community gatherings, from Israel to Washington, D.C., and videos of productions began circulating on YouTube. Churchill's text soon inspired a wave of copycat playlets, with titles like *Seven Palestinian Children*, *Seven Other Children*, and *The Eighth Child*—some of these curated into joint stagings with the original, others appearing only online. The authors of these new texts mimicked Churchill's form but replaced her dialogue with language reflecting their own perspectives. Within months, many versions of Churchill's play were in circulation around the world: geographically dispersed, but thematically connected. In other words, *Seven Jewish Children* is a play that, in the parlance of the digital age, "went viral."

Not only did *Seven Jewish Children* go viral. It was, I believe, designed to do so. The play's eloquent brevity, its sparse staging requirements, and its deliberate political provocations suggest that it belongs to a new species of performance, self-consciously created for rapid international circulation: viral performance for the twenty-first century. If Churchill could not have predicted how artists, audiences, and reading and listening publics would respond to her text, the play's form still suggested openness to rapid dissemination and radical reimagining. So did the terms under which Churchill offered other artists the production rights, which were openly available at no cost, as long as audiences were not charged admission and the producing artists collected funds for the organization Medical Aid for Palestinians.[1]

Understanding *Seven Jewish Children* not only as a play written for digitally dispersed publics, but more particularly as an instance of what I am calling "viral performance," places Churchill's drama in the company of a diverse collection of modern and contemporary projects that draw on theater's contagious possibilities to engage with audiences and to spread ideas, gestures, and images in live and mediated form. This book traces the contours of such a constellation of artistic works, charting a series of viral dramaturgies across the twentieth and twenty-first centuries. They range from the Living Theatre's revolutionary performances of the 1960s to the media-savvy ventures of the self-described viral artists General Idea, and from digital-age provocations by Eva and Franco Mattes to theatrical networks like the 2003 Lysistrata Project. The works I place in this category are almost always deeply political, seeking to mobilize spectators toward radical action or to engage them in considering the contagious properties of ideology in the culture at large. They also almost always harness the properties of emerging media forms in order to depict, but also create, fundamental shifts in the transmission of action, and especially actions meant to further social change and political critique.

The viral, a concept that has not yet been substantively applied to theater or performance, illuminates these artists' responses to some of the oldest questions in theatrical theory, and to a rapidly changing world of new media, new audiences, and new modes of public participation. Viruses, in their many forms—digital, biological, artistic—nearly always function as disruptions in the fabric of daily life, making them natural allies for generations of avant-garde artists who elevated rupture into the primary dramaturgy of radical change. Meanwhile, viral dissemination, with its implications of speed, simultaneity, and multidirectional spread, draws new technologies into service, and pushes to the fore assumptions about how and why we pass ideas, affects, and gestures to one another: out of revolutionary fervor or allegiance to ideologies, motivated by social critique or inchoate affective response. In creating viral works, these artists provoke profound questions about the politics of dissemination itself, asking whether media-fueled transmission can ever be democratic, or whether it always ultimately shores up systems of control. They engage with the politics of spectatorship, dismantling easy equations between participation and political efficacy, and between contagious dissemination and the loss of individual identity and choice.

Viral dramaturgies also challenge fundamental ideas about theater. They stretch performance time, rejecting compact dramatic structures in favor of the open-ended series, the expansive network, or the evolving process.

They upend relationships between actors and spectators, turning audience members into performers or placing the actions of viewers center stage. They unravel distinctions between live and mediated art, and between performance and its documentation. They draw attention to the invisible circulation and dissemination of emotion and affect. This book, by examining a series of works that are productively described in viral terms, argues for the necessary inclusion of the viral in dialogues about radical, political, and transmedial performance.

My exploration of viral performance begins by drawing together the many strands of theatrical and cultural theory necessary to come to terms with the stakes and dimensions of the viral. No singular theoretical framework can account for the artistic and cultural power that concepts of virality and contagion have held; for the ways they have evolved; or for their changing relationships to performance, media, and spectatorship. Instead, I invoke a diverse range of historical precedents, from Plato's foundational assertion of theater's contagious power, to Artaud, whose essay "The Theater and the Plague" set the terms for modern artists experimenting with viral modes. I draw on the history of new media forms, which have frequently been understood to wield contagious power, and I examine contagion's changing significance in affect theory and in postmodern philosophy.

Through such a wide-ranging introduction, I aim to offer the panoramic view of viral theory—and the performance histories it calls upon—that is necessary for the artistic close-readings that follow. My case studies are arranged chronologically, beginning in the 1960s with the Living Theatre's *Mysteries and Smaller Pieces* and *Paradise Now* and viewing the company's use of Artaudian principles as a point of origin for modern viral performance. Moving to the early 1970s in my second chapter, I juxtapose three dramaturgies of invisibility, all of which relied on spectators to perform in the near-absence of actors: General Idea's transmedial spectacles, Augusto Boal's invisible theater, and Marc Estrin's radical infiltrative theater. My story then proceeds into the 1990s, investigating artists who created work alongside the evolving internet, and who use large-scale public fictions to test the contagious properties of new media and performance: the collective Critical Art Ensemble; the duo Eva and Franco Mattes; and the German film and theater director Christoph Schlingensief. Finally, I explore the twenty-first-century advent of viral performance networks, examining both the dramaturgy and the artistic philosophies fueling the 2003 Lysistrata Project, Suzan-Lori Parks's *365 Days/365 Plays* Festival, and Churchill's *Seven Jewish Children*. I conclude with a meditation on "Virus in the Theater," a 2006 performance project that simultaneously returned to the origins of viral dramaturgy and suggested new directions in which the viral might venture.

In grouping these artists together—in many cases, artists who have not been considered side by side before—and in calling them viral, my goal is to recognize their shared participation in a set of theatrical strategies, and to build a case for the viral as a thematic and formal concept that has held profound meaning for many modern and contemporary theater-makers. I do not suggest that these theater-makers constitute an artistic movement, or that they represent a direct line of artistic influence (in fact, resistance to such linear modes of evolution is, for many of these artists, a motivating factor driving them to work in viral modes). I also do not presume to account for every artist who has created viral performance; my case studies are limited in number and in geographical and historical scope, representing a few of the many artists laboring in the aftermath of the European and American avant-gardes, and engaging, overtly or obliquely, with the legacies of Plato and Aristotle. Nor can I claim that every artist analyzed here has self-identified as a maker of viral or contagious work. Rather, I view the philosophical and artistic ideas explored in this book as multiple dimensions of a complex history: a series of linked schools of thought, adjacent lines of influence, and complementary modes of art-making that continue to permeate conceptions of contagious art, and of contagion itself. The artists described here challenge wider cultural assumptions about the meaning of "the viral," about the nature of a "virus," and about the ways ideas, feelings, and gestures spread.

I also deliberately avoid proposing a singular definition of the term "viral," or its close cousins: "virus," "contagious," and "infectious," among others. In biological terms, the virus is a modern discovery, emerging with the twentieth century. The word describes an agent that spreads infectiously, and that can only survive through the life of its host body. "Viral," whose emergence in the *Oxford English Dictionary* postdates "virus" by nearly fifty years, describes the mode in which such pathogenic agents spread. "Contagion" is much older, referring more broadly to the communication of disease from one body to another. Such meanings have offered profound metaphors and, in some cases, structural principles for the artists in this book. Yet holding too closely to biological analogies would limit analysis of the artistic works under discussion. This book is not about the relationship between performance and medical disease (indeed, many wonderful studies already take up that topic).[2] Rather, I seek out the changing cultural, artistic, and philosophical power that the concepts "viral" and "contagious" wield: their influence on radical theater's form, and on its terms of engagement with spectators and with media. I use the term "viral" flexibly, exploring the vocabulary of infection's evolving significance for ideas about cultural transmission, spectatorship, artistic power, and politics.

Such terminology—viruses and virality, contagion and transmission—is especially charged in the current era: our historical moment is a viral one. The advent of digital culture (as well as the evolving culture of technology that preceded it) has occasioned a seismic shift in the discourse surrounding contagiousness and the viral. "The virus," wrote artist and scholar Zach Blas in a 2012 essay, "is perhaps the major trope of the postmodern condition."[3]

In so saying, Blas joined a growing number of philosophers and scholars in fields ranging from media studies to affect theory who have identified the figure of the virus, and viral modes of transmission, as primary metaphors in the contemporary imagination. Viruses and virality make legible many of the political, social, artistic, and economic relationships in twenty-first-century culture. They describe the workings of digital-age capitalism, the strategies fueling new modes of political action, and the affective properties of emerging media forms.

Viral and contagious models of thought emerged in philosophy both before and alongside the development of digital technologies. As early as 1987, Gilles Deleuze and Félix Guattari proposed the concept of contagion as an alternative model for cultural and social transmission and development, one not tied to heredity or bound by capitalist-controlled channels of power. "We oppose epidemic to filiation, contagion to heredity, peopling by contagion to sexual reproduction, sexual production," they wrote.[4] While contagion here represented an escape hatch from constricted social systems and historical paradigms, in the decades that followed, the concept was increasingly linked to global capital and to digital technology. In 1996 Jean Baudrillard commented on the epidemiological power of the computer virus, writing, "The tiniest computer bacillus will soon create as much mayhem in our societies as the influenza or smallpox bacilli did among the Amerindians of the sixteenth century."[5] And in 2000 Michael Hardt and Antonio Negri declared, "The age of globalization is the age of universal contagion."[6]

By the first decades of the twenty-first century, scholars were looking back, tracing the advent of the viral, and looking forward to predict its evolution. Thierry Bardini's 2006 essay "Hypervirus: A Clinical Report" argued that it was in the early 1980s that philosophical concepts of the virus began to merge with ideas about the computer virus and about biological epidemic. "At the dawn of capitalism's fourth phase, the hypervirus awoke," writes Bardini—"hypervirus" referring, here, to the contagious spread of the viral concept itself (as Bardini puts it, "the 'virus' virus").[7] He continued, "From this point on, an explosive diffusion in 'postmodern culture' emerged, eventually it plateaued near saturation, redefining culture as a viral ecology."[8] The following year, the media scholar Jussi Parikka, in his study *Digital Contagions*, proposed the concept of "viral capitalism."[9] The year 2012 saw two significant works of scholarship dedicated to the concept of the viral: a volume of *Women's Studies Quarterly* entitled "Viral"[10] and Tony D. Sampson's *Virality*, which synthesizes theories of social contagion, examining the claim that "the age of networks is indeed the age of contagion."[11] Such assertions, made over the course of decades and across intellectual fields, aid in identifying the models of viral transmission practiced and questioned by the artists in this book, and testify to the recent proliferation of viral theories.

And yet: theater, in the cultural imagination, has always been contagious. Since Plato, philosophers have argued that stage actions can be infectiously transmitted to audience members—some viewing this as a source of theater's danger to society, others following Aristotle in seeing it as the reason why performance can serve as a form of moral inoculation against social ills. These classical modes of understanding theatrical reception have persisted: they remain, occasionally submerged, beneath centuries of anti-theatrical rhetoric, and they fuel defenses of theater's moral potential. They structure our understanding of how and why performance works in society—the contentious question of theatrical "efficacy"—and they inflect modern philosophies of audience reception and response, from the writings of Artaud to those of Rancière. They add dimension and stakes to questions of theatrical contagion, recurring in renovated form in modern and contemporary viral performance.

These models of thought register, above all, a continued and widespread belief—one held by artists, philosophers, critics, political leaders, even corporate marketers—that when people come into contact with one another, something spreads. Whether we plan it or not, whether we like it or not, whether it spreads through imitation or through difference, through deliberate copying or subconscious somnambulism, something spreads. Performance, an art form requiring and relying on live contact, renders such spreading visible, raises its stakes, gums up its works with fiction, and encodes it in dramatic structure and theatrical form. The artists explored in this book rarely attempt to disseminate their ideas or gestures as directly as a viral marketer, a political leader, or a computer hacker would. These artists' approaches to transmission, rather, tend to undermine such simplified concepts of contagion, to point out our susceptibilities to consumer capitalism and political slogans, to seek subversive forms of dissemination. Yet they also cannot help holding dialogue with the many strands of discourse, philosophical and popular, surrounding viral culture: all testifying to the viral's persistent appearance and reappearance, all directing our attention to the age-old instinct that—in some form, through some mechanism—when people gather, something spreads.

Platonic Foundations: Theater Is Contagious

If "going viral" is a twenty-first-century concept, the idea that theater is contagious is as old as Plato, who laid the foundations for describing performance in the language of infection, contagion, and inoculation. His theories prompted Aristotle's famous response in the *Poetics*, and structured anti-theatrical discourse for centuries to come. The historical distance separating these classical philosophers from contemporary artists like Eva and Franco Mattes and Critical Art Ensemble only deepens the significance of contemporary artists' choices (implicit or explicit) to create work that engages with spectators in Platonic and Aristotelian terms.

In the *Republic*, Plato, speaking through the figure of Socrates, famously banished poets from his ideal city, citing the dangerous effects mimesis might have on the unformed minds of the city's young leaders. Unflattering tales of gods and heroes could inspire morally muddled thinking on the part of listeners, and susceptible audience members might be persuaded to imitate the weak or immoral behavior they witnessed onstage. Actors, meanwhile, might absorb characters' bad qualities simply by playing them. Plato's initial discussion of the perils of mimesis occurs in book 3, where Socrates sketches a course of study for the hypothetical leaders of the new city. These unformed minds, Socrates declares, must listen only to stories in which gods and heroes are portrayed in the flattering light of virtue:

> For, my dear Adeimantus, if our young men listen to passages like these seriously and don't laugh at them as unworthy, they are hardly likely to think this sort of conduct unworthy of them as men, or to resist the temptation to similar words and actions.[12]

Even comedy is suspect, since Socrates links it directly to the expression of violent impulses, noting, "Indulgence in violent laughter commonly invites a violent reaction."[13]

Not only would it be dangerous for the Republic's guardians to witness examples of gods, heroes, or leaders behaving immorally; performance would also, as Jonas Barish notes in *The Antitheatrical Prejudice*, allow for a vertiginous freedom of thought that could lead citizens to question their predetermined roles in a heavily regulated society. Socrates argues that each person possesses narrow aptitudes, "which makes it impossible to play many roles well, whether in real life or in representations of it on the stage."[14] For the guardians' part, he says:

> If they do take part in dramatic or other representations, they must from their earliest years act the part only of characters suitable to them—men of courage, self-control, piety, freedom of spirit and similar qualities. They should neither do a mean action, nor be clever at acting a mean or otherwise disgraceful part on the stage for fear of catching the infection in real life.[15]

With the phrase "catching the infection," Plato directly links the concept of contagion to mimesis, bequeathing to future generations of anti-theatricalists the idea that performance is contagious, both to those who watch stage representations and to those who perform them.

The major classical counterpoint to Plato's idea—Aristotle's discussion of tragedy in the *Poetics*—envisions a different conduit from performance to morality. Rather than resisting the temptation to fall under imitative poetry's spell, Aristotle writes, audiences can experience catharsis by watching a tragedy that follows particular dramaturgical principles, and through catharsis, can eliminate violent and antisocial impulses. In the *Poetics*, Aristotle describes the combined effects of the elements of a tragic plot, proposing that "through pity and fear it achieves the purgation (catharsis) of such emotions."[16]

Aristotle wrote relatively little on the precise meaning of catharsis, and the concept has been the subject of intense debate among classical scholars.[17] In addition to the *Poetics*, the concept appears in the *Politics*, a work that cannot be assumed to employ "catharsis" in the same way, but which nevertheless offers additional description of the term. In the *Politics*, Aristotle suggests that listening to music, even music that conveys strong and dangerous feelings, can be morally beneficial, provoking a form of purgation in its audiences:

> An emotion which strongly affects some souls is present in all to a varying degree, for example pity and fear, and also ecstasy. To this last some people are particularly liable, and we see that under the influence of religious music and songs which drive the soul to frenzy, they calm down as if they had been medically treated and purged. People who are given to pity or fear, and emotional people generally, and others to the extent that they have similar emotions, must be affected in the same way; for all of them must experience a kind of purgation and pleasurable relief.[18]

Such concepts of purgation and relief represent one powerful strand of thought about how theater can be socially valuable, not in spite of its immoral or antisocial themes but because of them. Many of the artists I explore in this book see their work as a form of inoculation, presenting audiences with performances of social and political threat in order to, emotionally or ideologically, immunize them against the greater harms of ignorance and paranoia.

The Platonic attack on the theater, and the associated language of contagion, contamination, and inoculatory catharsis, reemerged repeatedly in the anti-theatrical debates that cropped up in times and places where performance played a vital role in Western culture. Such concepts recurred under the Roman republic and empire, in the writings of the early Christian philosophers Tertullian and Saint Augustine.[19] In the sixteenth century, Sir Philip Sidney's *Defense of Poesy* echoed both Plato and Aristotle;[20] in the seventeenth century, the Puritan William Prynne's *Histriomastix* condemned the English stage in tones that recalled Tertullian's,[21] while Jeremy Collier's *A Short View of the Immorality and Profaneness of the English Stage* took a Platonic view of theater's ability to influence the public.[22] In the nineteenth century, the language of contagion emerged in, for instance, the scandals surrounding such modern dramas as Ibsen's *Ghosts*, which was famously condemned as "a loathsome sore unbandaged; a dirty act done publicly."[23]

The Platonic fear of theater's moral contagion, and the Aristotelian hope in performance as social inoculation, have endured. For my purposes, in describing the works of modern and contemporary artists who have drawn on these ideas, it matters less whether recent artists' dramaturgies are precisely or consciously rooted in these philosophers' texts, and much more that Platonic and Aristotelian ideas, reshaped and renegotiated, have proven inspiring to artists over two millennia, and function particularly as grounding assumptions for artists creating viral performance. Such concepts reemerged with particular force in the late nineteenth and early twentieth centuries, when new types of media—which, in turn, demanded new types of spectatorship and public participation—inspired avant-garde artists to rethink the contagious properties of performance. During the same era, evolving alongside new media forms, a new school of philosophy, known as crowd theory and promoted by social theorists like Gabriel Tarde and Gustave Le Bon, began to explore the social transmission of ideas, actions, and emotions. Their thinking would have a profound effect on the emergence of viral and contagious concepts in the modern era.

Social Transmission and Contagious Crowds

"The age we are about to enter will in truth be the era of crowds," declared Gustave Le Bon in his 1895 *The Crowd: A Study of the Popular Mind*, one of the most vivid expressions of the late nineteenth century's fascination with the social transmission of affect, which was often viewed in contagious terms.[24] Indeed, in the late nineteenth and early twentieth centuries, concepts of cultural contagion reemerged forcefully in the schools of thought surrounding social transmission, particularly transmission in crowds. Such modes of thinking provide a context for modern artists' relationships to concepts of contagion: particularly Artaud, but more broadly, the many theater-makers in this book, such as the Living Theatre and Critical Art Ensemble, whose work engages with the transmission of feeling through live and mediated publics. (I am indebted to Kimberly Jannarone's work for my fascination with crowd theory and for connecting it to Artaud's ideas of contagion; more on this connection shortly.)

The French sociologist Gabriel Tarde's *The Laws of Imitation*, first published in 1890, preceded Le Bon in theorizing social contagion, viewing imitation as the driving force in the propagation of customs, ideas, emotions, and more. "Everything which is social and non-vital or non-physical in the phenomena of societies is caused by imitation," he wrote.[25] Tarde's theory offered several key interventions in the conceptualization of social interactions. He proposed dismantling distinctions between the natural and the cultural, a move that would later be echoed by many late twentieth-century philosophers, and particularly by the theorists of cultural evolution who, in the 1970s, began conceiving the field of memetics, a school of thought whose ideas would in turn fuel much twenty-first-century thinking about viral culture.[26] He also proposed that social imitation unfolds largely below the level of consciousness, that we adopt each other's phrases, gestures, and affects through unexplained volition rather than deliberate decisionmaking. "I shall not seem fanciful in thinking of the social man as a veritable somnambulist," he wrote.[27]

For later thinkers who invoked concepts of contagion—including Gilles Deleuze, who drew on Tarde's concepts of difference in *Difference and Repetition*, and Bruno Latour, who cited Tarde as a predecessor for actor-network theory—this model of social transmission proved foundational. Tarde's assertions that affects and behaviors spread in indirect, nonlinear fashions, that they are passed along unconsciously and sometimes involuntarily, and that they travel along the lines of affective affinities rather than overt cognition, offered a theory of social development that evaded the restrictive models of cultural evolution embodied by normative systems of power and deterministic models of heredity. Though few of the artists I examine would directly endorse a "somnambulist" model of affective transmission, many—the Living Theatre, Eva and Franco Mattes—have been profoundly invested in nonlinear and emotion-driven concepts of contagion, while others, such as the creators of the networked performances examined in chapter 4, structured theatrical projects around the inclusive, nonlinear dissemination of performances and texts.

During the decade when Tarde was developing his theories of social transmission, Le Bon founded the field of inquiry that would come to be known as crowd theory, later to be associated with the right-wing fascist movements of 1930s Italy and Germany, and reconceived in the 1960s by Elias Canetti. Le Bon's theories provide striking expressions of the power that ideas of social contagion, catalyzed by live presence, would assume in the twentieth century. For Le Bon, as for Tarde, transmission among the members of a gathered group occurred primarily at the subconscious level, and acquired its force from the loss of individual cognition that mass presence provoked. Both Tarde and Le Bon viewed social interactions as sites of involuntary contagious transmission; in Le Bon's paradigm, this offered evidence of crowds' ultimate malleability and their susceptibility to the seductions of powerful leaders:

> We see, then, that the disappearance of the conscious personality, the predominance of the unconscious personality, the turning by means of suggestion and contagion of feelings and ideas in an identical direction, the tendency to immediately transform the suggested ideas into acts; these, we see, are the principal characteristics of the individual forming part of a crowd. He is no longer himself, but has become an automaton who has ceased to be guided by his will.[28]

This vision of de-individuation, which also reflected racial and class-based anxieties about the changing populations of industrializing European cities, was understandably appealing to political leaders seeking to maximize their charismatic sway; Mussolini famously cited Le Bon as an important influence.[29] Le Bon was rightfully discredited in the mid-twentieth century and after, both for his association with fascist leaders and for the undisguised elitism and primitivism driving his thought.[30]

Even so, crowd theory proved transformative for creators of political theater during the early twentieth century, and its implications for social transmission inflect viral performance today. Early twentieth-century mass spectacles, as Erika Fischer-Lichte persuasively documents in *Theatre, Sacrifice, Ritual*, drew on assumptions similar to those of crowd theorists, incorporating large groups of spectators or employing vast numbers of performers. From the first modern Olympic Games to the large-scale Soviet spectacle *The Storming of the Winter Palace*, Fischer-Lichte argues that modern mass performances functioned as attempts to revive a fantasy of long-lost communal feeling. These temporary assemblies, she explains, appealed to artists and publics seeking an antidote to a growing sense of isolation and ennui that—as Emile Durkheim observed—had emerged as industrial society created increasingly mobile populations and severed individuals from traditional ways of life. New mass performances created narratives of national sacrifice and resurrection (as in the case of many Nazi performances) or mythologized moments of nation-building (as in the Soviet spectacles). In most cases, these mass performances used the excitement created by the gathering of many bodies to forge new national communities bolstered by utopian ideologies and eschatological narratives.

Central to the appeal of mass spectacles, Fischer-Lichte proposes, was the belief that feelings and ideas are particularly contagious among members of a live, gathered crowd. In mass spectacles,

> theatre appeared to be capable of transforming individuals into members of a community, albeit only temporarily, by focusing on the bodily co-presence of actors and spectators, on the physical acts of the actors and their capacity to "infect" the spectators as well as on the "contagion" occurring among the spectators.[31]

The suspicion that live co-presence lends itself to contagious feeling grew, and assumed deeper implications, in the wake of World War II. Elias Canetti's *Crowds and Power*, published in 1962 and often considered the landmark work of twentieth-century crowd theory, sought to understand the behavior of publics in Nazi Germany and Fascist Italy. Although Canetti was critical of the anti-populist anxiety displayed by writers like Le Bon, he likewise explored the ways that crowds changed their members' behavior and consciousness. "Few can resist its contagion," he wrote of the crowd; "it always wants to go on growing and there are no inherent limits to its growth."[32] Canetti's detailed analysis of mass behavior posited a taxonomy of crowds and argued for a specific sequence of events in the creation of a crowd—in particular, a watershed moment of "discharge," when members of a group relinquish their individual wills to fuse emotionally with those surrounding them. "This is the moment," Canetti wrote, "when all who belong to the crowd get rid of their differences and feel equal."[33]

The dramaturgical connections linking bodily co-presence, mass identification, and contagion famously reached an apotheosis in the writings of Antonin Artaud, who figures in this study as a central source of theory governing theater's contagious potential. In *Artaud and His Doubles*, Kimberly Jannarone's 2010 study of the French playwright, director, and philosopher's politics and aesthetics, Jannarone argues that Artaud's ideas about spectatorship align clearly and disturbingly with the strategies used by fascist regimes at rallies and mass performances. She demonstrates just how much early twentieth-century crowd theory, particularly as pioneered by Le Bon, has in common with the way Artaud envisioned spectators behaving at his ideal theater. Crowd theory, in turn, illuminates affinities between Artaud's theoretical plans for an all-consuming theatrical spectacle and the real spectacles created by the Fascist and Nazi movements of the 1930s. "Crowd theory," writes Jannarone, "helps us see that the Theater of Cruelty envisions the audience in many of the same ways people's theaters in Italy and Germany did . . . as a group of people they would make feel liberated and exalted while also keeping it under tight control."[34]

Few of the artists examined in this book share the political goals of either Artaud or the creators of fascist people's theaters. These artists, for the most part, engage with ideas of crowd-fueled contagion in order to complicate them—as in Critical Art Ensemble's *Radiation Burn*, which directly pitted an audience's susceptibility to contagious fear against its capacity for individual contemplation. Yet the principles of contagious social transmission have persisted through the twentieth century and into the twenty-first, recurring as artists test their limits and as theorists renegotiate concepts of cultural circulation. These concepts found their way into modern and contemporary theater most directly through the writings of Artaud.

The Theater and the Plague

Antonin Artaud's essay "The Theater and the Plague" is the best-known and most influential modern assertion of theater's contagious power. Echoes of the essay's convictions and refractions of its wild imagination recur in many of the works explored in this book, from the Living Theatre's efforts to directly embody Artaud's plague in *Mysteries* to Eva and Franco Mattes's experiments with digital contagion.

The diversity of works taking inspiration from Artaud's theatrical plague testifies not only to its influence but also to its ambiguity: the puzzle of just what he believed the plague was, how he believed it would spread, and how these things resembled the performance and reception of theater. His essay is steeped in medical terminology, yet disavows epidemiological science, at once detailing the theater's powers of transmission and distinguishing these powers from the biological principles of germ theory. "We must recognize," he wrote, "that the theater, like the plague, is a delirium and is communicative."[35] There could hardly be a more direct statement of theater's contagious power. Yet lingering alongside Artaud's repeated recourse to medical description is, always, a deep anxiety about the terms in which science would or could understand the mechanisms of contagious transmission. In relating a parable from the eighteenth-century outbreak of plague in Europe, Artaud emphasized the spiritual dimension of the plague's presence, its ability to communicate without physical connection. He described an incident in which a Sardinian viceroy, sensing the plague's proximity in a dream, refuses to let nearby ships dock in his harbor, intuitively averting an epidemic in his territory. "It cannot be denied that between the viceroy and the plague a palpable communication, however subtle, was established: and it is too easy and explains nothing to limit the communication of such a disease to contagion by simple contact," Artaud concluded.[36] Later, he elaborated on the distinction between medical infection and his own more flexible epidemiology. "If the essential theater is like the plague, it is not because it is contagious," he wrote, "but because like the plague it is the revelation, the bringing forth, the exteriorization of a depth of latent cruelty by means of which all the perverse possibilities of the mind, whether of an individual or a people, are localized."[37] This shift in the relationship between theater and plague—the revelation that contagion is not the point of connection, after all—gestures toward the philosopher's antagonism to modern science and medicine.

More importantly for this study, it also resists any temptation, on a reader's part, to draw a straightforward analogy between biology and art: a rejection that later makers of viral art will echo and revise. Artaud dismissed newfound scientific explanations of viral contagion, centered on the recently discovered microbe, and asserted, "Personally, I regard this microbe only as a smaller—infinitely smaller—material element which appears at some moment in the development of the virus, but which in no way accounts for the plague."[38] I join scholars such as Stanton B. Garner and Kimberly Jannarone in viewing these assertions not as a sudden disavowal of contagion's significance for theater, but rather as testaments to Artaud's desire to take the widest possible view of the plague's potential for physical and spiritual transformation. The idea of microbial contagion was never far from his thoughts; Artaud simply conceived contagion in broader terms than his scientific contemporaries would have. As Jannarone explains, scientific ideas of contagion offered important contributions to Artaud's metaphysics:

> The idea of the microbe had just entered into scientific thinking in the late nineteenth century, and while Artaud explicitly dismisses the medical importance of the microbe's physical body, he adopts a viewpoint that the microbe made possible: that the world is at all times awash in *le mal*.[39]

Indeed, Artaud frequently compared his ideas about contagion with the developing theories of early twentieth-century epidemiology, and his explicit denial of "contagion" as the scientific link between theater and plague only serves to underscore their broader relationship. Garner, in his article "Artaud, Germ Theory, and the Theatre of Contagion," suggests, "Through a logic at once assertive and self-repudiating, contagion and the body become the animating centers of Artaud's medical metaphysics at the very moment their clinical meanings are superseded or bracketed from consideration." He adds, "Freed from its narrowly medicalized definition, the relationship between the material body and its double—between the plague and its 'spiritual image'—reveals itself to be an essentially performative one."[40] Separating "plague" from, as Garner notes, a "narrowly medicalized definition" also serves an important function in opening space for the multiple modes of contagious transmission explored by the artists in this book. If "contagion by simple contact" is far too simple for Artaud, it is, too, for nearly every artist who has worked in a viral mode since.

In an essay titled "Cruelty and Cure," Jane Goodall offers a persuasive reading of this Artaudian contradiction, arguing that Artaud's plague is communicable, not through direct contact but through psychic transferal, traveling through thoughts, dreams, and emotions:

> The plague, Artaud asserts, is not virally transmitted. Its spread has nothing to do with contamination by contact. It takes hold only upon those in whom it finds the seeds for its growth already planted . . . the principle of quarantine with its associated stratagems of exclusion is useless against the plague, for it operates according to the principle of telepathy and thus in defiance of all physical boundaries.[41]

For Artaud, in this reading, the plague does not pass directly from one infected person to another: rather, it contains the power to provoke an eruption of the disease in a person for whom it is already present in latent form. This model of contagion offers powerful illumination of the contagious dramaturgies described in this book. From the Living Theatre, whose mode of emotional and affective contagion used acting technique to summon audience response, to the networked performances described in chapter 4, which mobilized theatrical communities already in existence, contagious performance tends to call forth action from those in whom, in Goodall's words, "the seeds for its growth are already planted"—artistically, politically, or both.

For Artaud, the theater and the plague were linked by their boundless powers of destruction; calling forth latent powers resulted, in both cases, in ruin. "Once the plague is established in a city, the regular forms collapse," he wrote. "There is no maintenance of roads and sewers, no army, no police, no municipal administration . . . Entire streets are blocked by the piles of dead. Then the houses open and the delirious victims, their minds crowded with hideous visions, spread howling through the streets."[42] For nearly every other artist under discussion here, though, theater's contagious potential is a source of social possibility. Whether seeking revolution or reform, promoting a sense of utopian togetherness or provoking skepticism and disbelief, the artists in this book put viral structures in the service of critique and change. Yet rather than viewing the appropriation of Artaudian aesthetics for non-Artaudian political ends as an artistic misfire or political misappropriation, I believe that such slippages simply testify to Artaud's abiding hold on the viral imagination. Indeed, viral dissemination—including, but not limited to, the kind Artaud theorized—is culturally significant not in spite of, but because of its availability and appeal to practitioners of widely disparate politics. Virality has been powerfully attractive to forces of rupture and revolution, repression, and radical inclusion alike.

Although Artaud's theatrical writings include very few ideas that could be construed as prescriptions for societal rehabilitation, his enthusiasm for destruction as a cleansing force bears affinities to later artists for whom viral performance can provide a social cure. "It appears that by means of the plague, a gigantic abscess, as much moral as social, has been collectively drained; and that like the plague, the theater has been created to drain abscesses collectively," he wrote.[43] This comparison of theater and plague is potentially restorative (and potentially Aristotelian): the draining of the abscess must, as Artaud describes elsewhere, release destructive forces, but it also leaves the body less contaminated than before. The idea of performance as a form of social cure—whether theorized as homeopathic remedy, imaginative inoculation, or social corrective—aligns with the theoretical approaches of more contemporary viral performance artists such as Eva and Franco Mattes, Christoph Schlingensief, and Critical Art Ensemble, who disseminate theatrical fictions in order to inoculate their societies against more dangerous types of infection. At the end of "The Theater and the Plague," Artaud wrote, "we can see, to conclude, that from the human point of view, the action of theater, like that of plague, is beneficial, for, impelling men to see themselves as they are, it causes the mask to fall, reveals the lie, the slackness, baseness, and hypocrisy of our world."[44]

Yet Artaud also shared affinities with the opposite point of view about the effects of mimesis on viewers—the Platonic perspective, which sees performance as a dangerous imitation of tangible realities, which are, in turn, imitations of their ideal forms, and thus an invitation toward realizing the acts of violence it depicts. Here is Artaud, describing the ways in which the realities felt in performance can exceed or overpower the realities of the external world:

> Once launched upon the fury of his task, an actor requires infinitely more power to keep from committing a crime than a murderer needs courage to complete his act, and it is here, in its very gratuitousness, that the action and effect of a feeling in the theater appears infinitely more valid than that of a feeling fulfilled in life.[45]

This view of performance's contagious possibilities bears more resemblance to Plato's fears—that the act of performing would engender real-world violence—than to Aristotle's more benevolent understanding of performance's possibilities. In Artaud's writings, both ideas are held in tension: the notion that performance can serve a purgative social function, and the idea that performed fictions can tip powerfully into reality. Both ideas are central to later dramaturgies of viral performance.

Artaud's theories of contagion also intersected with his engagement with broadcast media, particularly in his late radio play, *To Have Done with the Judgment of God*. The poetic drama, scheduled to be aired in 1948, suggests an intrinsic link between new technologies and viral performance, laying the foundations for later viral experiments. In fact, Artaud believed, radio broadcast was necessary for communicating the particular kind of plague envisioned by his final, apocalyptic, dramatic poem. In his writings on the radio play, he drew an explicit and rich connection between contagion and broadcast media despite the fact that *To Have Done with the Judgment of God* was never publicly aired. In February 1948, a day before it was slated for broadcast, the radio station director Wladimir Porché canceled the presentation of Artaud's drama. Artaud wrote a furious letter to Porché, demanding that the station director understand the significance of the piece he had presumed to remove from the public airwaves:

> And you are not unaware of the curiosity with which this broadcast had been awaited by the great majority of the public who looked to it for a kind of deliverance, counting on an auditory experience that would save them at last from the monotony of ordinary broadcasts.[46]

Later, in a letter to Fernand Pouey, a director of literary programming for French radio, Artaud repeated this view of the radio play's potential, insisting: "never/ has a broadcast been ANTICIPATED with greater curiosity and impatience by the great mass of the public who were specifically waiting for this broadcast to help them form an attitude to confront certain aspects of life."[47] The subject matter and artistic intentions embedded in *To Have Done with the Judgment of God* were, for Artaud, inextricable from its method of transmission. The dispersed public awaiting his words expected, in Artaud's thinking, not only that the play would offer an auditory experience entirely distinct from the usual radio broadcast, but also that it would be physically and spiritually transformative, that it would alter and correct their perspectives on the world, offering a kind of religious leadership.

For Artaud, such a vision of immediate, geographically dispersed psychic and spiritual transformation contributed directly to his larger, long-standing artistic project: he reportedly believed that the final recording of *To Have Done with the Judgment of God* constituted "a model in miniature of what I want to do with my Theatre of Cruelty."[48] In an article tracing Artaud's ideas about the relationship between sound and image on film, Denis Hollier argues that sound—the medium at work in Artaud's radio drama—stood at the center of the playwright's vision for audience interaction and even audience control. "Artaud's theatrical utopia," writes Hollier, "is primarily what I call a sound system."[49] And Artaud's theatrical utopia, of course, was a contagious one. He was not alone on either count. In the years before and during Artaud's theorization of the Theater of Cruelty, and his contagious vision for radio broadcast, a host of other artists and thinkers were imagining other equally vast implications for the contagious power of new media and technology.

A Vast System of Channels: Radio and the Politics of Transmission

In a very short play entitled *Madness*, written by the Italian Futurist Mario Dessy, the combination of performance and new media renders insanity irresistibly contagious. The play is set during a film screening in, Dessy writes, "a large, modern movie theatre." Onscreen, a protagonist is going mad. Gradually, other characters in the film begin to go mad, too. Soon, insanity breaches the movie screen and begins to spread through the audience. "The public becomes uneasy," writes Dessy, and before long

> *everyone is disturbed, obsessed by the idea of madness that comes over them all. Suddenly the spectators get up screaming . . . gesturing . . . fleeing . . . confusion . . . MADNESS.*[50]

This brief drama, written entirely in stage directions and occupying less than half a page, is rich with implications for a theory of viral performance. First, the scene reads as if it had been ripped from a Platonic nightmare. Performers in a film, screened for a live audience, infect their spectators with mental and spiritual illness, with a madness that manifests in physical and emotional loss of control. Dessy's onstage spectators are scripted and choreographed, cast as the agents of contagion, a theatrical strategy that would be echoed by later viral artists, from the Living Theatre to General Idea.

In Dessy's play, it is not just performance that proves contagious, but also the presence of a new media form, since the unnamed protagonist inspires infectious madness by breaching the barrier of a cinema screen. For the Italian Futurists, as for a host of their contemporaries, new forms of media offered new ways of transmitting performances and reaching larger audiences more swiftly than previously imaginable. The story of twentieth-century viral performance unfolds alongside, and in dialogue with, the histories of new media and media culture, which have offered form and subject matter for makers of viral art. They have also put pressure on the politics of performance: the relationship between theater and media is an especially important one for viral dramaturgy because the viral—in representing the most prolific forms of dissemination and amplification, as well as the most participatory types of performances—also forces the question of political orientation. Is viral dissemination inherently democratic, participatory, or even subversive, as it is for many of the artists I describe? Or is it just as readily an agent of government or corporate control? Such questions recur in each chapter of this book, and while I avoid posing a singular answer—believing that the absence of a singular answer testifies to viral performance's significance and complexity—these questions register the political significance of new media for the performance works under discussion.

The adjacent histories of new media and contagious performance overlapped on October 30, 1938, when Orson Welles's Mercury Theatre on the Air began to broadcast what sounded like a dance-hall music program. Before long, the songs were interrupted by a series of announcements from "reporters," who began to describe an odd meteorological occurrence involving several violent explosions on the surface of Mars. These news bulletins gave way to increasingly urgent local reports from a New Jersey farm, where, to the reporters' apparent astonishment, a group of unidentifiable metal cylinders had crash-landed. Extraterrestrial monsters began emerging from the spacecraft, and soon a disaster of national proportions was underway. As the tale unfolded—this was, of course, Welles's infamous *War of the Worlds* broadcast, adapted from H. G. Wells's novel of the same name—reporters related the unfolding emergency without identifying it as fiction:

> The monster is now in control of the middle section of New Jersey and has effectively cut the state through its center. Communication lines are down from Pennsylvania to the Atlantic Ocean. Railroad tracks are torn and service from New York to Philadelphia discontinued except routing some of the trains through Allentown and Phoenixville. Highways to the north, south, and west are clogged with frantic human traffic. Police and army reserves are unable to control the mad flight.[51]

This is a scene of technological and communications systems disrupted, a nightmare scenario staging the breakdown of the very networks that enabled

Welles's broadcast to take place. Such communications networks are also, in a deeper sense, context for the real-world response that Welles's program provoked: contagious panic that turned the broadcast into one of the legendary media events of the twentieth century.

I invoke *War of the Worlds* as an early study in media contagion, a half-accidental convergence of theater, infectiousness, and technology that forecast many such overlaps to come. Hadley Cantril's sociological study of the broadcast, written in 1940, asserts—almost certainly hyperbolically, but not without basis in truth—that "people all over the United States were praying, crying, fleeing frantically to escape death from the Martians." Cantril adds, "At least six million people heard the broadcast. At least a million of them were frightened or disturbed."[52] Cantril's survey of responses to the Welles broadcast identifies social influence—the coercive force of others' belief—as an important factor in inducing listeners' panic. He writes:

> One of the things we would first suspect is *the corroboratory effect of other people's behavior: the contagion of other people's fear*. A person who was told to tune in by a frightened friend would listen under different conditions than someone who tuned in for other reasons. If the person who called him was someone whom he had confidence in, he would be particularly apt to accept that person's opinion, tune in with a pre-existing mental set, and have his attitude confirmed.[53]

Credulousness was contagious, spreading first through radio and then through social networks. The print media, Cantril contends, compounded public anxiety (even after the broadcast had been revealed as fictional) by running endless "human-interest stories relating the shock and terror of local citizens."[54] Welles's tale of Martian invasion spread infectiously, and then continued to circulate as the media marveled at its own vertiginous powers of contagion.

In *The Citizen Audience*, a history of the American media consumer, the scholar Charles Butsch describes a phenomenon he calls "media panic." Sudden and deep anxieties, he explains, have followed the introduction of nearly every form of communications technology—radio, television, internet—as public perception recoils from unfamiliar modes of watching or listening, simultaneously embracing each new paradigm for consuming information while also worrying that it will corrupt minds and unravel society. As early as the 1930s, Butsch writes, parents were switching off radios, declaring their children "radio fiends." In the 1950s, publications warned that too much television viewing could send well-intentioned citizens down the path to family disintegration and financial ruin.[55] Cantril's study of *War of the Worlds*, written when memories of the public response were fresh, offers a description of radio's power that exemplifies the concept of "media panic":

> Radio has inherently the characteristics of contemporaneousness, availability, personal appeal and ubiquity. Hence, when we analyze this panic, we are able to deal with the most modern type of social group—the radio audience—which differs from the congregate group of the moving picture theatre and the consociate group reading the daily paper. The radio audience consists essentially of thousands of small, congregate groups united in time and experiencing a common stimulus—altogether making possible the largest grouping of people ever known.[56]

Radio's power was, for many, not just a source of general social or moral anxiety; it also provoked specific fears about the potential for new media to aid in the rise of authoritarian powers. In a previous study, *The Psychology of Radio*, Cantril had described radio as "an agency of incalculable power for controlling the actions of men,"[57] predicting that "the day cannot be far off when men in every country of the globe will be able to listen at one time to the persuasions or commands of some wizard seated in a central place of broadcasting, possessed of a power more fantastic than that of Aladdin."[58]

Welles's program constituted perhaps the most infamous instance of contagious radio broadcasting, but other artists shared Cantril's instinct that this relatively new form of communications technology held immense potential for the infectious transmission of idea and emotion. At the forefront of such thinking were the Italian Futurists—including but not limited to Dessy—who embraced the new technology as the herald of performance modes that could address previously unimagined publics with previously unimagined speed. The Futurists' obsession with the communicative power of new technologies makes them an important predecessor for later viral performance artists. In a 1933 manifesto, "The Radio," Futurist leader F. T. Marinetti critiqued the radio programming of his day—still under the sway of old dramaturgies and stagnant social mores—and laid out a series of principles governing "Radia," his term for "great radio events."[59] Radia would include "compressed dramas comprising an infinite number of simultaneous actions," all of them to be broadcast concurrently around the globe. "The possibility of picking up radio broadcasts from stations in different time zones, together with the absence of light, destroys the hours, the day, and the night," he wrote. "Reception and amplification, by means of thermoionic valves, of light and of voices from the past, will destroy the concept of time."[60] The heady impulse to "destroy the concept of time" registers simultaneity and speed as central dimensions of the Futurists' political and artistic program.

Such fascinations were timely. Speed, considered broadly, had generated increasing attention from artists and philosophers throughout the early twentieth century, as newly mechanized workplaces were created, city streets filled with automobiles, and an array of new technologies accelerated the activities of daily life. During this era, as Stephen Kern eloquently observes in *The*

Culture of Time and Space, higher speed limits allowed for faster automobile travel, efficiency experts such as Frederick Winslow Taylor sought to speed up and standardize industrial production, and journalists began using the telephone to increase the pace of reporting.[61] Speed would recur in the early twenty-first century as a fundamental characteristic of viral culture: the instantly shared internet meme, the split-second YouTube fad. It is also, more specifically, a central element in most modern viral dramaturgies (digital or not), which tend to test the pace of perception and participation, and the potential for images and ideas to circulate through public space long after a particular performance has ended.

Other elements of Marinetti's vision for radio performance were formulated in direct dialogue with conventional theater, and challenged Aristotelian dramatic structure. Declaring that "radio has killed off the theater," he proposed that Radia would eliminate "unity of action" and "the theatrical character"—as well as, crucially, "the audience, in the sense of a judgmental mass—self-electing, systematically hostile and servile, always antiprogressive and backward-looking."[62] The ambition to remove any "self-electing" element of spectatorship constitutes perhaps the most radical element of Marinetti's vision for contagious radio performance, and the one with the most profound implications. It not only reflects Futurism's well-known authoritarian leanings; it also suggests the stakes of viral dramaturgies in relation to the wider publics they address. Intentional participation is, arguably, a defining element of any listening or viewing public, as Michael Warner argues in his landmark book *Publics and Counterpublics*, which asserts that public speech is constituted through its intention to address not only specific listeners (or readers) but unbounded and unidentified others, and that those listeners become a public through the act of paying attention.[63] Contained within Marinetti's invocation of involuntary spectatorship is the desire to create performance that can circumvent the conscious agency of those who spread it. Such a prospect places Marinetti in a history of both artists and philosophers imagining forms of involuntary transmission, reaching back to Tarde's concept of social somnambulism and forward to thinkers conceiving the meme as a self-perpetuating unit of cultural evolution. Contagion, with its threat of uncontrolled, involuntary circulation, will surface again and again as a descriptor of performances that try to spread through affect, emotion, or unintentional transmission, from the Living Theatre's embodiment of plague to Eva and Franco Mattes's viral media experiments.

Even as Marinetti and his collaborators envisioned employing radio to create newly coercive modes of performance, others were exploring the possibility of employing radio to foster new modes of participation and exchange. Though many artists, writers, and philosophers were investigating such questions, I focus here on the radio theory of Bertolt Brecht, both because it offers particularly striking opposition to Marinetti's approach, and because of Brecht's foundational importance to later artists working in viral modes:

the Living Theatre, Boal, Critical Art Ensemble, and Caryl Churchill. Indeed, Brecht's theory permeates the case studies in this book nearly as thoroughly as Artaud's does, if less explicitly in many cases. Walter Benjamin, describing Brecht's theatrical theory, wrote: "'Making gestures quotable' is one of the essential achievements of epic theatre."[64] Viral dramaturgy, in all of its forms, strives to do precisely that: to make gestures quotable, to make spectators quote them.

Brecht began experimenting with radio in the 1920s, shortly after it was introduced in Germany.[65] He adapted the texts of *Macbeth* and *Hamlet* as radio plays in 1926, and adapted his own plays *The Life of Edward II of England*, *Man Is Man*, and *Saint Joan of the Stockyards* for broadcast between 1926 and 1932.[66] He was also immediately critical of the discourse surrounding radio, and of the uses to which the new medium was being put. Brecht believed (as did Marinetti) that directors of radio stations were squandering the medium's particularities. "From the beginning the radio imitated practically every existing institution that had anything at all to do with the distribution of speech or song,"[67] he wrote in his essay "The Radio as a Communications Apparatus." "This was the radio in its first phase," wrote Brecht, "as substitute: a substitute for theatre, opera, concerts, lectures, coffeehouse music, the local pages of the newspaper, etc."[68]

Radio—in Brecht's view—could be useful only if it fulfilled its potential as a medium of exchange, rather than of straightforward dissemination. He wrote:

> when a technical invention with such a natural aptitude for decisive social functions is met by such anxious efforts to maintain *without consequences* the most harmless entertainment possible, then the question unavoidably arises as to whether there is no possibility to confront the powers that exclude with an organization of the excluded.[69]

Brecht worked, in his experimentation with radio, to orchestrate such a confrontation, as in, for instance, the 1929 staging of the *Lehrstück Lindbergh's Flight* as a radio play at the Baden-Baden Festival for German Chamber Music. Thus a play already built on the armature of participatory spectatorship (the *Lehrstücke* form) became material for exploring the radio's participatory possibilities. As Marc Silberman writes in an introduction to Brecht's writings on radio, Brecht was "not only thematizing the radio in a broadcast presentation but suggesting how the medium itself can transform social communication through its technological advantage: the ear is to become a voice."[70] In his own writings, Brecht used *Lindbergh's Flight* to articulate an ambitious theory of radio: "*The Flight of the Lindberghs* is not intended to be of use to the present-day radio but to *change* it," he declared. "The increasing concentration of mechanical means and the increasingly specialized education—trends that should be accelerated—call for a kind of *rebellion* by the listener, for his mobilization and redeployment as producer."[71] To effect such a renegotiation of power, Brecht wrote,

> radio must be transformed from a distribution apparatus into a communications apparatus. The radio could be the finest possible communications apparatus in public life, a vast system of channels. That is, it could be so, if it understood how to receive as well as to transmit, how to let the listener speak as well as hear, how to bring him into a network instead of isolating him. Following this principle the radio should step out of the supply business and organize its listeners as suppliers.[72]

Brecht concluded by observing that his ideas for the repurposing of radio were "unrealizable in this social order but realizable in another"[73]—a testament to how deeply new technologies' forms reflect the societies that produce them.

Later artists, and later theorists of new media, would take up this very question, asking whether new communications technologies such as radio could ever be oriented toward mass participation, toward democratic discourse, toward countercultural agendas and anticapitalist messaging, or whether "one-sided" communications and capitalist ideologies were inherent aspects of the new technologies the twentieth century had made possible. Even as emerging media forms evolved from radio to television, and from television to the early stirrings of the internet, Brecht's formulations continued to guide philosophers writing on this question. In 1971, the German Marxist philosopher Hans Magnus Enzensberger would return directly to Brecht's 1932 essay to argue for a repurposing of all modern communications technologies for public participation and revolutionary agitation. Jean Baudrillard responded to Enzensberger with the argument that new technologies contained, within their modes of working, the capitalist ideologies that had given them birth. Reactionary media, Baudrillard warned, could never serve revolutionary messages.

In the meantime, of course, in the decades between Brecht's essay and Enzensberger's essay, media theory had emerged as a field of inquiry and mode of analysis in its own right, due largely to the 1964 publication of Marshall McLuhan's *Understanding Media*. McLuhan's foundational observations about the power of media forms to shape the meanings those media disseminate, about the relationships among various media forms and the human body, and about the types of systems that could be productively analyzed as "media," from radio to the postal service, proved formative for many of the artists analyzed in this book—most directly, for General Idea, but more broadly for all of the artists working at the intersection of performance and media technology. McLuhan's largely formal analysis provoked responses, in turn, from Marxist philosophers like Enzensberger, who advocated for more attention to the politics embedded in media form—a debate that would recur with the dawning digital age.

The Advent of Viral Culture: Media, Memes, and Mobs

In the 1960s and 1970s, as dialogues about the politics of media continued to evolve—and as the dramaturgies described in the first two chapters of this book were beginning to flourish—cultural studies also saw the advent of a series of schools of thought that used viral and contagious models to describe the evolution of culture. These models, mixing biological, social, and cultural modes of change, took inspiration from the foundational philosophies of social imitation and crowd theory pioneered by Tarde and Canetti and emerged fully with the publication of evolutionary biologist Richard Dawkins's 1976 *The Selfish Gene*. In his study, Dawkins proposed the influential concept of the "meme" as a cultural analogue to the biological unit of the gene. The meme was, as he wrote, "a unit of cultural transmission,"[74] which replicates itself in a manner analogous to the way genetic material spreads. Dawkins derived his term from the concept of mimesis—his initial idea for the new word was "mimeme"—and in his description, he explicitly linked the "meme" to imitation:

> Examples of memes are tunes, ideas, catch-phrases, clothes fashions, ways of making pots or of building arches. Just as genes propagate themselves in the gene pool by leaping from body to body via sperms or eggs, so memes propagate themselves in the meme pool by leaping from brain to brain via a process which, in the broad sense, can be called imitation.[75]

In proposing imitation as a central component of cultural dissemination, Dawkins implicitly connected performance to cultural contagion. His insight about the proliferation of culture also laid the groundwork for later observations, particularly those made by cultural critics such as Douglas Rushkoff in the dawning digital age, about the media-enabled circulation of memes.

Dawkins's meme theory helped to launch the field of memetics in the decades that followed: scholars explored the possibility that culture, ideas, ideologies, and customs could be analyzed using the model of the meme and the principles of biological evolution. Such thinking took shape in works like Aaron Lynch's *Thought Contagion* (1996), Susan Blackmore's *The Meme Machine* (1999), and Kate Distin's *The Selfish Meme* (2005), in which Distin expands on Dawkins's theory of memetic evolution, arguing that "the evolutionary processes—replication, selection, and variation—are present in culture"[76] and that "*memes* provide the mechanism for that evolution."[77] Social transmission, so significant for crowd theory, played an equally important role in memetics, and, as Tony D. Sampson notes in his recent book *Virality*, some scholars have claimed Tarde as a predecessor for this field.[78]

Though memetic theories coincided historically with the artistic trajectory of this book, most of the artists whose work I explore would disavow the directness of the biological analogy memetics draws upon. In fact, despite its potential appeal as an elegant way of applying biological models to cultural evolution, memetics was also attended by discomfort nearly from the start. The uncertainty of what, exactly, constituted a "meme" lingered—after all, cultural "units" cannot be viewed in isolation or scientifically compared to one another as genes can. Scholars noted that the biological analogy fit culture uncomfortably, or not at all, and were troubled by the possibility that genetic comparisons could subject our understanding of culture to a model of deterministic progress precluding multiplicity, simultaneity, and variety. Tony Sampson describes the pitfalls plaguing the field of memetics in particularly persuasive terms:

> Memetics treats social encounter as the passive passing on of a competing idea. By attributing this level of intentionality to the fidelity, fecundity, and longevity of the meme itself, the theory crudely consigns the by and large unconscious transmission of attitudes, expectancies, beliefs, compliance, imagination, attention, concentration, and distraction through social collectives to an insentient surrender to a self-seeking code.[79]

I join Sampson in searching for a more flexible means of understanding cultural and artistic contagion. Memetics is as illuminating for its limitations as for the revelations it has produced.

Yet memetics, for all its logical constraints, has persisted into popular discourse, holding double significance as a model for understanding contagious consumerism, and as a tool for propagating radical, often anticapitalist politics. Viral marketers attempt to sell products—and affective identities linked to those products—through the proliferation of memes, while activists create political memes to spread subversive slogans. The meme's contested meaning, its capacity to serve both Wall Street and Occupy Wall Street, demonstrates how viral transmission operates in multiple and contradictory ways, opening questions about the politics of transmission itself.

Many of the artists described in this book probe precisely these contradictions and tensions, which continued to evolve simultaneously in scholarly and popular writing and in art-making. In 1994, novelist and media scholar Douglas Rushkoff's study *Media Virus!* heralded the advent of a radical new media culture, fueled by the viral spread of images, ideas, and gestures, which—he argued—were disseminated through the newly democratic communications networks that new technologies made possible. Yet, only five years later, Rushkoff published a follow-up study, *Coercion*, lamenting the speedy corporate adoption of viral tactics. In 2001, Malcolm Gladwell's bestseller *The Tipping Point* offered an epidemiological approach to understanding the dissemination of social habits and culture, from crime to fashion. In 2009, Bill Wasik's *And Then There's This: How Stories Live and Die in Viral Culture* surveyed what Wasik described as a new landscape of media-savvy, semi-amateur creators of culture—reporters, video bloggers, musicians—who attracted brief, dramatic spikes of popular attention before vanishing from public view. "The 'viral,' whether e-mail or website or song or video, was gradually emerging as a new genre of communication, even of art," he wrote, adding, "A marginal genre only a few years ago, the intentional viral has become central as this decade malingers on."[80]

Wasik's book not only described viral phenomena he had observed, but also detailed his own efforts to provoke a viral phenomenon: the "flash mob" series he engineered in the summer of 2003, sending cryptic, anonymous emails to groups of acquaintances, intended to produce a contagiously popular gathering. During that summer, Wasik organized mobs at the Grand Hyatt Hotel on Forty-Second Street, in Macy's rug department, and in Central Park. In each case, an anonymous email, passed along by increasingly eager recipients, advertised the event, and a large group of strangers converged upon Wasik's location at an appointed time. Frequently, he assigned participants to perform a single action—arranging themselves around the railing of a hotel lobby mezzanine, then applauding for precisely fifteen seconds; bowing to a giant toy *Tyrannosaurus rex* in the Times Square Toys"R"Us—before disbanding and disappearing back into the streets. (I participated in the Grand Hyatt mob, responding to an anonymous email passed along by a friend.) By the end of the summer, flash mobs were everywhere. In an electronics store in Minnesota, which happened to be playing *The Lord of the Rings* on display televisions, a flash mob gathered and collectively requested popcorn.[81] In London, hundreds of people performed odd ritual movements, brandishing umbrellas and bananas, near the London Eye. In Toronto, a group of about fifty people hopped up and down "like frogs" in a Toys"R"Us store, then performed jumping jacks in a gym.[82] In Moscow, a flash mob gathered on the steps of the Bolshoi Theater, perused newspapers for several minutes, then dispersed on cue.[83] Wasik's flash mobs—mass performances minus the historical narratives and political aspirations of early twentieth-century spectacles—demonstrated a belated revival of interest in crowd thinking and crowd behavior. They hinted at the format of the political demonstration without actually demonstrating, and gestured toward contagious consumption while rarely consuming much.

In the years that followed, scholars, pop-culture writers, and marketers continued working to reverse-engineer viral popularity. In 2013, Karine Nahon and Jeff Hemsley published *Going Viral*, an attempt to analyze the process of twenty-first-century flash popularity in detail. That same year,

Jonah Berger published *Contagious: Why Things Catch On*, which, like Gladwell's and Wasik's studies, sought to dissect the evolution of contagious cultural phenomena in order to help others construct them. Viral popularity had become an elusive but heavily sought-after phenomenon, its unpredictable nature imbuing anything that successfully "goes viral" with a sense of authenticity and truly widespread appeal.

This book is not about viral marketing, or about memetics, popular YouTube videos, or brief, violent Twitter storms. Yet the discourse around contagion and virality that emerged over the last decades of the twentieth century and the early years of the twenty-first reveals much about the shadow these concepts cast in theater and performance of the period. The ubiquitous urge to "go viral" testifies to the mysterious potency still held by the concept of cultural contagion, a power glimpsed not only in what might be considered "successful" viral phenomena, but more broadly and perhaps more significantly in the sheer volume of writing on the subject, the effort fueling our continued, largely futile struggle to understand popular viral phenomena (whether political, cultural, artistic, or consumerist) and to create them. The artists described in the chapters that follow do not, largely, seek to control viral phenomena, and do not view contagion as a linear, unidirectional force. Rather, they explore the politics and theatricality of contagion, the viral possibilities inherent to their art form.

Affect and Emancipation: Theories of Spectatorship and Transmission

Viral thinkers, whether philosophers or marketing gurus, hold in common the belief that in social gatherings, something spreads. For many contemporary philosophers, this contagious force is both impossible to isolate from its channels of transmission, and also resistant to linear models of change over time. Yet it is, nevertheless, palpably present, and essential to understanding the social circulation of ideas, feelings, and behaviors. In this section, I describe a succession of overlapping theories of contagion—all testifying to the viral's increasingly important role in our assumptions about social transmission—and then connect these ideas with models of audience response and participation particular to theater.

Even as Dawkins and his fellow travelers were developing the field of memetics, Gilles Deleuze and Félix Guattari were dismantling such models of evolution in their philosophy, placing contagion in direct opposition to heredity as a model for understanding change. The philosophers declared, in *A Thousand Plateaus*:

> Bands, human or animal, proliferate by contagion, epidemics, battlefields, and catastrophes . . . Propagation by epidemic, by contagion,

> has nothing to do with filiation by heredity, even if the two themes intermingle and require each other. The vampire does not filiate, it infects. The difference is that contagion, epidemic, involves terms that are entirely heterogeneous: for example, a human being, an animal, and a bacterium, a virus, a molecule, a microorganism.[84]

For Deleuze and Guattari, contagion offers a way out, a way around restrictive linear models of growth, change, and evolution. Its primary characteristic is less the involuntary nature of spread, and more its power to connect beings who are fundamentally different, and who do not need to become the same in order to participate in transmission and circulation. This includes, in their famous example, the wasp and orchid, who "become" each other—forming what the philosophers call an assemblage—without becoming the same as one another. In the case studies examined here, this model of heterogeneous transmission applies, most directly, to the relationship between actors and spectators, who transmit affects and behaviors to one another without necessarily erasing the distinction between them.

The philosophers' assemblage theory, with its focus on fluid relationships, heterogeneity, and constant flux, has offered an important model for later thinkers of viral and contagious transmission. In Sampson's *Virality*, assemblage is foundational for a flexible understanding of contagion: for viewing contagion as an element of both power and subversion, political systems and the resistance to them. Such flexible modes of thinking are important for the types of contagion explored by makers of viral art. The contagious image or gesture, in viral performance, is rarely transmitted in literal or linear terms (although some projects, especially those by Critical Art Ensemble and Eva and Franco Mattes, explicitly critique the perniciously unidirectional contagions that viral media and infectious paranoia can promote). Rather, virality takes complex shapes: finding form as imitation with repetition (as in *Seven Jewish Children*), dissemination through networks (as in *365 Days/365 Plays*), and repeated mass choreography (as in the work of General Idea).

Or, as in the Living Theatre's *Mysteries* and *Paradise Now*, contagion finds form through the spread of historically and culturally specific affective states. Affect theory, emerging in the 1990s after psychologist Silvan Tomkins's *Affect Imagery Consciousness*, took up the question of contagion as part of a larger investigation of affective circulation. For some, contagion became a primary model for understanding emotional transfer: "Bodies can catch feelings as easily as catch fire: affect leaps from one body to another, evoking tenderness, inciting shame, igniting rage, exciting fear—in short, communicable affect can inflame nerves and muscles in a conflagration of every conceivable kind of passion," wrote Anna Gibbs in 2001.[85] In 2004 Teresa Brennan argued for a broad, and bodily, understanding of affective spread, asserting that

> The transmission of affect, whether it is grief, anxiety, or anger, is social or psychological in origin. But the transmission is also responsible for bodily changes; some are brief changes, as in a whiff of the room's atmosphere, some longer lasting . . . The "atmosphere" or the environment literally gets into the individual.[86]

Brennan's work, one of the most significant and thorough investigations of affective circulation, views transmission in broader and more complex terms than a literal or mimetic understanding of contagion would allow.

Other thinkers, likewise advocating for variety and complexity, have argued directly against contagion as a model for affect. Sara Ahmed, in *The Cultural Politics of Emotion*, distinguishes between her own account of emotional circulation, and the school of affect theory that views feelings as explicitly contagious:

> In this model, it is the emotion itself that passes: I feel sad, because you feel sad; I am ashamed by your shame, and so on. In suggesting that emotions pass in this way, the model of "emotional contagion" risks transforming emotion into a property, as something that one has, and can then pass on, as if what passes on is the same thing.[87]

For Ahmed, "what passes on" is rarely contained or stable, rarely a "thing" that reaches a recipient in the same form it left the sender. The same is true for the majority of artists described in this book. The circulation of affects, emotions, and passions is central to viral dramaturgy, from the Living Theatre's efforts to transmit revolutionary ecstasy to the feelings of communal connection inspired by *365 Days/365 Plays*. The artists in this book imagine affective circulation in complex terms, viewing contagion as a primary model for cultural and artistic spread. In doing so, they reimagine contagion into a richer, more complex means of thinking about transmission than it has sometimes been presumed to be.

This is, among other reasons, why I employ concepts of affective transmission in combination with theories of theatrical spectatorship and public participation, ideas about the particular ways emotions spread, transform, and provoke action among audiences. Many of the projects described in this book address themselves, directly or indirectly, not only to live audiences but to wide, dispersed publics, and so I draw on Michael Warner's 2002 *Publics and Counterpublics* for insight about the nature of public speech. Foundational to Warner's book is the belief that publics are not necessarily generalized and all-encompassing, but rather, can constitute particular audiences and readerships summoned up by the nature of a work of literature or art. "*The* public is a kind of social totality," Warner writes. On the other hand, the form of "public" he theorizes is "the kind of public that comes into being only in relation to texts and their circulation."[88]

This, too, is the kind of public I examine: the kind that performances call into being, the kind that artists ask participation of, and the kind that responds, both in ways that creators invite and in ways that are unanticipated or unintended. Contagious artworks are, usually, inherently intended for wide and continuing distribution, aiming to reach broad publics, and to expand those publics as they circulate. The reliance of viral media on the viewers, listeners, or consumers who disseminate it aligns with Warner's idea of a public that is created by attention (and, frequently, by active response). A viral public, as I see it, is a public created not only by attending to a particular work of art, but also by engaging in some way with its spread.

This engagement is always politically fraught. The viral imagination can—under the long shadow of philosophy that views contagion as an involuntary mode of transmission—risk eliminating individuality and choice from its understanding of spectatorship. So, too, can creators of viral art risk equating participation with political action, a stance famously dismantled by Jacques Rancière in his 2009 essay "The Emancipated Spectator." Much of modern theater, Rancière writes, especially political artists working in the wake of Brecht and Artaud, is constructed on a series of faulty assumptions: that spectatorship is equivalent with passivity; that only by eliminating traditional notions of "audience" can theater avoid perpetuating nefarious social relations (such as the alienation that Guy Debord decried in *Society of the Spectacle*, an extension of the passivity and separation induced by traditional spectatorship).

Artists who have made this critique, Rancière writes, often believe, further, that live performance alone (as opposed to film, television, or other media) brings audiences together as a communal entity, and therefore that live performance alone has the power and the obligation to rouse spectators to action. "Theatre accuses itself of rendering spectators passive and thereby betraying its essence as community action," writes Rancière. "It consequently assigns itself the mission of reversing its effects and expiating its sins by restoring to spectators ownership of their consciousness and their activity."[89] He argues for a reconsideration of the distinction between passive spectatorship and active participation and advocates for the identification of members of live audiences as intellectually engaged individuals. "Being a spectator is not some passive condition that we should transform into activity," he writes. "It is our normal situation."[90]

These indictments of the false binary between action and observation, passivity and participation, illuminate the work of many of the artists described in this book, most of whom have labored under the sign of Brecht, Artaud, or both: the Living Theatre, attempting to rouse spectators to revolutionary action; Marc Estrin, seeking to go "beyond audience"; and Augusto Boal, striving to turn spectators into "spect-actors." Yet, though such artists attempt to provoke participation, my argument here is not that viral performance falls into the trap of unthinking allegiance to participation as political salvation—but, rather, that viral dramaturgies hold productive dialogue with Rancière's terms. Many viral dramaturgies invite the active engagement of spectators, and many also address their audiences collectively, in the form of gathered crowds. In this sense, viral performance might be considered the limit case of the fallacy that Rancière describes. And yet viral performance also, almost always, creates the possibility for spectators (or spect-actors) to respond as individuals. Critical Art Ensemble hopes to change individuals' assumptions about contemporary sources of political anxiety one viewer at a time—as did Boal, who believed that mass participation could never have the deep political effect that engaging with a single spectator could. Eva and Franco Mattes work to instill small seeds of doubt in their spectators' minds, hoping that audiences will become skeptical of even the Matteses' own performances. *Seven Jewish Children* went viral as individuals rewrote Churchill's contagiously provocative script, displaying individual beliefs as they did.

Not only do viral dramaturgies challenge the distinction between active and passive forms of participation; they also challenge distinctions between participatory and non-participatory performances. In her 2012 study *Artificial Hells*, Claire Bishop offers an analysis of socially engaged participatory art that is guided by the idea that participation means "people constitute the central artistic medium and material." Bishop investigates, specifically, works of art dedicated to "the creative rewards of participation as a politicised working process."[91] These concepts are frequently at play in the projects I examine in this book, since many of the artists who make viral performance view some form of active audience engagement as the link between art and social change, understanding theater either as a microcosm for a larger public arena (in the case of the Living Theatre) or as a provocative rift in the fabric of public life (in the case of Eva and Franco Mattes). Yet other projects—for instance, Suzan-Lori Parks's *365 Days/365 Plays*—embody social formations more obliquely, engaging with community politics through their producing strategies without demanding direct audience participation on stage. Viral performance thus represents, at once, a kind of limit case for audience participation, and a broader, conceptual dramaturgy: a set of ideas that can guide the producing strategies, thematic concerns, and politics of theatrical projects, without requiring that audiences leave their seats.

Case Studies

The chapters in this book, although unfolding chronologically from the mid-1960s to the early twenty-first century, are also organized by dramaturgical affinity, linking artists and works that deploy the concept of viral performance in (sometimes unexpectedly) similar ways. I will, in some cases, be tracing lines of influence: from Artaud to the Living Theatre, for instance, or from the Living Theatre to Critical Art Ensemble. In other cases, no such direct artistic dialogue exists, yet the viral dramaturgies in question emerged at similar times, and found similar significance in the possibility of contagious performance. Such is the case with, for instance, the artists described in chapter 2: General Idea, Marc Estrin, and Augusto Boal. All of these artists, I argue, conceived of themselves in viral terms, seeking to choreograph audiences in the absence of performers, yet none of them worked, to my knowledge, with an awareness of the others' artistic practice. In such cases, I argue, the emergence of similar dramaturgies at similar historical moments testifies to the continued potency of the viral concept, particularly for artists creating politically radical performance that is often in dialogue with new forms of media.

Chapter 1, "Performing Plague," examines the Living Theatre's revolutionary performance works of the mid- and late 1960s through the lens of one of the company's central influences, Antonin Artaud. Artaud's writings, and especially his famous essay "The Theater and the Plague," proved profoundly transformative for the Living Theatre. I parse the underlying questions of affective transmission and media circulation that undergird the theatrical strategies of both. This chapter employs affect theory and related concepts of historically specific emotion—Raymond Williams's "structures of feeling"—to reexamine the company's use of Artaud's plague as a model for acting, and examines closely (and, to my knowledge, for the first time) the Dilexi Series's 1969 televising of "The Rite of Guerilla Theatre," an infamous sequence from *Paradise Now*.

In the 1970s, a constellation of artists drew on their experiences with radical 1960s performance and the emerging field of media studies to create viral performances that relied not on overwhelming presence (as Artaud and the Living Theatre did) but on absence, invisibility, and the carefully orchestrated actions of spectators. Chapter 2, "Towards an Audience Vocabulary," examines the work of the American artist Marc Estrin, who coined the concept of "infiltrative theater"; Augusto Boal, who created invisible theater as a means of prompting spectators to engage in social change; and General Idea, a Canadian-American artistic trio who self-identified as a viral force within the art world, creating queer, media-savvy performances structured around the contagious choreography of their spectators. These artists drew on contemporary ideas about circulation and transmission to stage politically subversive performances that invoked the participation of spectators in making theatrical gestures spread.

Chapter 3, "Germ Theater," brings my argument about the viral into the dawning digital age—beginning with a moment in the early 1990s when concepts of contagious spread acquired a host of new meanings, from runaway capitalism to newly instantaneous information transfer to the anxieties of biological contagion wrought by the HIV/AIDS crisis. The works in this chapter combine viral performance strategies with thematic explorations of contagion, virality, and contamination. They include Critical Art Ensemble's and Eva and Franco Mattes's playfully subversive provocations; and German director Christoph Schlingensief's 2000 *Please Love Austria!*, which confronted the Viennese public with its own paranoia through the intertwining of live performance, new media, and social action. The performance projects described here frequently take the form of large-scale public fictions: theatrical sleights-of-hand staged in public places and borrowing narratives or performance strategies from the institutions they seek to criticize—megacorporations, militaries, the mass media.

Chapter 4, "Everything Is Everywhere," examines a series of twenty-first-century performance projects created by women artists, each of which summoned into being a dispersed, virtually linked network of theaters and theater-makers: the 2003 Lysistrata Project, Suzan-Lori Parks's 2006–7 *365 Days/365 Plays*, and Caryl Churchill's *Seven Jewish Children*. These networks—which relied, I argue, on conceptions of digital-age viral dissemination for their inspiration and their spread—were envisioned as structures for making theater radically inclusive, or for political intervention in protest of violence and war. In dialogue with these projects' decentralized, dispersed performance structures were the material experiences of local performances, with artists' bodies at their centers. These performance projects registered the intimate connections between networked structures and the viral, and demonstrated the political potency of theatrical networks.

In my conclusion, I return to the virus's origin: a stage, an audience, a performance fiction ruptured in real time. Joanna Warsza's 2006 piece "Virus in the Theater" employed a pair of performance artists to disrupt (or "virus") a conventional play, stepping onstage to stop the action and announcing their intentions to act on behalf of the audience. This performance testifies to the continued significance of the viral metaphor, not just in performance but also in the theater itself. "Virus in the Theater" offers a glimpse of the viral's evolving importance for theater, politics, and media, and, in looking back, also looks forward to a moment when the viral might leave the digital world behind, but continue to invade the theater.

Chapter 1

✦

Performing Plague

The Living Theatre and Antonin Artaud

Partway down the San Francisco–based television station KQED's list of scheduled broadcasts for the year 1969, an unusual item appears. Among works by dance, video, and visual artists to be aired as part of an ongoing project called the Dilexi Series, KQED reports broadcasting a segment entitled "Rite of Guerrilla Theater," with Julian Beck and the Living Theatre listed as its creators. This twenty-five-minute program, which aired on May 28, 1969, depicted an "orientation of the audience," performed by the avant-garde theater troupe in an auditorium at Mills College in Oakland, California. The Living Theatre would accomplish this in three steps: by first "infiltrating [the audience], then imparting some '60s wisdom, then requesting participation from the gathered hordes."[1]

The Rite of Guerilla Theatre was, even then, legendary. This sequence of events comprised the opening moments of *Paradise Now*, the Living Theatre's late 1960s ritualistic spectacle, which was intended to launch a nonviolent, anarchist-pacifist revolution through the power of ecstatic audience participation. Mills College was one of dozens of universities, community institutions, and theaters to host the Living Theatre during their tour, and the audience of undergraduates and community members there was representative of the spectators who gathered to watch, cheer, join, scorn, and protest *Paradise Now* across the United States and Europe. What was different, here, was the medium. The Living Theatre would not only perform live for the audience at Mills College: their performance would be broadcast—and was shaped to be broadcast—for television spectators following along at home.

The Living Theatre's choice to stage their Rite for broadcast is striking because it appeared, initially, to contradict many of *Paradise Now*'s central artistic principles, and to undermine the company's expressed attitudes about the politics of media in general and of television in particular. In the early 1970s, Julian Beck objected strenuously to the mode of attention that he believed small screens inevitably encourage. "It always makes the people weak," he wrote of television, adding, "It takes away their power, it always makes them passive spectator [*sic*], it never takes them to another life, another perception, dots and all, cool aspects and all, it diminishes awareness."[2] *Paradise Now*, perhaps more than any other piece the Living Theatre had made, engaged the power of intensive live presence, close confrontation, and bodily contact between performers and spectators. How could the aims of the Rite of Guerilla Theatre—a scene designed particularly to heighten spectators' awareness of unseen restrictions all around them—be communicated through the barrier of a television screen? How could the Rite summon and choreograph audience emotion, as it aimed to do, without the benefit of bodily presence? Would its dispersed audience be inspired to join the revolution, or simply to change the channel?

Yet the Living Theatre repeatedly engaged with television broadcasting as a medium for their work during these years. In May 1968, while *Paradise Now* was in rehearsal, Judith Malina, Beck, and Carl Einhorn traveled to Paris with plans to film a television special for the French state television company ORTF. The program, Malina noted in her diary, would feature improvised outdoor performances: "it was being called street theatre, but among ourselves we referred to it as guerilla theatre," she wrote. (The TV special was never filmed, in the end, due to the student and worker protests that engulfed Paris that month.)[3] In 1969, the company filmed the "Plague" sequence from *Mysteries and Smaller Pieces* for a California television broadcast. On the same day, they staged the Rite of Guerilla Theatre for producers Jim Newman and John Coney of the Dilexi Series, shaping a resolutely live creation into a half-hour piece for a television audience.

I open with this interlude from the Living Theatre's famous tour, and analyze the KQED broadcast later in this chapter, as a way of entering a conversation about the Living Theatre's philosophy of contagious art and its relationship to radical political action. Such philosophies were transformative, not only for the Living Theatre, but for radical performance and its audiences for decades to come. During the mid- and late 1960s—an era when radical social change through widespread participation seemed increasingly imminent in both the United States and many parts of Europe—the company offered a template for the mobilization of spectators, participants, and publics that generations of countercultural artists would revive and renegotiate. This model of contagious revolutionary performance took shape through the careful orchestration of audiences' emotional and affective responses to radical theater, and such strategic engagements with spectators' emotions emerged especially clearly in the Dilexi broadcast's filmed staging. Mediation demanded that the artists clarify and condense their approach to working with live spectators. It also—like the use of stage fictions in *Mysteries*' Plague scene, as I will detail shortly—created productive distance between revolutionary performance and the real revolution: a gap that allowed spectators to inhabit roles as performers, and that allowed emotion to more readily circulate.

The Dilexi broadcast also brings into focus the Living Theatre's role in this book. The company's work represents the least overtly mediated approach to theatrical contagion of any artist, in any chapter. Yet the company also set the tone, in fundamental ways, for most of the case studies to come. In translating Artaud's philosophies into stage action, they created a vision of theatrical contagion that was both emotional and bodily, but which defied, as Artaud did, easy equations between biological transmission and artistic dissemination. The company offers a reminder that even as viral performance has become more closely identified with the cultures of media and technology, the body has remained ever-present, in complex ways. So, too, does their exploration of viral emotion predict other artists' experiments with contagious affect, in a variety of different emotional registers. For the Living Theatre, the emotions and affects onstage included ecstasy, rage, and confusion; for later artists discussed in later chapters, they included fear, anxiety, or joy. Finally, the broadcast, because it shows the Living Theatre teaching their spectators to perform—offering a lesson in viral acting—also registers viral dramaturgy's propensity to influence other artists as much as, and sometimes more than, its spectators.

The Living Theatre sought to construct theatrical scenarios so irresistibly open to audience participation that spectators would not only join in the action but would also spread it outside the theater and into the public at large. Yet contagious performance, for the company, was never a matter of straightforward emotional transfer, of evoking the same emotions in spectators that the actors themselves were portraying. Rather, in pieces such as *Mysteries* (1964) and *Paradise Now* (1968) the company employed passions, affects, and emotions in strategically layered ways, summoning feelings in their audience members that captured, in condensed form, the larger emotional tensions of the era's radical politics. Taken together, these two performance pieces, and the emotionally complex forms of audience participation they summoned, offer a road map, of sorts, to the emotional landscape of late-1960s revolutionary change.

The relationship of feeling and emotion to radical social change was being widely theorized during this period: by American artists and philosophers, and perhaps most directly by the writers and artists associated with French situationism. Situationist writings—which emerged before and during the period that saw both the Paris uprising of May 1968 and the creation of *Paradise Now*—explored the connections between the individual internal landscape and larger psychological geographies of power. In situationist philosophy, as well as in the overlapping, burgeoning field of the philosophy of everyday life, the literary scholar Rita Felski explains, "the everyday is seen to harbor inchoate impulses and unconscious desires that foreshadow an incandescent future of revolutionary upheaval."[4] Shifting, half-formed affective states can thus lead—not directly, but in associative and contradictory ways—to revolutionary action. In an unpublished collection of writings entitled "Messages,"

Beck and Malina likewise situated the impetus toward large-scale revolutionary change not in knowledge but in emotion. They wrote:

> The Historic Process. Marx. That's what we're in. To find out where you're at in the midst of the Historic Process. To observe it. Then to decide what to do about it . . . But Intellectual Awareness is not enough. It is necessary to decide what to do *guided and impelled by feeling*.[5]

To be guided and impelled by feeling, Beck and Malina knew, was a theatrically and politically complicated matter, made more complicated by the shifting spectrum of sensations that comprise what we call "feeling" and "emotion," and by the unstable relationship between onstage emotions and those felt by spectators.

Scholarship theorizing affect and emotion—by writers such as Philip Fisher, Raymond Williams, Sara Ahmed, and Sianne Ngai—thus provides useful context for understanding the Living Theatre's theatrical project. In his 2002 study *The Vehement Passions*, Fisher describes the networks of vocabulary that are commonly marshaled to describe inner states, noting that each of these terms is politically and socially charged. "The feelings, the affections, the sentiments, and the passions are not alternative ways of talking about the same matters but language used in the service of quite distinct politics of the inner life," he writes. These varying concepts, in different ways, "participate in the communal act of installing and defending one or another design within psychological life."[6] Both *Mysteries* and *Paradise Now* took part in such communal acts, staging and reflecting the emotional landscapes of radical political action in their moment. Each piece, in different ways, evoked the emotional pitfalls pockmarking the fields of radical action, circled the cul-de-sacs of emotional epiphany and affective confusion, and tested for emotional pathways toward political change.

Both Artaud and the Living Theatre relied, in their conceptions of contagious performance, on the prospect of eliciting profound emotional responses in their spectators through strategic acting choices, and on the possibility that those responses would propel spectators to action. "Communication"—the concept, and the word itself—recurs repeatedly in the writings of both. Yet, though both had viral visions, neither conceptualized emotional communication in performance as a simple or straightforward transfer. In this book's introduction, I cite Sara Ahmed's important observation that affective transmission is far more complex and multifarious than a linear or mimetic model of contagion would allow (though I persist in seeing contagion as an important term for understanding such circulation). For Ahmed, emotions, feelings, and affects mutate as they spread, calling up other emotions, feelings, and affects in those perceiving them. The same was true for the artists described in this chapter.

In the Living Theatre's rehearsal rooms, particularly in the months when they were creating, and then touring and performing *Paradise Now*, they returned regularly to conversations about the particular types of emotional expression and affective response that would attend the mode of revolutionary action they sought. They parsed the significance and the efficacy of ecstasy, passion, and anger. They canvassed the repercussions of evoking in spectators smaller, less obviously transformative feelings like passivity and scorn. Drawing on Artaud, they returned repeatedly to the idea of pain—physical and emotional—as the source of the actor's emotions onstage. Drawing on Marx, they envisioned themselves as caught in, and promoting, a particular kind of historical change through the performance and summoning of emotion. *Mysteries* forged connections between vehement passion and collective action, while *Paradise Now* staged the gulf between performances of revolutionary rage or ecstasy, and the materialization of real-world change. This disjuncture is especially significant, both because it reveals the complexities of emotional contagion onstage, and because it is the source of many critiques of the Living Theatre, past and present—critiques that I rethink here.

Such emotional and artistic disjunctures were not the Living Theatre's alone, but characterized the contradictions at the center of radical political performance. In the introduction to his 1971 edited collection *Guerrilla Street Theater*, Henry Lesnick critiqued the prevalence of performance acts that participated in the visual and emotional discourse of social change, without actually creating that change:

> The politics of put on, of play, has an undeniable appeal for everyone whose primary experience of the contradictions of society is one of boredom and a sense of stultification. Their weakness is obvious. They have no strategy for effecting change (they were doomed once they failed to levitate the Pentagon), and consequently offer no program that addresses itself to the basic needs of the great majority of people. This weakness is behind the Cleaver faction of the Panthers' recent split with the Yippies. Urinating on the Justice Department may be both gratifying and eloquent, but it doesn't generate the kind of struggle necessary to obtain decent housing or jobs or to get rid of dope pushers.[7]

For Lesnick, the actions of groups like the Yippies, no matter how thrilling, were emblems, depictions, or portraits of revolutionary change. They were not the change itself. Even more so performances like *Mysteries* and *Paradise Now*, which took place in theaters, on stages, using actors in roles and testing, but not fully eliminating, the boundaries of stage fiction. This aspect of the pieces, particularly of *Paradise Now*, has frequently been disparaged as a theatrical misfire, a misunderstanding of the relationship between theatrical fiction and radical real-world action. I view it somewhat differently, seeing the Living Theatre's choices, rather, as a direct expression of the emotional problems inherently embedded in performing revolution, and as a strategic use of theatrical contagion as a form of acting.

Concepts of contagion did not emerge for the Living Theatre in a vacuum. Instead, in conceptualizing their performances of contagious revolution, the company drew on Artaud's ideas about the transformative powers of theatrical action, and particularly his foundational essay about the theater and the plague. The Plague scene from *Mysteries*, as well as, more broadly, the Living Theatre's approach to audience interaction in *Paradise Now*, remain in many ways some of the clearest and most direct attempts by any artist or artistic group to find theatrical form for Artaud's writings about the contagious nature of performance. Aspects of the Living Theatre's Artaudian project are known: that the company intended to stage the infamous plague; that they viewed it as a necessary means of provoking revolutionary action among their spectators; that, to them, Artaud's radical voice aligned with, and served as endorsement for, nonviolent anarchist-pacifist revolution. Known, too, is how deeply the company's attachment to Artaud was based on a misapprehension of the French writer's own politics. In *Artaud and His Doubles*, Jannarone describes the Living Theatre as a particularly prominent example of the artistic impulse to appropriate Artaud's ideas for non-Artaudian political and theatrical ends; the company, she also notes, long monopolized the conversation over Artaud's artistic legacy in the United States. "They interpreted Artaud's cosmic rage as a call to revolution against the coercive effects of government, repressive society, and personal inhibitions," she writes.[8] Jannarone's study, in particular, is an important corrective to the temptation to take the Living Theatre at their word in their use of Artaud. *Artaud and His Doubles* powerfully demonstrates how wide the gulf really was between the anarchist-pacifist revolution that Beck and Malina sought to provoke, and the deeply violent, quasi-fascist ideology underlying Artaud's writings.

Consciousness of this tension also propels, implicitly or overtly, many of the most prevalent critiques that were received by the Living Theatre during their tour of *Paradise Now*, and that have been aimed at them since. These critiques imply, frequently, that the company's Artaud-inspired works were not really Artaudian—and also that they were too Artaudian, that by drawing on the French writer's theatrical ideas they also inadvertently embodied his reactionary political beliefs.[9] Robert Brustein, Jannarone notes, thought *Paradise Now* "overwhelmed the spectator in a manipulative, Wagnerian way," and that "the 'freedom' with which audiences sometimes responded represented repressive chaos and not the beautiful liberation the Living thought it did."[10] Such criticisms, familiar by now, argue that beneath the Living Theatre's calls for freedom lay dictatorial coercion; that the language of beautiful nonviolent anarchism was fundamentally incompatible with the vocalizations of hostility and irrepressible wrath they sometimes offered onstage; that the plague was not what the Living Theatre imagined it to be.

Performers and spectators during a performance of the Living Theatre's *Paradise Now*. Photo courtesy of Thomas S. Walker, Living Theatre Archivist, and the Yale Collection of American Literature, Beinecke Rare Book and Manuscript Library, Yale University.

But audience members were not always overwhelmed, nor were they automatically manipulated. Rather, the Living Theatre's contagious performances summoned a spectrum of audience emotion, resulting in a spectrum of audience behavior. What I aim to articulate here is how the plague manifested onstage: what it meant for actors, in stage directions, in a scripted play in a theater. Because, despite the rhetoric of *Paradise Now* as a "real" protest action, revolution, or historical-communal event—a description of the piece promoted by the company, a description both inaccurate and sincere—*Paradise Now* was, above all, a play. I view the company's use of Artaud as a set of strategic acting choices, a way of theorizing the ensemble's performance of revolutionary affect and emotion, and capturing, in the relationship between performer and spectator, the particular affective mode of their own revolutionary moment. Rather than parsing the "real-world" effects of *Paradise Now*—rather than seeking out the revolution that wasn't, a term of measurement implicitly present in many critiques of the piece—I examine here the theatrical particularities of performing plague. I attempt to trace the company's use of Artaud's concept to find an acting vocabulary for staging revolution, and to create and recruit more actors who would do the same.

Viewing the Living Theatre's works of the mid- to late 1960s explicitly as acting exercises—grounded in (counterintuitively enough) modes of theatrical realism, and bounded by forms of fictive cosmos—offers an alternate means of understanding the striking emotional and affective provocations that *Mysteries* and *Paradise Now* represented. Central to nearly every account of the Plague scene from *Mysteries* and the Rite of Guerilla Theatre from *Paradise Now* (the scenes on which I center my analysis) is the question of how and why these performances called up feelings in their spectators—and how and why they failed to. In the case of *Mysteries*, audiences reportedly empathized so deeply with the company's enactment of Artaud's plague that they joined in the action, dying in heaps alongside the performers. During the Rite of Guerilla Theatre, by contrast, spectators witnessed performances of revolutionary rage, but frequently experienced feelings of theatrical frustration.

Understanding the Living Theatre's approach to contagion primarily in terms of an acting exercise removes the easy binary of failure and success from our historical understanding of them. It means that they were not "failures" for not having uncomplicatedly mobilized massive numbers of audience members to join their rituals onstage or to start the revolution offstage. It means, rather, that a significant part of the legacy of viral performance—like much avant-garde theater—includes works that are vastly ambitious in their quest for audience response, and whose primary influence is, ultimately, on other artists.

Although Artaud infused much of the Living Theatre's practice from 1958 onwards, I focus here on two scenes from the company's body of work: the Plague scene that ended *Mysteries*, and the Rite of Guerilla Theatre that began *Paradise Now*. These were the two scenes that, by most reports, lingered in audiences' minds and inspired them to respond—in excitement, sympathy, irritation, and confusion—and that garnered the attention of critics and reporters. They were, among other sequences, the sections of the Living Theatre's work that most made them targets for the police (in addition to the street procession concluding *Paradise Now*). Both scenes were deliberately intended to "communicate"—to spread charged action or emotion to spectators—and they represent twin poles of communication, the Plague scene regularly inspiring spectators to spontaneously join the action onstage, and the Rite of Guerilla Theatre instead provoking confusion, annoyance, and apathy. (In other words: one really was contagious, in an obvious sense, while the other was infamously not.)

There is also evidence suggesting that the company itself considered the two scenes paradigmatic of its larger revolutionary project, and separable from the works in which they first appeared, subject to reimagining and reuse. The Plague scene, after serving as the culminating action of *Mysteries*, reappeared on its own as a street theater protest piece. It surfaced in a May 1972 protest outside the ITT building in New York City, and as the first section of *Six Public Acts*, a prologue to the company's epic *Legacy of Cain* cycle, performed throughout the mid-1970s. Like the Rite of Guerilla Theatre, the Plague scene was also chosen for broadcast: on March 8, 1969, the same day they played the Rite for KQED, the company staged the Plague for another television broadcast in San Francisco.[11] Later that year, performing outdoors for a crowd of thousands in Toulouse, France, the company chose to show just three sequences: the Rite of Guerilla Theatre; the Plague scene; and the Toulouse sequence, the section of *Paradise Now* that was rewritten to address specific conditions in the city where the piece was currently being performed.[12]

Closely reading these elements of *Mysteries* and *Paradise Now*, before returning to the 1969 Dilexi broadcast, helps to frame the Living Theatre's vision for politically radical emotion in performance, and suggests the ways they imagined that emotion spreading. The transformation of Artaud's plague into revolutionary contagion was not so much a radical expectation layered on top of acting, directing, scenography, and audience participation. Rather, it was materially constructed out of those things. Beck and Malina not only aspired to staging Artaud's plague—they did stage the plague, beginning in the early 1960s and continuing in different forms for a decade or more.

The (Living) Theatre and the Plague: *Mysteries*' Audiences

Artaud was famously transformative for Malina and Beck, who first encountered his ideas in 1958, when Mary Caroline Richards was completing the first English translation of the essay collection *The Theater and Its Double*. Malina, when I interviewed her in person many decades after the fact, remembered experiencing an epiphany upon reading Artaud: "The moment we read it," she said of *The Theater and Its Double*, "we were overwhelmed with the reality that Artaud showed us, that theater is about the relationship of cruelty to art, of art to cruelty, of our political position and our dramatic position being equivalent."[13] Artaud's insistence that unraveling the modern human psyche was a prerequisite to reinventing society echoed in the Living Theatre's efforts to influence its audiences' spiritual lives, even as they evinced far more interest than he did in engaging with the realities of political struggle. To the Living Theatre, the theories of Artaud and the politics of anarchist revolution were unmistakably intertwined: "Artaud is political and who masks his politics misrepresents his theory," concluded Beck.[14]

The Living Theatre first staged Artaud's plague in the collaboratively created performance piece *Mysteries and Smaller Pieces*, rehearsed and performed during the early months of the company's multiyear European tour. *Mysteries* was a theatrical collage, sampling memorable scenes and images from the company's previous productions—*The Brig*'s harsh military choreography made several appearances—and combining them with new movement sequences and performances of poetry and ritual. (Some of these, in turn, became the seeds of sequences in *Paradise Now*.) But by far the most iconic scene from *Mysteries* was its final scene, inspired by the plague Artaud had envisioned thirty years earlier. In *Mysteries*, the plague unfolded as violent choreography. Members of the company dispersed themselves through the auditorium, then pretended to gruesomely expire in close proximity to the audience: writhing, suffering paroxysms, and collapsing, sometimes in spectators' laps. When all "life" among the acting company had been extinguished, two performers moved through the crowd, picking up the stiff bodies and stacking them in a pyramid onstage.

The Plague scene directly followed a sequence entitled "Sound and Movement, Called Lee's Piece,"[15] a movement exercise that would now be recognizable as a common rehearsal game. (It was not inspired by Artaud: Joseph Chaikin is credited with its creation, Lee Worley with teaching it to the company.) Sound and Movement did not take place within the framework of an overtly contagious model of acting, or within any fictive cosmos. Yet it too modeled a version of transfer, of communicability, of transmission of sound, gesture, and affect in performance that offers an instructive contrast with the Plague scene. Sound and Movement was an exercise in gestural and vocal free-association: a performer gestured, then "sent" that gesture to another performer in the room, who would transform the movement and send it to a third. Repeating this sequence, performers added sounds as instinct and inclination dictated, and altered their positions in the room according to the same principles. "The piece is about communication," the description of this scene concludes. "It unifies the community."[16]

It is difficult to know how effectively the Sound and Movement piece "unified the community," because accounts of *Mysteries* in performance focus almost exclusively on audience response to the scene that followed, which was also about communication: about the communication of deadly disease as a metaphor for the contagious circulation of communal pain. In the latter scene, though—the Plague scene—the Living Theatre actors inhabited a fictive cosmos, a world in which Artaud's plague manifests as a highly specific biological reality:

> Fever. Fatigue. Nausea. Blisters. Vomit. Gangrene. Congestion. Boils. Pus. Around the anus. In the armpits. The skin cracks. Gall bladder. Soft and pitted lungs. Chips of some unknown black substance . . . Hideous visions. Howling through the streets. The brain melts, shrinks, granulates to a sort of coal-black dust. Death everywhere.[17]

Following these instructions, the stage directions enjoin, "Each performer chooses his/her role and acts it out."[18] Such insistence on the specificity of acting choices suggests that fictional, interiorized acting was not just compatible, but in some ways was necessary for achieving the form of frenzied contagion the Living Theatre aspired to create. Straightforward transmission of sound and gesture was not contagious; highly specific, internally driven acting, based on fictional scenarios, was. And the Plague scene was perhaps the most straightforwardly contagious scene of any the Living Theatre created. Across Europe, as the company toured *Mysteries* to theaters, universities, community centers, and other public spaces, spectators were enthusiastically "infected" with the company's plague. Audiences performed illness, dying alongside the performers and joining them in the growing body pile onstage.

Saul Gottlieb, a friend and follower of the Living Theatre, recounted a succession of infectious responses to the scene as *Mysteries* toured Europe:

> The plague scene has had a most violent effect on audiences. Most people get out of their seats, mill about, laugh, cry, shout, touch the bodies of the actors, pull and push them, and even sometimes beat them. Some people die with the actors, and permit themselves to be put in the body-pile—in Brussels, fifty people took part in the scene. In Trieste the show was banned after one performance, which included the nude appearance of one actor for three seconds during the tableaux vivants, as well as the audience's refusal to leave the theatre on the orders of police while the plague-deaths were going on. It was also banned after the first performance in Vienna's elegant old Theater An Der Wien, when the fire department rang down the curtain in the middle of the scene because twenty Viennese student-actors had gone on stage to join the dying. In Rome, a fist-fight and general pandemonium broke out during the scene. Most recently, police in Venice had to stop a brawl between pro- and anti-*Mysteries* people in the audience.[19]

Judith Malina's diaries report vivid responses to the Plague scene in cities across Europe. During a 1969 performance of *Mysteries* in Besançon, France, spectators threw eggs and fruit at the performers as they lay in their "body pile," making the experience of playing dead, Malina wrote, very difficult, an endurance test involving "waiting for the crash and the splash and the pain."[20] (One actor, she noted, chose to smear his body with the raw egg, later receiving a charge of indecency from the French police.) Spectators thus did not always participate in the ways the Living Theatre hoped they would—they protested, scorned, threw things and tried to drown out the actors as often as they joined in with them—but they almost always participated.

The Plague scene's appeal was, likely, partially because of the scene's metaphorical availability and deliberate ambiguity. Though less explicitly tied to a vision for social change than the scenes of contagion that the company would develop for *Paradise Now*, the images of helpless corpses heaped onstage, and silent spectators looking on, suggested all sorts of political allegories. "In Europe," Malina told Richard Schechner, in a 1969 *TDR* interview, "it is always assumed to be Auschwitz or Hiroshima. Except in Vienna, where, of course, they thought it was a sex orgy."[21] "Here," Schechner replied, "nobody died with you because Americans don't really like to think of death." (Rather than joining the body pile onstage, he remarked, American audiences tended to spring up and attempt to comfort the "dying" performers—likewise creating a scene of mass participation, if less violently than European audiences did.) American spectators, too, saw a broad social commentary in the scene. In his essay on the Living Theatre's late 1960s tour, in which the company presented *Mysteries* alongside *Frankenstein*, *Antigone*, and *Paradise Now*, Richard Gilman pointed to the social implications of *Mysteries*' concluding gesture:

> The last piece of action, a long mimesis of our social despair and the horrors of our impersonality, in which members of the group "die" in agony at various points in the theater and are carried stiff and strangely remote by others in the company to be piled in a pyramid on stage, was solemn and affecting, and, what's more, a true theatrical action, a new one.[22]

Part of the scene's participatory ethos, then—part of what made it irresistibly catching—was that it could be Hiroshima in Brussels, the Holocaust in France, and the alienating angst of American politics in New York.

Philip Fisher's observations about the literary and philosophical significance of the passions—as distinct from affects, feelings, or emotions—are helpful in illuminating what was particular about the Plague scene. "Unlike the feelings, the affections, or the emotions, the passions are best described as thorough," Fisher writes. "They do not make up one part of a state of mind or a situation. Impassioned states seem to drive out every other form of attention or state of being."[23] Following this line of thought, and citing the philosophy of Stanley Cavell, Fisher further points out that the passions, perhaps alone among the various models of interior states, hold the power to radically disrupt the everyday states of being that contribute to social and political inertia: "it is in the moment of repudiating the hold of the ordinary and the everyday," argues Fisher, "that an impassioned state begins."[24] Impassioned states are states in which radical change becomes possible.

In the annals of physically and emotionally contagious performances, the Plague scene from *Mysteries* ranks among the most clearly and theatrically infectious. I propose that this is not only because of the scene's flexible stage fiction, but also because it was physically—to use Fisher's term—thorough. The scene asked performers and audience members to imagine a set of symptoms that were first and foremost physical, and through inhabiting such extreme physical states, to find a route to the most extreme emotional states, the passions. In exploring what he calls the "vehement passions," Fisher cites debates among philosophers on which of the classically recognized passions—for instance, terror and rage—were the most thorough, the most all-consuming. He quotes Lucretius's description of fear, which reads, in part:

> When the mind is excited by some more vehement apprehension, we see the whole soul feel in unison through all the limbs, sweats and paleness spread over the whole body, the tongue falter, the voice die away, a mist cover the eyes, the ears ring, the limbs sink under one; in short we often see men drop down from terror of mind . . .[25]

For my argument about the Living Theatre's work, it matters less whether terror or rage is the more vehement or all-encompassing passion, the passion that most completely takes possession of the one feeling it, forcing other forms of thought and sensation from consciousness. What matters is that such an account of fear, which roots the emotion in specific physical symptoms—in the weakening of the limbs and the misting of the eyes, in paleness and perspiration—closely resembles Artaud's description of the plague, which the Living Theatre drew upon as stage directions for the final scene of *Mysteries*. Fisher's study offers a reminder that the passions are forces of extremity, beyond everyday affect or emotion. "Only terror and other vehement states saturate the body as a whole and the soul or psyche as a whole," Fisher observes.[26]

The Plague scene was catching because it was grounded in physical saturation, in fictive but obsessively specific vehemence—which was to lead in turn to highly specific performances on the part of both actors and their audiences. Indeed, it wasn't only an exterior physical commitment to reenacting Artaud's plague that the Living Theatre looked for; they were seeking, in their company and in their spectators, emotional dedication as well. Describing the company's initial development of this scene, Malina and Beck explicated an approach to performing plague that sounds surprisingly reminiscent of Stanislavsky (or, in fact, the acting approaches of the American Method teachers Stella Adler and Lee Strasberg, who were among the faculty at the New School where Malina had studied):[27]

> BECK: We keep talking about the plague, for instance, as an exercise in locating the pain and watching the pain travel around the body, feeling it . . .
>
> MALINA: The first time we did it, it was just as intense [as in later public performances]. There were some people who didn't do it well and we worked with them . . . Mostly they were not finding specific enough pain or not taking it out far enough.[28]

In conclusion, Malina adds, the Living Theatre, which was then attracting a steady stream of would-be company members, sought only to recruit "a certain kind of person; that kind of person can do this dying."[29] In fact, as *Mysteries* toured, Beck, Malina, and their collaborators began to employ the scene as a barometer of sorts, measuring the readiness of the Living Theatre's audiences to join corporeally and emotionally in the stage action. "We have a test for them," Malina told Schechner. "We pick them up by the neck and ankles. If they're stiff, they get carried up [to the stage]; if they fold, then we put them down."[30]

Only those spectators who not only sympathized with the Living Theatre's broad theatrical and political goals, but also possessed the physical stamina and the rigorous emotional presence to enact the Living Theatre's scene on a moment's notice, were allowed to join in the action, as the pile of stiff "corpses" onstage grew and grew. In other words: philosophies of rigorous emotional and physical acting, inflected by, among other sources, Malina's training at the New School, lay beneath the apparent spontaneity of *Mysteries*' Plague scene. Acting theory fueled the company's performances and contributed to the Living Theatre's thinking about what performing the plague meant for them. The plague was not so much an uncontrollable force emanating from the company's commitment to revolutionary upheaval as it was a repeatedly rehearsed and carefully calibrated acting technique rooted in the physicality of the passions.

The plague not only predated *Paradise Now*, but also outlived it. Two instances from the Plague scene's later life suggest the continuing significance of the scene, and the theatrical principles on which it operated. On May 10, 1972, the Living Theatre took part in a public protest outside the International Telephone & Telegraph (ITT) building on Park Avenue in Manhattan, voicing outrage at numerous American actions: recently, President Nixon's escalation of the war in Vietnam, and more particularly, the role of ITT in abetting CIA action internationally. In her diaries, Malina noted that she was drawn to the protest particularly because it was organized with an eye to multiple layers of performance: "it is not a rally with speakers, but a 'die-in,' " she wrote, "a theatrical action in which both civil disobedience and dramatic action accompany the rallying and picketing."[31] Amid multiple forms of protest and street theater, including a play linking the production of Wonder Bread to the production of bombs, and the tape-recorded sound effects of shells and screaming, the Living Theatre performed the plague. This choice to perform an acting exercise, with an internalized fiction, registers, once again, the Living Theatre's prioritization of layered theatrical communication over straightforward political action. Meditating on the many forms of protest that erupted across the country that spring, Malina noted: "I don't ask, 'What does this *mean*.' It's perfectly clear to me what it means—what's not certain enough yet is what it communicates." She added: "This communication must get/is getting clearer and clearer."[32]

The Plague scene resurfaced again in 1975, this time as the first section of the company's piece *Six Public Acts*, a prologue to the company's larger work *The Legacy of Cain*. *Six Public Acts* premiered in Pittsburgh, as part of the company's multiyear exploration of the situation of workers, and was performed in numerous site-specific locations in other American cities as well as in multiple European countries, including Germany and Italy. The piece consisted of a preamble and six acts or "Houses," structured thematically around objects of protest—Money, War, Property, the State—and building toward the final "House of Love," in which, following a series of dialogues on the ways money, tradition, the state, and other external forces work to stifle love, the performers tied each other up with rope and waited for spectators to set them free.

By the time they staged *Six Public Acts*, the Living Theatre had weathered a significant identity shift, splitting into smaller collectives and dispersing internationally to pursue multiple, distinct goals—some of them artistic and others spiritual or political. And yet, even after such fundamental change, the Plague scene still figured as a central element of the company's theatrical approach to the performance of politics, spectatorship, and social change. During the piece's first section, titled the "House of Death," the company performed a reinvented version of the Plague scene. Performers and spectators gathered in front of a building chosen for its significance in promoting destructions of various kinds: the selected site could be "any company with heavy investments in the death culture (armaments, pollution, 3rd world exploitation, worker enslavement)."[33] At the University of Michigan, for instance, the performers selected the Engineering Building because "research is done here which has led to the development of Napalm and the electronic battlefield."[34] Once the company arrived at its location, while two designated "Shamans" described the building as a center of "death culture," the performers began enacting the plague. This was a formalized and carefully rehearsed procedure: as the script explains, "the people begin to dissolve from their procession tableau positions into a rapid (3 minute) plague death. When all are dead the six doctor-shamans rise and begin the building of the body pile."[35]

Even as the scene from *Mysteries* surfaced, in *Six Public Acts*, as part of a formalized, outdoor processional performance, accompanied by painted signs and timed to the ringing of gongs, the tug toward realistic acting of the plague itself persisted. In a series of rehearsal notes on the scene, from November 28, 1976, the directors[36] remind the company to locate and play the pain with attention to physical and emotional detail. "Everybody," the notes read, "please try to make sure your plague scene is based on a real awareness of your body and its death—don't play for effect—the risk of melodrama is that it's funny."[37] Street theater here was still compatible with an internalized vision of the plague. In fact, street theater required it.

While the Plague scene opened *Six Public Acts*, the piece concluded with a complementary sequence that likewise included participation and required performers to submit to collective physical restraint. This time, rather than stacking their bodies, as in the Plague scene, performers bound each other with ropes, continuing until the only remaining performer requested that a spectator take over and restrain him or her. Once tied up, the performers simply waited for spectators to take action and free them. "The liberation will begin," asserts the script with confidence, "eventually it will happen."[38] So important was it that the performers refrain from initiating any act toward their freedom that a separate typewritten reminder, signed by Julian Beck, asserts:

> The Act of Untying—at the end of the House of Love—is to be done by the public. It should NEVER be initiated by a member of the collective. It is for the public to do. It may mean that the actors/actresses wait 20 minutes or an hour+: but eventually THE PEOPLE will make the revolutionary choice—action—and they will do this without being led, without being shown how—the action, *the discovery*, the rush, belongs to them; and the whole play was made for that moment.[39]

In his study *The Theater Is in the Street*, Bradford Martin suggests that this final sequence in *Six Public Acts*—the House of Love—constituted the true culmination of the company's quest for spontaneous audience participation. "The Living Theatre's 1970s productions, such as *The Money Tower* and *Six Public Acts*, synthesized the company's long-standing aims to involve the audience, revitalize the form of theatrical events, and express political ideas through theater,"[40] he argues. Below a photo of *Six Public Acts*, he writes: "Fulfilling *Paradise*'s promise."[41]

Such an approach does much-needed service to the long history of the Living Theatre's quest to catalyze radical social change through audience participation, removing *Paradise Now* from historical isolation as both the high-water mark and death knell of the radical avant-garde. But it also operates within the same bounded terms of artistic efficacy as any of the indictments of the Living Theatre's approach to audience participation. Martin's logic suggests that the sheer fact of audience-initiated action—outside of an explicit fictional scenario, and without explicit instructions from performers—represents a greater degree of theatrical radicalism than the more explicit "acting" of *Mysteries* or the heightened confusion and alienation of *Paradise Now*. It implies that stage action operates as a direct microcosm for a larger political landscape, and that spectators' participation in the theatrical event is a means of reflecting or even provoking their participation in any form of radical social change.

I take the opposite approach: not seeing the Plague scene (or the Act of Untying, for that matter) as training for revolution, but seeing both, rather, as training for actors, training that drew on the complexities of fictional, physically specific emotional states to create contagious action. Viewing the company's use of Artaudian contagion as a matter of rigorous training and rehearsal—not only for company members but also for spectators—assists in removing the false expectation of spontaneous radical action from the Living Theatre's work. The Living Theatre's staging of Artaud's plague demonstrates how radical contagious performance was not only compatible with the mediating layers of fiction, but flourished because of those layers, which offered a route into the performance of vehement emotions. "Fulfilling *Paradise*'s promise," to borrow Martin's phrase, was less a matter of getting audience members to participate—and more a matter of getting them to perform.

Five Hundred People a Night: *Paradise Now* and the Emotions of Radical Change

Three and a half years after premiering *Mysteries*, the Living Theatre gathered in an off-season tourist resort in Cefalù, Sicily, to begin conceiving and rehearsing the piece that would become *Paradise Now*. This development period, in the spring of 1968, coincided with a high point in radical protest action, culminating in, among other events, the general strike and related protests of May 1968 in Paris, in which Malina and Beck took part. Performance's power to spark widespread radical action was more important to the company than ever, and as the collective debated dramatic structure, acting technique, and theatrical subject matter, their attention was ever-focused on the recruitment and engagement of audience members.

By the time the Living Theatre created *Paradise Now*, the language of Artaud had thoroughly permeated the company's artistic and political consciousness. The paradigm of plague as a model for performance, as well as the prospect of a link between the physical and the metaphysical, manifested frequently in the company's thinking from this time period and suggest that Artaud's ideas about infectiousness—both in the theater and in the wider world of performative politics—lay beneath the surface of many of their performance strategies and artistic philosophies. Beck's *The Life of the Theatre*, comprising meditations on the company's work from the early 1960s to the early 1970s, is littered with discussions of trance states and ritual, plague and alchemy. Recalling Artaud's essay "The Alchemical Theater" as well as "The Theater and the Plague," Beck described *Paradise Now* as "the search for alchemical formulae":[42] "those mysterious changes, metabolic, electrochemical, flow of blood, glandular, neurological."[43] Such phrases might as well have come directly from *The Theater and Its Double*. Indeed, in "The Alchemical Theater," Artaud parses the relationship between theater and alchemy through the lens of transformative efficacy—the transmutation of lead into gold, but also of theatrical action into the real world. And Beck was not the only one drawing on Artaudian ideas of infectiousness and plague during the rehearsals of *Paradise Now*. On March 12, 1968, for instance, company member Echnaton asked whether someone in the group could "do a lecture on effective [*sic*] athleticism."[44] Later that month, Malina remarked, "We would have to signal thru/ the existing flames."[45] "Signaling through the flames" maintained a consistent presence on the list of actions the company planned to do during their new piece.

I invoke the consistent, insistent, detailed presence of Artaud in the conversations surrounding *Paradise Now* as a way of suggesting the significance his ideas held for the Living Theatre—not only as generalized inspiration but as specific, granular performance strategy. The company's new piece may have diverged from Artaud's politics, but it was deeply inflected by his ideas about theater. "We want to find something that will change 500 people a night," announced the actor Rufus Collins to his collaborators in February 1968.[46] In another rehearsal, Collins declared: "I want them [the audience] to be trapped into it," adding that "I think that in 6 minutes the A[udience] will be in a point of hysteria."[47] William Shari, another performer, agreed that the actors' primary objective in *Paradise Now* was to "infect the people nearest you to do something."[48] When performer and company member Jenny Hecht announced that she hoped the new piece would move beyond the format of *Mysteries*, another actor, Henry Howard, proposed that it could do so by striving "not just to be/ but to communicate/ to make it catching like the plague."[49] It strikes me as significant that for these creators, the hope was that *Paradise Now* would be even more "catching" than *Mysteries*, a piece that already explicitly and literally staged Artaud's plague, and that asked audience members to rise up and do the same.

Even more striking is Howard's comment that he hopes the piece will "communicate." Both the concept of communication and the word itself recur frequently in the Living Theatre's rehearsal discourse, in Malina's and Beck's diaries and notes, and particularly in their theories of acting. In a January 1969 conversation about the problems involved in integrating audience members into *Paradise Now*, Collins[50] suggests: "In *Paradise Now* there is a time when there is a large conglomeration of people on the stage and we get them to come off the stage and get the people in the audience." Here, Beck interjects: "and find ways to communicate with each other."[51] These terms invoked not only the discourse of bodily contagion, but also contagion's dual relationship to bodily presence and to media technology. In February 1969, in a short essay extolling the uses of the tape recorder for both political and artistic purposes, Beck linked the company's consistent emphasis on acting as "communication" with his new thinking on the politics of media:

> We are no longer interested in winning, but in communication. Communication is winning. This is why media are, McLuhan told us, the controlling influence of our behavior. Seize the media. Communicate.[52]

Beck's decision to invoke McLuhan, the powers of recording, and technology's significance as a means of transmitting ideas, reveals the complexity that the concept of "communication" held for the company at this time. Here, communication meant seizing the apparatus of information transfer.

In rehearsal, communication meant speaking and listening. And in performance, communication meant infectiously transmitting revolutionary ideas and revolutionary feelings.

The concept of communication also drives Beck's writing on acting during this time period, when he wrestled repeatedly with the legacy of Stanislavskian theory, and with the Living Theatre's departure from what he referred to as the "theater of fictions." Beck's diary from January to July 1969 provides a running commentary on the differences between the type of acting commonly practiced in studios and on stages across the United States, and the type of acting he envisioned for his own company. In a brief essay titled "How to Act," he instructed:

> Acting is earnest communication of everything you are with the people who have earnestly assembled to be guided through the mysteries. Whatever you know of the mysteries must now be transmitted. The actor, whatever school he derives of, must be engaged in this, no? In communicating what he has learned and his experiences during his psychic voyages into the recess of space and time, his physical voyages into the anatomy of life and space, his voyages into the unknown. Your life depends on communication.[53]

To call for theater that "communicates" is to invoke both physical and emotional transfer, to suggest the double implication of communicable disease and communicable ideas.

Whether intentionally or not, the statement is also a citation of Artaud, who asserts in his famous essay: "First of all we must recognize that the theater, like the plague, is a delirium and is communicative."[54] Curiously, though, this statement does not appear "first of all," or even close to the beginning of "The Theater and the Plague," but instead near the end, in one of the many contradictory passages describing the mode of contagion in which his theatrical plague would participate. I return here, briefly, to Artaud's description of how the plague would spread—and how it would *not* spread (addressed in my introduction)—as a means of better understanding the Living Theatre's own vision for theatrical communication. Among several counterintuitive swerves in "The Theater and the Plague" is the assertion that for all the qualities that the theater and the plague may share, contagion is not actually one of them. "If the essential theater is like the plague, it is not because it is contagious,"[55] insists Artaud. Elsewhere, he states, "it is too easy and explains nothing to limit the communication of such a disease to contagion by simple contact."[56] Too easy—despite Artaud's assertion, elsewhere in the essay, that theatrical catastrophes should "discharge themselves into the sensibility of an audience with all the force of an epidemic."[57] These tensions within Artaud's own conception of the plague recur, in different form, in the Living Theatre's version of theatrical contagion—where, too, performance discharges itself into the sensibility of an audience, but, likewise, in far more mediated ways than "contagion by simple contact" could account for.

Jane Goodall's assertion, quoted in full in my introduction, helps to illuminate the plague's manifestation in the Living Theatre's performances. Arguing that the plague is less a direct physical contagion than a psychic transfer, Goodall recalls the reader to Artaud's description of the plague's eruption among those in whom the "seeds" for such infection had already been planted. For the Living Theatre, these people were primarily other actors—whether those who already identified as such or those who became actors in order to join in the Rite of Guerilla Theatre or to join the company as a whole. For audience members who engaged with *Paradise Now* as spectators, the piece frequently disappointed, presenting an emotionally charged, quasi-fictional portrait of contagious revolution rather than a truly infectious spectacle. But for audience members who took up Living Theatre's invitation to perform—not as political revolutionaries but as stage actors—the plague frequently called up something theatrically potent.

My analysis of *Paradise Now* focuses on the first few minutes of the piece, the Rite of Guerilla Theatre: the section that came to paradigmatically stand in for the problems of the piece as a whole, for the contradictions faced and embodied by the company more broadly, and for the challenges attending radical theater in the late 1960s. I choose this not only because it was the most famous, the most frequently attacked, and one of the most provocative sections of *Paradise Now*, but also because, like the Plague scene from *Mysteries*, the Living Theatre viewed it as a performance piece in its own right, separable from the rest of the four- to five-hour show. During the Rite, performers approached audience members, gazed into their eyes, and made a series of increasingly frantic declarations: "I am not allowed to travel without a passport"; "I don't know how to stop the wars"; "You can't live if you don't have money"; "I'm not allowed to smoke marijuana." When spectators responded (if they did), performers ignored them, spoke over them, screamed louder, and ranted harder. The scene typically culminated not in dialogue between performers and spectators, but in one of many moments titled "Flashout" in the published text (which was compiled and edited after the company had been touring *Paradise Now* for some time, with authorship attributed to the collective). Flashouts, the company specified, were moments when "the actor by the force of his art approaches a transcendent moment in which he is released from all the hangups of the present situation."[58]

Critiques of this enraging, seemingly counterproductive, confused and confusing scene abounded, and still do. "With all their devotion and righteousness, The Living Theatre is a community theater which pretends interest in dialogue but tolerates only dogma; pretends interest in art but creates events; pretends participation but exercises punishment," complained a 1969 review of *Paradise Now* at Yale University.[59] Erika Munk, in an essay on the

Living Theatre and its audiences, summarized the infuriating effect of the piece's first few minutes:

> The opening "Rite of Guerrilla Theater" . . . became every critic's paradigmatic, usually enraging, Living Theatre moment . . . Reading the description, one can easily imagine a true communication of the impossibility of communication. What occurred instead, not only the three times I saw it but from all reports at most performances, was a psychodrama of scorn and hostility.[60]

Though he did not cite the Rite of Guerilla Theatre by name, Richard Gilman's assessment of this element of *Paradise Now* objected, in similar terms, to the disjuncture between the performers' rhetoric about participation and the actual dynamic that spectators experienced in the auditorium. He balked at what he referred to as the company's "pompous, self-righteous, clichéd talk," which he described as

> talk that separates and kills as effectively among leftists and radicals as among the "enemy," the talk that reinforces complacency at the very moment it's trying to unsettle and prod, that brings the darkness closer through its utter blindness to the political and social realities, that says what we already know, what we've found useless *as talk*.[61]

The range of scholarly and critical responses includes many more such critiques. "The actor's relation to audience response is entirely one-sided: no matter what the audience does, the actor will use the audience to produce a predetermined emotion," writes Marianne DeKoven in her 2004 analysis of *Paradise Now*, adding that "the production must move forward, oblivious to the nature of audience response."[62]

Stefan Brecht, in his report on the Living Theatre's American tour, in which they played *Frankenstein*, *Antigone*, *Mysteries*, and *Paradise Now* in repertory, offered a detailed and revealing description of the Rite's effects on spectators:

> For example, though the rite of Guerrilla Theater in *Paradise* consists of a theatrically *acted* crescendo of horrified plaints as to what the members of the Company (I, we) are not allowed to do, each of which the first time around is delivered as sincere *intimacy* to a spectator (who mostly responds by one of 2 or 3 shitarse cracks), the performers with absolute rigidity refuse response even to "sincere" rejoinders, continuing their routine as rite. When at other times they do engage in dialogue with spectators—with evident disinterest in the interlocutor & responding to his points only with the concern

> to make the ideology prevail—their design is to make the dialogue an act which will appropriately move third parties, the surrounding audience.[63]

The key word here—for Brecht and for me—is "acted." If critiques of the Rite align in any way with the company's own explicit vision for the scene, it is precisely in this agreement that the performers were playing rehearsed, scripted material, that their confrontations with audience members were never intended to be dialogues, that the scene comes closer to establishing a fictive cosmos than to tearing one down. "If the spectator addresses him, he listens to the spectator but repeats only this phrase," state the published stage directions, referring to whichever of the five selected phrases a performer is voicing at the moment. "He is obsessed with the meaning of the prohibition and by the ramifications of the prohibition. He cannot travel freely, he cannot move about at will, he is separated from his fellow man, his boundaries are official: the Gates of Paradise are closed to him."[64]

As if to underscore that the Rite's emotional charge was rehearsed, the stage directions included in the published text include overtly Stanislavskian terminology. "At all points in the performance the actor's superobjective is to further radical action demonstrating the futility of violence and the joyous quality of non-violent revolutionary action," the text enjoins. "At all points the superobjective is to work for the changes that diminish violence both in the individual and in the exterior forms of society."[65] Since the company had been performing *Paradise Now* for some time before creating the final performance text, the stage directions are likely some combination of observations made in rehearsal and performance, and aspirations as to actors' behavior during this section of the piece. Such recourse to Stanislavskian structures is, I argue, not an accident but a reflection of the ways the company constructed the piece from the beginning: as a play with a fictive cosmos, characters, and its own internal, shifting reality. (It is also, of course, a reflection of Malina's New School training, which deeply influenced the company's acting work.) The concepts of "further[ing] radical action" and "work[ing] for the changes that diminish violence" only appear ludicrously out of step with the concept of the superobjective if we hold *Paradise Now* to a different standard of realism than any other fictional play. The language of superobjectives testifies to the specificity of acting technique, and thinking about acting technique, that was at work in the Rite and in *Paradise Now* more broadly.

Stanislavsky—and his legacy, broadly considered—remained the paradigm against which Malina and Beck conceived their approach to acting. His name, his theory, and his way of understanding the actor's work surface again and again in the pair's writings. A short passage from their "Messages" series announces: "When an actor asks a question there are always 2 (two) answers: 1. Specific details as to immediate action and motivation. 2. A discussion of 'what is the meaning of this play.'" Malina and Beck then inquire,

"How is this different from Stanislavsky's beats and super-objectives?" and assert: "Not at all."[66] The Living Theatre's commitment to dismantling what they repeatedly called the "theater of fictions" did not, for them, preclude the use of realist acting models as a means of summoning and channeling emotion in performance. Rather, the Rite of Guerilla Theatre (and the company's acting work more broadly in the mid- to late 1960s) constituted an attempt to merge Stanislavsky with Artaud.

Mingling with Stanislavskian superobjectives, throughout the company's writings on acting, were observations about the centrality of pain to the actor's work. Pain was, of course, the primary sensation at play in the Plague scene, and the performance of pain was the primary indicator of whether an actor was ready to become part of the company. In Beck's notebook, he asserted that "whatever the actor does, whether he is playing a character in the theatre of fiction or whether he is playing life in the theatre of life, always has to be expressing the pain."[67] "Messages," too, contains multiple meditations on the subject, including one entitled "The Theatre of Pain," which notes that "when the spectator begins to feel the pain, then the actor begins to accomplish a vivid purpose: to heighten awareness."[68] The Theatre of Pain was Artaudian, but Stanislavsky fueled its performance onstage.

The company's acting choices were provocative at the time, not only for the emotions they summoned in their spectators, but also for contemporary thinking about acting itself. In his 1972 essay "On Acting and Not Acting," Michael Kirby invokes *Paradise Now* as a new midpoint on a spectrum running from "not-acting" to "acting." The company's approach, for Kirby, represented a form of "emotional" acting that did not involve playing fictional characters but nevertheless was distinct from any straightforward presumption of spontaneity or reality. His analysis is so revealing that it is worth quoting in full:

> At times in "real life" we meet a person that we feel is acting. This does not mean that he is lying, dishonest, living in an unreal world, or that he is necessarily giving a false impression of his character and personality. It means that he seems to be aware of an audience—to be "on stage"—and that he reacts to this situation by energetically projecting ideas, emotions and elements of his personality for the sake of the audience. That is what the performers in *Paradise Now* were doing. They were acting their own emotions and beliefs.[69]

It is notable, first, that Kirby singled out the performers in *Paradise Now* as representative of an unfamiliar, highly particular form of acting. For Kirby, the Living Theatre's actors occupied a position between familiar forms of acting—stable characters inhabiting a stable fictive cosmos—and ordinary behavior or "non-acting." The idea that they were "acting their own emotions and beliefs" (rather than those of a fictive character) still implies an interior mode of performance, driven by internal emotions and objectives rather than by spontaneous interaction with spectators. As realist actors would do, the performers in *Paradise Now* sought to give the impression that their carefully rehearsed speech was driven by spontaneous, sincerely felt emotion.

If the performers did not, in Munk's words, create a "true communication of the impossibility of communication" during this section of the piece—if that was never the intention anyway—the feelings they did communicate, by most accounts, were frustration, skepticism, confusion, and annoyance. Such sensations are what Sianne Ngai might categorize among the "ugly feelings" she describes in her study of that name, where she analyzes envy, irritation, and paranoia, distinguishing such "weak" emotions from their more celebrated counterparts: passions like rage and ecstasy. Drawing on the writings of Brian Massumi and Lawrence Grossberg, Ngai also describes the distinction between affect and emotion, citing the oft-presented idea that while emotions typically have subjects, affects do not—and, perhaps more significantly, that affective states, unlike emotions, are "neither structured narratively nor organized in response to our interpretations of situations."[70] Ngai invokes such categorical distinctions partially in order to dismantle them: the "intentionally weak" feelings she analyzes challenge such categorization. So do the responses that audience members reportedly felt while watching the Rite of Guerilla Theatre. They did not feel rage or fear, emotions that Ngai categorizes as "grander passions," nor did they feel empathy or catharsis, emotional responses on which theatrical relationships between audiences and performers are built. Spectators at *Paradise Now*, I argue, arrived open to feeling emotions—open to the ecstasy of revolt, to the joy of radical communion—but frequently experienced affect instead. They were waiting for the exultant rage of the revolutionary, but instead experienced the maddening confusion of the needled audience member. Expecting big feelings, they experienced an overwhelming series of small ones.

Such disjunctures between expected or anticipated emotion, and actually felt affective state; and between molecular personal change and sweeping societal restructuring, are, I argue, representative of the emotional state of the aspiring revolutionary in this late 1960s moment. Henry Lesnick, in the critique of guerrilla theater cited at the beginning of this chapter, suggested that displays of extreme rebelliousness, though thrilling, did little to promote actual political change, arguing that the "politics of put on, of play, has an undeniable appeal for everyone whose primary experience of the contradictions of society is one of boredom and a sense of stultification." In identifying the sensations of "boredom" and "stultification" as the affective enemies that radical guerrilla performance sought to vanquish, Lesnick captured the Rite's tendency to veer vertiginously between global, high-stakes targets of protest and those that risk appearing more trivial. "I don't know how to stop the wars" competes, in this section of *Paradise Now*, with "I'm not allowed to smoke marijuana." Despite the company's assertion that such destructive societal forces are inextricably linked, it's not only the difference in significance and scale, but also the ease with which the second complaint is satisfied—and the impossibility of altering the first—that causes political vertigo.

Lesnick's analysis also reflected the gap between spectators' anticipated emotions and the ones they reportedly really felt during the Living Theatre's opening Rite. It's not that boredom was the only affective expression driving the Rite of Guerilla Theatre. To the contrary: the emotions portrayed by the Living Theatre's actors during this section of the piece included rage, panic, and desperation. But small feelings—boredom, annoyance, confusion—were commonly the affective expressions it produced. To me, this effect represents neither a deliberate attempt to exasperate spectators, nor evidence of theatrical failure. Rather, the gap between immense passions and small feelings is indicative of a larger emotional gap that pervaded the performances of revolutionary and radical theater during these years—an emotional gap that can be revealingly understood as an instance of what Raymond Williams called "structures of feeling." In his essay in *Marxism and Literature* (a collection that emerged out of the social and political upheaval of the 1960s), Williams describes the ways that fixed social forms, such as educational paradigms and verbal habits of argument, frequently fail to encompass or account for all of the communal experiences, conversational tenors, or shared emotions in a given historical moment. He writes:

> There is frequent tension between the received interpretation and practical experience. Where this tension can be made direct and explicit, or where some alternative interpretation is available, we are still within a dimension of relatively fixed forms. But the tension is as often an unease, a stress, a displacement, a latency: the moment of conscious comparison not yet come, often not even coming.[71]

For Williams, what distinguishes a structure of feeling from other possible descriptions of a given period's style, cultural practices, or social relationships is its location in the present tense. Structures of feeling cease to be so when they are fixed, codified, or even precisely named. He chooses the word "feeling" over "experience" for his new term specifically because of the risk that "experience" implies events that have already taken place.

For spectators present at the Rite of Guerilla Theatre, the dual eruption of boundless passion embracing vast historical change, and of confusion, boredom, and irritation in the moment of performance, constitutes such a tension between emotion as articulated and emotion as felt. That numerous spectators shared the second category of affective responses suggests its public and communal nature; that it could not be framed within a politically revolutionary context—that it, in fact, contradicted such a context—suggests it as a "structure of feeling." This tension operated not only at the level of emotion in the Rite of Guerilla Theatre sequence, but in a larger sense throughout the performance as a whole: in the tension between opening space for audience participation and moving the performance inexorably along; in the tension between the symbolic depiction of revolution and the real-world, practical embodiment of it; and in the tension between the images that merged onstage and the feelings that refused to coalesce in the audience.

The Rite of Guerilla Theatre, I argue, manifested a structure of feeling particular to the late 1960s radical movement: a tension between depicting the revolution and living it. Such feelings were importantly at stake for radical artists throughout this period. In an essay titled "Some Notes in Defense of Combative Theater," Charles Brover observed, "In every crucial area of personal life—love, friendship, work, family, language, and even dream—there was demanded a thoroughgoing transformation. The process of personal change was so rapid that one could not simply trust oneself. The struggle for a liberated future became temporarily a struggle against unconscious subversion."[72] Lesser emotions, even unconscious or unnameable feelings, were thus crucial to the revolution, forces that could undermine sweeping social change or be marshaled into its service.

The company's rehearsal notes and writings suggest that a central aspect of *Paradise Now* was an attempt to evaluate the specific passions, emotions, and affects that should accompany their particular political moment. A brief meditation in the "Messages" text, titled "Passion, Anger, Sadness, Weeping," observes: "When the actors cry out against the pain, our detractors say: 'They are filled with hate.' Imagine! They can't tell the difference between passion and anger."[73] Other conversations suggested that neither passion nor anger would be effective in performance. In a February 1968 conversation during *Paradise Now* rehearsals, Malina argued against revolutionary rage, not just as a mode that was inappropriate to their performance, but also as a mode that was unproductive for their historical moment. "I do not think this is the play to arouse people to anger," she said. "In fact historically I don't think this is the time to arouse people to anger. The Revolutionary Act has to be so cool. I'm a radical Revolutionary, I want to get to the hot act. But this is the time for the cool."[74] It is no accident, then, that they repeatedly included television—the paradigmatic "cool" medium according to both Beck and McLuhan himself—in their repertoire of revolutionary performance during this period.

The company's thinking about emotion infused many of *Paradise Now*'s scenes, but especially the Rite of Guerilla Theatre. An early draft of the performance text contains a typewritten script of the Rite, in which copious instructions and ideas about emotion, absent from the typescript, are instead handwritten in the margins. For instance: in typewritten text following the actor's instruction to announce, "I am not allowed to travel without a passport," the stage directions instruct the actor that "if a spectator addresses him, he listens to the spectator but repeats only this phrase." Following this injunction, a handwritten insertion adds: "The spectator may be passive, sympathetic, superficial, witty, profound, cynical, hostile. The actor uses this response to increase his expression of the frustration of the taboos and inhibitions imposed on him by the structure of the world around him."[75] Such handwritten insertions are scattered through the margins of this page, and nearly every insertion adds detailed emotional information to stage directions and dialogue. Another explains that the actor "experiences the spectators' growing frustration at the sense of a lack of communication."[76] In the updated third draft incorporating corrections, these emotional additions are integrated into the text.[77]

However this means the text was created—whether these stage directions carefully choreographing emotions were conceived separately; were always present but simply overlooked in the first typescript; or were observations made in performance and then deemed important enough to include in the final text—the copious insertion of emotional information into the draft, and its inclusion in subsequent versions of the scene, testifies to the overwhelming significance of emotion here. What's more, the specific affective states attributed to audience members in the early draft's marginalia—passivity, wittiness, hostility, superficiality—align closely with the (to use Ngai's phrasing) "weak feelings" spectators really reported experiencing during the scene.

The disjuncture between major passions and minor affects remained a constant for both performers and spectators. After performing *Paradise Now* for about eight months, Malina recorded in her diary one of the frequent responses the Rite elicited from spectators.

> There's this dumb-bunny selfishness, that means to change the world with a specious argument.
>
> i.e.:
>
> —"I've found a way, I can travel without a passport."
>
> —"Therefore you can do likewise."
>
> —"Therefore I *am* allowed to travel without a passport."
>
> As if the good example of a few smart-ass radical beauties could work the wonders for the war-torn and the starving and the jailed and the wage-slaves. That the scene is about Revolutionary Outcry escapes them in their feelingless notion that "we are beyond that."[78]

For Malina, this moment in the performance was not about the logistics of traveling without a passport, but about something larger and more symbolic. It isn't that the Living Theatre didn't want to create real revolution, with all of its attendant practical concerns; to the contrary, their seriousness about large-scale political change emerges continuously through *Paradise Now*. Spectators were invited to form revolutionary cells, to liberate the prisoners in local jails, to exchange phone numbers in order to continue political action once the company left town. But *Paradise Now* was at its most Artaudian, its most fascinatingly contagious, not as a direct embodiment of political action but as a layered study in revolutionary feeling (indeed, she critiques the confused spectators as "feelingless"). Malina's response to her audiences suggests that the scene was never so much about literal action as it was about locating and embodying—in other words, performing—the emotional landscape of radical change.

Televising *Paradise Now*: The Dilexi Broadcast

This landscape emerges finally, fully, in the televised portions of *Paradise Now*, in the Dilexi broadcast, where the contagion of Artaud and the contagion of broadcast media merged, and where the company's approach to choreographing audience emotion and transmuting it into acting becomes clear. Viewing Artaud and the Living Theatre as companions in making mediated performance is itself somewhat counterintuitive: the accepted lines of influence connecting Artaud with his heirs at the Living Theatre do not usually run through the terrain of broadcast media, and his major experiment with broadcast, *To Have Done with the Judgment of God*, appears, at first, unrelated to *Paradise Now*. Yet, placed side by side, Artaud's radio play offers resonances with the Living Theatre's utopian vision. Both plays connect the granular dynamics of everyday living to the largest questions of human society, spirituality, and seismic historical change. Both contain eschatological historical visions: Artaud's desperately dystopian, the Living Theatre's, anarchically utopian. Both offer worldviews deeply informed by the apparently unending nature of global warfare, and both assume the mantle of indigenous groups' spiritualities. The scale of vision, the fascination with diagnosing global geopolitical orders, and the availability of impending and totalizing new forms of being obliquely echo each other.

For Artaud, broadcasting offered a possible means of expanding his theater of cruelty with more immediacy, more visceral power, and more universal reach than could ever be achieved by gathering spectators together in a theatrical space. For the Living Theatre, it offered a means of incorporating audience members by teaching them, step by step, how to perform the company's infamous Rite—and demonstrating, too, to all of the potential performers following along at home. It is in this concentrated effort to shape the Rite of Guerilla Theatre for television that the company's approach to contagious performance—to performing Artaud's plague, to launching revolution—is at its clearest and most direct.

The Dilexi Series was itself a pioneering exploration of the medium of television, devised by the San Francisco gallerist Jim Newman as an opportunity for experimental artists in a variety of media to work with the relatively young format of the television broadcast. Yvonne Rainer contributed a video entitled *Dance Fractions for the West Coast*, aired in June 1969, in which a group of thirty dancers performed mass choreography followed by, among other things, a discussion by Rainer on "the virtues and problems of snot."[79] Andy Warhol offered for broadcast the *Paul Swan Film*, a thirty-minute portrait of 83-year-old dancer Paul Swan, who danced and recited poems on camera. Both of these, and many of the other contributions to the series, explicitly explored the properties of film and video. Rainer's piece contained "electronic effects" that were "keyed over the basic imagery"; Warhol's consisted of a single take that was "painful," "more for Swan than the viewer." A performance broadcast in late June, by the artists Kenneth Dewey, Don Harper, and Marie Zazzi, claimed to explicitly build on "Marshall McLuhan's idea that television is the new family hearth" by staging a conversation with a group of Happenings artists around a real campfire, into which a television eventually intrudes.[80]

The Living Theatre staged its Rites of Guerrilla Theater, as the broadcast was titled, at Mills College on March 8, 1969.[81] In *The Living Theatre: Art, Exile, and Outrage*, John Tytell mentions the broadcast event in passing, noting that the company members staged the Rite for TV only because they needed "extra money, afraid now that escrow funds for the return trip to Europe did not exist."[82] Yet a glimpse at Malina's diary from that day suggests that the decision to film the Rite was not so casual as all that. Her diary reflects that it was not so much the broadcast that was motivated purely by a need for funds, but rather the number of events the company scheduled into a single performance day, which included not only the Mills College staging, but also a staging of the Plague scene from *Mysteries* for a different television station, as well as a regular performance of *Paradise Now*.[83]

It's no accident that although the Rite is listed in the singular in the published text of *Paradise Now*, the Dilexi broadcast is titled Rites, in the plural. The Living Theatre stages, at Mills College, a three-part sequence that repeats the Rite multiple times. First, the company performs the Rite for its spectators; the actors then hold an informal seminar of sorts to discuss its strategies and intended effects; and finally, the Living Theatre restages the Rite using audience members as the primary performers. In other words, the performance piece created for Dilexi is a how-to guide, a training session, a rehearsal, not of the Living Theatre, but of their audiences.

The performance of the Rite itself takes less than a third of the twenty-five-minute video. Spectators fill the rows of a college auditorium, murmuring quietly in anticipation. Some appear young—students from the Mills campus—while others are, perhaps, faculty or community members there to see the already legendary company perform. Actors enter from multiple doors and begin addressing audience members, quietly at first, murmuring the now-familiar plaints: "I'm not allowed to travel without a passport"; "You can't live if you don't have money"; "I'm not allowed to smoke marijuana." As in most performances of the Rite, these incantations proceed from quiet observations to desperate, terrified cries. Soon, Malina is wailing, "I

Paradise Now. Spectators performing the Rite of Guerilla Theatre at Mills College for the Dilexi broadcast, produced by Jim Newman and John Coney. Image used with permission of Jim Newman and courtesy of Pacific Film Archive.

don't know how to stop the wars!" She clutches her temples and leans into a spectator in the second row, who smiles sympathetically, knowingly, but does not speak. Throughout, the performers treat the cameras as if they were live spectators too, sometimes speaking directly to the broadcast audience and, at other times, giving us a sidelong glance or part of an angry phrase en route to delivery somewhere else.[84]

Then, as if by mutual agreement, the actors stop, quietly holding their ground throughout the auditorium. Julian Beck hoists himself onto the edge of the stage and perches there, a cool professor leading a class. "The purpose of the Rite of Guerilla Theatre," he says, "is to assault the culture, to assault you, to assault ourselves, and to establish the facts and the feeling of where we are right now. And so, like obsessed nuts, maniacs, because in fact we are obsessed nuts and maniacs, all of us, we move around among you, repeating five of perhaps a hundred phrases . . . which define the prohibitions, five of the prohibitions of this prohibitionary society . . . in which we live." He talks his audience through the five statements that comprise the Rite and fields questions from spectators about the company's intentions in performing them.

Then—and here is where the broadcast gets especially compelling—the Living Theatre asks their audience to take a turn performing. "Let us be aware that what is happening here today is a high seminar in brain damage repair," announces performer Steve Ben Israel, shirtless, wild-haired, close to the camera, turning to look at the spectators in their seats. After Beck explains that the company would like their audience members to act the Rite of Guerilla Theatre, performers give specific directions to spectators. Ben Israel instructs them:

> We shall start out low, and we shall build to the point where we shall scream, but let us try to scream all at the same time, by listening to each other as we rise individually and collectively, let us begin to say the first line, which is "I am not allowed to travel without a passport," and you can stand out of your seats and begin to move, and say this for two minutes and then scream.

Such clear physical and emotional instructions offer the spectators an entry point into the Rite that audience members at the "regular" performances of *Paradise Now* didn't have. Spectators mill around the auditorium, confronting other, seated spectators, at first timidly and then with increasing fervor. One spectator-performer carries a baby in her arms, shyly declaring, "I am not allowed to travel without a passport." Someone giggles hysterically in the background. "I am not allowed to smoke marijuana," bellows a spectacled man, moving through the crowd. "I'm not allowed to smoke marijuana!" insist two young women, confronting a man in sunglasses who exhorts them, "Yes, you can! You can!" The paradigmatic objection to *Paradise Now*, the obsessively derided tactic of shouting in audience members' faces—and then ignoring them when they attempt to shout back—is transformed in this moment, when the Rite becomes the acting exercise it always was.

"The Living Theatre's greatest transformative effect occurred among the numerous individuals who joined the company after first experiencing it as audience members," writes Bradford Martin in *The Theater Is in the Street*.[85] DeKoven echoes this idea in her analysis of *Paradise Now*, arguing that the performance piece, ostensibly open and inclusive to its audience, in reality included only those audience members who transformed themselves into actors:

> Later in the performance, near the end, the audience is much more actively and directly included, but by that time they have become honorary or temporary members of The Living Theatre and are expected to do more or less what the rest of the actors are doing. They are included only insofar as they have achieved the prescribed state of consciousness.[86]

Observations like these suggest that the company's "transformative effect" was small, and that such transformations were ultimately failures—that true revolutionary theater would turn its audiences into revolutionaries, not into actors.

But transformation was always a matter of acting, revolutionary feelings always a matter of performance technique. Malina's brief, but revealing, notes on the Mills College performance underscore such an interpretation. "It went well," she wrote, "with the eager-eyed girls doing a good thing when it came their turn to play the Rite of Guerrilla Theater. And some good outbursts—all getting more and more positive in response to the need."[87] The students here are evaluated primarily as actors playing a scene: a scene for which they have been trained and prepared over the course of the preceding twenty minutes. At the end of the students' performance, Malina recalls, "a tiptoed exit by the actors leaves them to their own devices."[88] The Living Theatre thus taught its audience how to perform the scene, and then disappeared so that the new "company" could continue: not continue making revolution—not immediately, anyway—but, rather, continue acting. For the Living Theatre, working in the wake of Artaud, revolutionary performance was at its most contagious when channeled through rigorous acting technique, emotional complexity, and rehearsed choreography. Neither fiction nor mediation disrupted the performance of revolution, or inhibited its infectious spread. Rather, stage fiction and viral performance worked hand in hand to point actors—and spectators who became actors—toward a distant vision of the revolution itself.

Chapter 2

✦

Towards an Audience Vocabulary

Marc Estrin, Augusto Boal, and General Idea

In an unpublished manifesto titled "Target Audience," the Canadian artistic trio known as General Idea described the swift transformation of a hypothetical audience, from passive observers to animated participants. Jorge Zontal, Felix Partz, and AA Bronson, the three artists comprising General Idea, envisioned the following rapid choreography:

> [The audience] started with ordered applause that soon filled the space and then rose en masse to a more militant stance. Electricity sparked the air in evidence of short circuiting. The volume continued to rise. The audience collectively took things into their own hands. They crossed the well-defined and defended footlight borderline. They occupied and claimed the vacuum between stage and seats. They became the performers while remaining their own captive audience . . . on one hand, and on the other their new status was echoed in their colliding palms.[1]

At first glance, this fantasy of spectatorial passion, of an audience ecstatically merging into the theatrical scene, appears to echo the Living Theatre's contagious ethos, or Artaud's. So irresistibly compelling are the gestures onstage, the emotions they incite, that spectators cannot help but join in.

And yet: a closer look reveals subtle but significant differences in General Idea's vision for a contagiously mobilized audience. These distinctions illuminate the viral mode of performance that they, and the other artists described in this chapter, began creating in the early 1970s, in the wake of pathbreaking 1960s works like *Paradise Now* and also in distinction from them. Where the Living Theatre's work frequently envisioned the total fusion of playing space and audience area, General Idea employed the language of military invasion to reinforce awareness of this "borderline," even as their imagined spectators transgressed it. Spectators, here, are "militant," then "captive"; the stage is territory to be "occupied" and "defended." The powerful impulses passing

General Idea's *Towards an Audience Vocabulary*, 1978. Photography by General Idea. Image courtesy of Esther Schipper, Berlin, used with permission of AA Bronson.

between and among spectators are compared to the rapid transmission of electric current. Here is a world of technological circulation, a world where performing is an infiltrative action and every audience member a potential guerrilla fighter.

Perhaps most significantly, General Idea's imagined spectators do not reiterate the gestures of performers. In fact, actors barely register in this description at all. Instead, the riotous audience aggressively repeats the gestures that spectators habitually make, from "ordered applause" to "colliding palms." This audience spreads and circulates performance *as an audience*. The imagined performance thus contains not contagious acting but contagious spectating. "From this vantage point," wrote General Idea of their spectators, "they are no longer acting in mere response to stimuli of situation or action. They were creating their own parts and the performance would last as long as they desired."[2]

If the Living Theatre envisioned passing revolutionary gestures from performers to audience members through affect and emotion, a new series of contagious performance works, created in the 1970s, aimed to keep the virus but alter the relationship between stage gesture and audience response. These artists, and these new contagious dramaturgies, explored the choreography of viral transmission among spectators, rendering performers secondary in significance or absent altogether. Marc Estrin, an American theatermaker, conjured "infiltrative" scenarios, pieces that were both performance fictions and real protests, to register dissent over the Vietnam War and an array of other social and economic issues. The Brazilian playwright-director Augusto Boal created invisible theater—performances staged in public settings and not overtly marked as fictional—as a means of drawing spectators into direct confrontation with economic inequality and other social injustices. Meanwhile, General Idea led its audiences in carefully rehearsed physical choreographies, as part of a series of "rehearsals" leading up to a much-anticipated, perpetually deferred performance. All three were deeply invested in testing the circulation of action and emotion, both in performance and in performance's afterlife, and all constructed theatrical models that moved performative gestures off the stage and into the bodies of their spectators. Politically, these artists employed viral dramaturgies not in the service of large-scale revolution, but rather, to fuel molecular-level social change, provoking radical action one subversive gesture at a time.

This chapter deliberately places the work of three disparate artists and artistic groups in conversation. These performance-makers did not create their work in dialogue with one another, and their practices have not been examined alongside one another before.[3] Yet the affinities among the three can be revelatory, illuminating the significance of viral thinking in each of these artists' works, as well as the implications of ideas about circulation and transmission permeating performance cultures of the early 1970s. Then, too, their apparent differences often conceal subtle parallels. General Idea's overt engagement with media technologies and popular culture helps to unearth similar, often overlooked impulses within the work of an artist like Boal. And Estrin's explicit dedication to employing performance as a means of effecting social change allows for the recognition of a subtler politics embedded within the playfully satirical performances of General Idea.

All three of the artists or groups under investigation here share the inheritances of radical 1960s performance and claim a common point of inspiration in the mode of contagious theater exemplified by the Living Theatre and explored in the last chapter. Both Boal and Estrin were deeply influenced by their viewings of *Paradise Now*, and General Idea more broadly by what the group understood as the eventual failures of radical performance in the wake of the utopian protest actions of 1968. All three were in deep sympathy with the Living Theatre's revolutionary work, while forging distinctly different models of transmission and circulation in their own practices. No longer would mass, overwhelming presence serve as a source of contagion. No longer would art confront life with the roar of revolutionary rage. Instead, performance would make playful use of absence and visual sleight-of-hand, would lurk in the peripheral vision of unsuspecting spectators, and would blend indistinguishably into everyday existence. At the same time—even as they created viral dramaturgies distinct from those of the Living Theatre and Artaud before them—these artists, like their predecessors, engaged with questions of affective contagion, individual agency, and emotional control.

The contagious dramaturgies explored in this chapter took up dialogue—implicitly or overtly—with the emerging fields of communications and media studies, which had been recently founded by scholars such as Marshall McLuhan and Harold Innis. Works like Innis's *The Bias of Communication* (1951) and particularly McLuhan's *Understanding Media* (1964) provide an important backdrop to the theatrical practices I describe here, both in the cases of artists who were explicitly engaged with media form and format, like General Idea, and also in instances where such engagement was subtler, as in the work of an artist like Boal. Viral dramaturgies not only investigated the possibilities offered by screens, recording devices, and communications networks, but also reflected these scholars' broader insights about the relationships among meaning, material form, and political power. McLuhan, for instance, proposed that, while societies governed by print media (as with the Western world, he argued, since Gutenberg) had liked to imagine themselves primarily visual and linear in both thought formation and cultural circulations, the new "electric age" would be governed by nonlinear and nonvisual circulations of thought, extending beyond rationality and consciousness.[4] Though they did not necessarily endorse such cultural dichotomies—instead frequently finding links between linear and nonlinear transmission—these "electric" modes were, in many cases, precisely the kinds of circulation to which the artists described in this chapter aspired.

For artists like General Idea, such revelations were foundational, and much of the trio's early performance work involved the systematic testing of McLuhan's concepts. But my argument here is that questions of material circulation and transmission just as importantly underlie the dramaturgies of Augusto Boal and Marc Estrin (and by extension, other politically interventionist performance artists whose work does not make obvious use of media channels). From Boal's use of recording technology to amplify an "invisible" performance to Estrin's insistence that his infiltrations should reverberate in news headlines, these architects of live intervention repeatedly invoked media culture in their theatrical works. McLuhan's text offers a reminder that media can be a much wider category than it is often given credit for. Not only does he devote sections of his study to expected media and information technologies such as radio, television, and telegraph; there are also chapters describing less likely candidates for inclusion: housing, clocks, money, clothing, and numbers.[5] Media, here, includes any system for circulating ideas, affect, or action; it need not take the form of a printed page or a glowing screen.

McLuhan also takes up Elias Canetti's ideas about communicability (discussed in my introduction), viewing live transmission as an essential part of a complex media ecology. In a section of *Understanding Media* devoted to "numbers," McLuhan finds direct inspiration in Canetti's *Crowds and Power* (published just two years before *Understanding Media*) and declares: "Just as writing is an extension and separation of our most neutral and objective sense, the sense of sight, number is an extension and separation of our most intimate and interrelating activity, our sense of touch."[6] McLuhan links the concepts of crowd, number, touch, and communicability, asserting that such forces should be considered technologies in their own right:

> The mysterious need of crowds to grow and to reach out, equally characteristic of large accumulations of wealth, can be understood if money and numbers are, indeed, technologies that extend the power of touch and the grasp of the hand.[7]

Virus, Zach Blas observed in 2012, is a form of "becoming-number";[8] McLuhan and Canetti, half a century earlier, had already imagined what "becoming-number" might mean, drawing on the connections among media, technology, and the circulation of affect within a gathered crowd.

These hypotheses about affective communicability—even if not direct inspirations for Augusto Boal—provide context for his approach to theatrical transmission, particularly within the viral form of invisible theater. Boal did not seek the transmission of affect among crowds of live spectators, but he did aspire to the continuous extension of what McLuhan called the "power of touch." For Boal, mainstream media and mass communications were futile in provoking members of the public to rethink their assumptions about social and economic injustices. "Big rallies are for people who are already convinced," he wrote. "The other way, like doing invisible theatre, reaches very few people. But it modifies people's opinions. That man whose opinion was changed goes home and talks to his family, and he goes to a bar and talks to his friends."[9] Mass communications, to Boal, were ineffectual compared to the communicative power of a single personal conversation. "Becoming-number" was achieved one audience member at a time.

McLuhan, fascinatingly, includes avant-garde art alongside his discussion of mainstream media channels, endowing its formal innovations with predictive power: "in experimental art," he wrote, "men are given the exact specifications of coming violence to their own psyches from their own counter-irritants or technology."[10] Avant-garde forms of representation, he suggests, reflect back to us the modes of communication that lie largely invisible beneath the surface of our daily interactions. Such a project describes precisely Marc Estrin's approach to communicating with his public, particularly through his strategic manual *ReCreation*, which offers instructions for inserting minute reminders of injustice into daily life.

Beyond an engagement with media studies, two theatrical strategies—both likewise linked to these artists' ideas about circulation and dissemination—recur importantly in the works discussed in this chapter. The first is invisibility, and the second is the overt framing of performances as rehearsals rather than as finished pieces. While only Boal created a form explicitly titled "invisible theater," Estrin's infiltrative scenarios and General Idea's use of the present-but-absent figure of Miss General Idea also attempted to inspire audiences to action through performances that weren't complete, visible, or even perceptible onstage (or in which no stage was employed in the first place). In this chapter, I contend that it is not only the overwhelmingly present—as with Artaud and the Living Theatre—but also the ostensibly absent that can spread with viral abandon. In the cases of the artists examined here, it is invisibility rather than hyper-visibility that fuels contagious performance.

Theatrical invisibility has been theorized before, in ways that offer useful counterpoints to my project. In his study *Dark Matter: Invisibility in Drama, Theater, and Performance*, Andrew Sofer argues that offstage characters and unseen but important spaces and forces constitute the "dark matter" of the theater, pressing urgently against the visible world onstage. His examples, though, are fundamentally different from mine, since he considers primarily dramatic texts with fictional worlds, which Estrin, Boal, and General Idea explicitly avoid. Closer to viral invisibility is the mode of performance proposed by Laura Levin in her 2014 *Performing Ground*, which examines artistic works that attempt to blend into their environments: embedded performances, camouflaged installations, pieces whose power comes from their unannounced presence in the wider landscape. Such a mode bears similarities with the viral performance strategies practiced by all three of the artists and groups in this chapter.

But while Levin's discussion of "embedded" performances emphasizes the relationships between performers and their surroundings, viral performance's aim is, rather, to employ invisibility as a means of triggering interactions between performers and spectators. Viral performance may blend into the background, but only as a means of expanding more thoroughly into its audience's gathered consciousness, and ultimately, their performing bodies. The artists in this chapter necessitate the conceptualization of a third kind of invisible performance, the kind in which there is no onstage fiction subject to encroachment by unseen forces, and where blending into the background is only the first step. For Boal, "invisible" performance does not expand the bounds of a fictional world, but instead brings the performance fiction as close as possible to a spontaneous real-world event. For Estrin, "infiltrative" scenarios are intended to inspire double-takes, and then active intervention. And for General Idea, deferring and then preemptively canceling the 1984 Miss General Idea pageant was a means of replacing stage fictions with theatrical absences and placing emphasis on the spectacular performances of their spectators.

These artists frequently withhold not only performance fictions, but also any final, finished version of the performance at all: absence is temporal as well as visual. They emphasize process, transmission, and circulation rather than climax or resolution, and as a result, they frequently imagine their pieces as "rehearsals" for a final performance that might never take place. For Boal, each performance that drew "spect-actors" into active participation in debating socioeconomic questions or resolving injustices was a "rehearsal of revolution."[11] Marc Estrin wrote scenarios for ongoing theatrical "infiltrations" that might extend for years with no narrative resolution or curtain call in sight. For General Idea, the entire performance series staged between 1974 and 1978, including pieces such as *Blocking*, *Towards an Audience Vocabulary*, *Hot Property*, and *Going Thru the Motions*, were designed as "rehearsals of the audience" for the mythic 1984 Miss General Idea Pageant, which never came to pass.

Conceiving of these performances as rehearsals in which spectators could perfect their participation allowed the artists to, imaginatively, keep their stage images in continual circulation, without placing them inside the temporal boundaries of a conventional performance. This approach toward time arises in many of the viral dramaturgies analyzed in this book, from the Living Theatre, instructing its spectators to continue the revolution after their performances ended, to Suzan-Lori Parks's yearlong cycle *365 Days/365 Plays*. Estrin, Boal, and General Idea thus provide a point of departure for considering such dramaturgies of expanded performance time, replacing bounded dramatic structures with continuous, mutating transmissions and circulations.

Getting beyond Audience: Marc Estrin's Infiltrative Acts

"Art has become a contained mental thing and it has a very detrimental effect on the way we look at the world," Julian Beck wrote in his memoir *The Life of the Theatre*. "Therefore, yes, it's no longer a matter of being an artist, it's a matter of infiltrating into being, into the world, into the people."[12] If *Paradise Now* rebelled against all boundaries—stage fictions, scripted texts, physical theaters, legal injunctions, and historical narratives—Marc Estrin took a complementary approach: infiltrating rather than overwhelming, creating performances intended to subtly permeate everyday life rather than raucously overtake it. Estrin studied directing at UCLA in the early 1960s, where, like Beck and Malina, he became enamored of Artaud's writings. Moving to Washington, D.C., in 1965, Estrin and a collaborator, technical director Dennis Livingston, established the American Playground Theater, which would take inspiration from the Living Theatre and would be dedicated to mixing performance with social and political critique.

Estrin's affinity for the Living Theatre began when he saw the company's 1961 production of *The Apple*, a second theatricalist venture from the writer Jack Gelber, whose play *The Connection* had been a formal breakthrough for the company in 1959. During intermission at *The Apple*, Estrin encountered an actor from the company in the bathroom, and after beginning a conversation with him, realized that the performer was still in character—even offstage, even without the promise of spectators to watch him and acknowledge his work. This revelation, Estrin recalled during an interview, vividly demonstrated to him that the border between theatrical fictions and offstage reality could be viewed as porous and unstable, available for experimentation and renegotiation.[13]

When Estrin founded the American Playground Theater and began making infiltrative performances, he hoped that the new company's experiments would succeed in breaking down the barrier between actors and audience, which he believed hindered the real-world efficacy of most of the political theater he saw. He recalled that

> the infiltrative theater was a direct assault on the idea of "audience" itself. There was something very protective [about being "audience"]—you put on your Teflon coating by buying your ticket, and it seemed like a high level of bullshit to me, given the exigencies of the political time that we were in. The idea was, how do you get beyond "audience"?[14]

"Getting beyond audience" ultimately served as a central element of Estrin's dramaturgy. Like the Living Theatre, Estrin attempted to recruit bystanders for his audiences, then to turn them into revolutionary actors. But Estrin went further than the Living Theatre had in seeking spectators from daily life: his audiences were composed largely of unsuspecting passersby, impromptu spectators who had not intended to see a performance and who sometimes never realized they were watching one.

Though Estrin cites Artaud, Beck, and Malina as primary influences, his work also emerged alongside a spectrum of artists who shared strategies and approaches—particularly the international Fluxus and Happenings movements, which provide instructive comparisons with Estrin's work. Artists affiliated and associated with Fluxus had been making transmedial performances, merging everyday life with artistic form, since the early 1960s. Fluxus performances, especially American ones, frequently made use of public space and engaged audience members in scenarios that, structurally, Estrin's infiltrative theater resembled. In a retrospective essay on the form, for instance, Dick Higgins recalls a performance by Fluxus artist Ben Patterson, which "took place in New York's Times Square, on the edge of a red-light district. He stood on street corners, waiting until the lights turned green, and then simply followed the light to the next corner. Several young women—they appeared to be prostitutes—watched him do this for a while, and then they joined in."[15] Like Fluxus, the performances loosely labeled Happenings merged the materials and experiences of everyday life, seeking to effect subtle shifts in spectators' and participants' perception. In some cases, too, Happenings were likewise invisible, as in, for instance, Allan Kaprow's *Self-Service*, a "piece without spectators" performed in Boston, New York, and Los Angeles in 1967. Kaprow instructed participants to select from among a range of activities that melded the everyday with the surreal: leaving a banquet along the side of a highway, handing out flowers to passersby with "pleasant faces."[16] One task—Kaprow suggests tucking transistor radios playing rock music among the food on grocery store shelves—is structurally akin to one of Estrin's scripts for social change, which suggested supporting the 1965 Delano grape-growers' strike by placing photos of Mexican children's faces among the bunches of grapes on the supermarket shelf.

Yet the distinction between Kaprow's and Estrin's chosen props also reveals how "infiltrative theater" differed from Happenings and Fluxus, and suggests the reasons I've chosen to foreground Estrin's work in this chapter. Happenings and Fluxus were deeply engaged with the politics of everyday life, but infiltrative theater was protest art, political intervention, a series of attempts to elicit specific actions from spectators, oriented toward specific policy objectives. Estrin sought to infiltrate everyday life rather than to merge with it, imagining performers as sources of spreadable images and gestures that would alter the political landscape.

The American Playground Theater's scenarios for infiltrative theater are available primarily in a book called *ReCreation*, an out-of-print manual edited by Estrin and published in 1971, which comprises instructions for promoting social change, texts for subversive performance, revolutionary poetry, and recipes for socially progressive art. Some of these documents are, as Estrin has described them, "detritus" rescued from trashcans and bulletin boards: protest letters to local Selective Service offices, practical suggestions for establishing food co-ops and underground newspapers, flyers of every kind, mimeographed and pasted together to construct a clamorous scrapbook of blueprints for radical change.

Alongside these curated texts, Estrin published his own scripts for various kinds of theatrical infiltrations: spectacles erupting out of mundane situations, confrontations in streets and classrooms and public parks, all intended to mobilize audience members unaware that they were viewing a work of art. Estrin's infiltrative performances—even, and especially, his solely hypothetical ones (to be discussed shortly)—constitute an important model for politically radical, personally infectious live performance, emanating from Estrin's foundational ambition to create a complete commingling of the real world and the theater. In his introductory note to *ReCreation*, Estrin declared that there should be "no limit to the number of people directly involved in THE RECONSTRUCTION OF THE WORLD WHICH IS THEATER."[17] For Estrin, conceiving of the world as theater, and of theater as a means of directly affecting the world, demanded the creation of a performance mode in which staged scenarios could not be readily distinguished from spontaneously occurring events.

Estrin frequently referred to his creations as scenarios for "guerrilla theater," a term that was under debate in this era, and whose implications are profoundly meaningful for parsing infiltrative theater's viral implications.

The phrase "guerrilla theatre" entered American artistic conversation in a 1966 *TDR* essay, titled "Guerrilla Theatre," by R. G. Davis of the San Francisco Mime Troupe (Davis credited his collaborator Peter Berg with coining the phrase). Drawing on the Mime Troupe's own work, Davis offered a succinct set of guidelines for using low-budget, politically direct performance to raise consciousness and inspire audiences to action. But, although Davis quoted Che Guevara at the beginning of his essay ("The guerrilla fighter needs full help from the people of the area"),[18] he did not suggest that actors should disappear into the landscape that surrounded them, or that staged performances would be more effective if they gave the impression of being spontaneous events. To the contrary, Davis's guerrilla theater relied on the appeal of colorful, easily understood scenarios, drawing on street performance traditions such as the commedia dell'arte.[19] Davis's "guerrilla theatre" attempted to emulate guerrilla fighters' ethos of close connection to local communities, and their scrappy, flexible survival strategies. In a 1970 article about the form, Richard Schechner echoed Davis's formulations, noting that "it is called 'guerrilla' because some of its structures have been adapted from guerrilla warfare—simplicity of tactics, mobility, small bands, pressure at the point of greatest weakness, surprise."[20]

But Estrin saw the connection between guerrilla warfare and guerrilla theater from a different angle, one that significantly alters the relationship between an audience member and a performer. In an introduction to his "Four Guerrilla Theatre Pieces," published in *TDR*, Estrin rejected any performance mode that called itself guerrilla but remained recognizable as art:

> The term *guerrilla theater* is beginning to be thrown around quite loosely . . . I suggest restricting its use to that form of theater which, like the Viet Cong, does not identify itself as such. Theater which does not present itself as "performance." Theater which IS a reshaping of reality.[21]

Unmarked performances, for Estrin, would inspire action because their stakes appeared to be those of real events.

In a written scenario representative of this vision—a durational piece in which politics reshapes artistic representation—Estrin proposed that a painter set up an easel near some prominent national landmark (he suggests staging the piece in Lafayette Park, opposite the White House). Day by day, the artist should establish himself as a congenial local fixture, chatting with police and passersby while sketching a blandly realistic portrait of the monument at hand—until, inexorably and incrementally, the painting mutates from an innocuous image into, Estrin writes,

> a scene appropriate to the subject matter. On the White House balcony babies are napalmed, from the roof ICBMs emerge. Fragmentation

> bombs are exploded on the lawn maiming the (black) visitors. A grotesque Nixon and Laird oversee the operations.[22]

Out of an unassuming work of art, true horrors were to burst forth—the painting's mutation from apparent truth into shocking "reality" doubling the infiltrators' permeation of everyday America to reveal underlying social truths.

If this scenario had been performed (and Estrin says that, to his knowledge, it never was),[23] "The Painter" was not to conclude with the metamorphosis of the painting, but was intended to mutate again, turning into a public scandal over the controversial work of art. Estrin envisioned that once the painting's subject matter became dark and confrontational, local police, who might previously have welcomed an unassuming artistic presence, would turn on the painter and perhaps even evict him from the area. Local newspapers would then run stories and print images of the offending work of art on their front pages, and the artist himself would give interviews everywhere he could, employing the mainstream media as a conduit for subversive messages.

Such a suggestion underscores the inextricable link, for Estrin, between infiltrative scenarios and their afterlives in spectators' consciousness and in the media ecology. The painting's mediated public is as significant, and much larger, than its live audience. To design a performance intended to provoke disruption, scandal, and notoriety is to imagine the newspaper headlines as an integral element of the piece, no less than it would be if Estrin had worked in the age of the viral video and scaled his performances to fit the white frame of the YouTube page. And Estrin's plan for circulating his message didn't stop with media coverage. Finally—and perhaps most significantly—Estrin wrote, "Money from the sale of the now-famous painting is donated to the Movement."[24] "The Painter" thus, in a series of three steps, was intended to infiltrate everyday reality and then alter it. Most importantly, such notoriety, or so Estrin hoped, would increase the painting's monetary value, attracting a high price that could subsequently be used for revolutionary purposes. The performance's message, initially confined by the painting's frame, could be converted into the ever-circulating commodities of headlines and cash.

Some of Estrin's infiltrative scenarios attempted to even more thoroughly inhabit everyday circumstances, escaping detection as artistic work completely. Estrin counts among his most successful interventions into everyday life an "invisible" performance in San Francisco's City Lights Bookstore. Founded in the 1950s by the poet Lawrence Ferlinghetti, the bookstore had long been a gathering place for countercultural communities, some members of which felt that books should never be sold for a profit, and therefore that it was only fair to "rip off" bookstores and seize communal knowledge for free. Accordingly, Estrin observed, a few countercultural activists began stealing from not only mass chain establishments, but also independent stores like City Lights. "This seemed like a typical example of Movement bullshit—brothers undoing each other in the name of 'liberation' or conflicting ideologies," wrote Estrin in an unpublished document describing the piece, "so we decided to explore our own and the customers' attitudes toward ripping off City Lights."[25] The performance consisted of seven "beats," beginning when a participant unobtrusively stashed a book in his pocket, to the outrage of several witnesses. Customers observed the confrontation, unaware that they had become spectators to a planned performance. Estrin took the part of a defender for City Lights, demanding to know why the "thief" didn't shoplift from corporate chain stores instead. The piece, performed on multiple occasions, concluded with a showdown at the store's front desk, its results dependent on the whims of whoever stood behind the cash register on any given day.

Spectators, Estrin believed, could not be relied upon to join in collective action if that action were advertised in advance; provocations could be more contagious if they were unexpected, their ontology unclear. When Estrin published four scenarios for infiltrative theater in *TDR* in 1969, he included, besides "The Painter" and a quirky plan for flying "Viet Cong" kites in a public park, two blueprints for radicalizing classrooms and conventions, which offer useful illustrations of the fraught relationships between contagious dramaturgies and live audiences. In "A Piece for Conventions," which Estrin performed with a group of collaborators, he described a strategy for forcing sluggish, inertia-bound institutions to confront pressing political problems. Estrin and his collaborators "infiltrated" an annual convention of college newspaper editors, hoping to provoke the timid group into addressing the Vietnam War.

"Before the conference began," Estrin recalled, "we hung giant white screens from the balconies of the ballroom."[26] These large drapes dangled there, innocuously—like the bland painting in the park—until, during a debate over whether to address the Vietnam War as a group, the leadership of the convention decided to shut down discussion and pass a motion to "table the question." Estrin and his collaborators were outraged, and their outrage provided the impetus they were seeking. He recalled:

> Table Vietnam!! At that point, we cut the lights and began a barrage of six simultaneous atrocity films and tracks: battle scenes, LBJ, Rusk, napalm, a homecoming parade, dead children projected on the hanging screens . . . After three minutes, the lights were switched on, the films cut off, and a voice boomed over the great loudspeaker system of the grand ballroom. It was our "police voice" announcing that the films just shown were contraband North Vietnamese films, shown without State Department approval, and were being confiscated. The meeting was declared illegal and was ordered adjourned.[27]

This subterfuge worked. The assembled newspaper editors, believing they had just watched an impromptu screening of illegally acquired propaganda films, were suddenly cast in the roles of countercultural rebels. And once cast, their reluctance to discuss "politics" evaporated, and they were inspired to play the parts they'd been given. Estrin and his collaborators convinced the members of the convention to disband into small discussion groups, all of which began actively debating the question of how student newspapers should respond to the Vietnam War.

The performance's fictional elements remained concealed until they'd been rendered irrelevant, the invisible actions of Estrin and his collaborators prompting highly visible responses from their spectators. "The way the films were stopped, the nature of the sound, the previous emotionalism all created a credibility which might not have prevailed in a more rational context," he wrote.[28] In other words, despite Estrin's avowed allegiance to a mode of performance that so completely permeated the real world that there was no difference between spectator and actor, some of the most successful "infiltrations" relied precisely on that difference. Here again, as in "The Painter," Estrin's live performative infiltration was the first step in a larger infiltration of the media ecology. While such a move might constitute a familiar performance strategy in the age of hidden cameras and the Yes Men, for Estrin to conceive such a mode of infiltration in a pre-internet age testifies to a longer history of viral media, and a wider range of viral media forms, than is frequently assumed to exist.

This performance strategy also recalls the ontological and ethical debates faced by Estrin's influences, the Living Theatre and Artaud. Estrin's dramas of invisibility (and Boal's, as I will discuss shortly) relied on stirring up the same emotions of surprise, outrage, and frustration that key sections of *Paradise Now* inspired, and on the intensity of emotion that Artaud envisioned as a means of propelling charged ideas from the stage into the audience. For Estrin, as for the Living Theatre, the prospect of shifting action from performers to spectators relied on the changeable nature of the boundary between the two. While the Living Theatre hoped to spread revolution through overwhelming emotional presence, Estrin hoped to spread subversive change through his strategic employment of absence. And, like the Living Theatre before him, Estrin faced accusations of emotional manipulation. In his case, the charge was that his infiltrative scenarios, by withholding their status as performance, were coercive and condescending to their audience members, that the very elements Estrin imagined could make these pieces infectious were also what made them unjust.

This critique was expressed particularly clearly in a letter to the editor of *TDR*, by a reader named Martin Trueblood who objected to Estrin's "manipulative techniques."[29] Trueblood argued that Estrin was undermining political theater's mandate to enlighten rather than deceive, by infiltrating rather than demonstrating and by favoring surreptitious fictions over straightforward advocacy. Estrin responded by drawing comparisons between his own manipulations and those of the corporate and government agencies he intended to unsettle. "Not all manipulation is necessarily evil," he wrote, adding,

> Manipulation by Madison Ave., manipulation by the press, yes. But the manipulation in the Classroom Piece? We are dealing here, I think, with a different sort of thing . . . The critical question: does the "audience" emerge from the experience with more options or less? Have the degrees of freedom been increased or decreased? The guideline I have formulated for myself is: *if people emerge with more options, more freedom, go ahead and do it. If people emerge with fewer, watch out—it's fascism.*[30]

The emotional manipulation of spectators—even the emotional confrontation of spectators—was acceptable to Estrin because it could provoke the audience response he was seeking. Like *Paradise Now*, Estrin's "Convention Piece" sought to transmute audience frustration into audience enlightenment, to avoid direct conversation and rational exchange in favor of the more contagious theatrical elements of surprise and outrage.

Some of Estrin's most fully "infiltrative" ideas were never performed, and yet offer provocative models for an invisible viral dramaturgy. Such is the case with "A New Family Moves In," another scenario directly inspired by the Living Theatre, in this case *Paradise Now*, which, Estrin, recalled, "was a real breakthrough paradigm"[31] in its staging of spectatorship and participation. After attending a performance of the Living Theatre's revolutionary extravaganza, Estrin did precisely what the company hoped their spectators would. He conceived a "restaging" of *Paradise Now*'s revolution, to take place outside the theater.

In the *Paradise Now* passage that had stayed most clearly in Estrin's imagination, actors bludgeon each other with verbal signifiers of difference: "You're young!" yells one; "You're old!" comes the reply. "You're tall!" cries another; "You're short!" is summarily lobbed back—and on and on, invoking race, gender, body type, and other criteria of social division. Musing that "there is really no end to potential divisions among people," Estrin imagined mounting a real-life assault on social barriers, in what amounted to a socially motivated version of a reality TV–style apartment swap:

> Two families—one from each side of a conflict—are needed to cooperate in the making of this piece. Each must agree to move into the other's home. The experiments then proceed simultaneously.[32]

Estrin imagined participating in a "redneck-hippie" version of the exchange, seeing himself driving a "battered '37 Chevie van, painted in psychedelic colors" into a conformist suburban neighborhood, then proceeding to live according to his "hippie" habits, while simultaneously maintaining "the most open and communicative life style possible."[33] The "spectators" would be unsuspecting neighbors, and the performance's duration undefined: "The time scale of the piece would relate to the intention," Estrin explains. "Whatever happened, life would be different afterward for all concerned."[34] The performance idea, put another way, is simply a social vision for more fully integrated neighborhoods, which would in turn encourage more open-minded communities.

This scenario—most of all among Estrin's theatrical ideas—can be understood as an example of what Laura Levin calls "embedded performance," projects that often involve "the strategic embedding of self into environment as a mode of socio-political critique."[35] Levin's examples range from visual artists posing for photos in complex costumes that render them indistinguishable from their backdrops, to pranksters like the Yes Men, who pose as representatives of the organizations they critique. Embedded performance, she argues, can function in a variety of ways: it can highlight the insider's perspective within the "frame" of a landscape or social situation, can reveal unexpected affinities between performers and environments, and can allow performers to gain entrance to usually restricted sites.[36] Levin argues that embeddedness, which has been accused of fostering a biased, insider's perspective, can, on the contrary, be "a performative strategy used by artists to work *against* a dominant perspective and the obfuscating frames produced by media and state."[37] Embedded performers alter the background—sometimes, simply by making it visible.

Estrin's "A New Family Moves In" can be viewed as just such a project. Performer-participants are physically embedded within the frame of a social setting in which they do not obviously belong, as a means of critiquing assumptions about belonging itself. But here—and in viral performance as a whole—the emphasis is subtly but revealingly different from Levin's embeddedness. Viral performances focus not only on the relation between a performer and her environment, but also importantly on the relationship between a performer and her spectator, who is assumed to be in ideological flux, open to a shift in perspective, able to alter the environment as well. Embedding performers in an environment is the first step for Estrin, while provoking spectators into action is the necessary result.

"A New Family Moves In," perhaps his most ambitious script for "infiltrative theater," is limited in many ways, most significantly by the near-impossibility of staging it. (The more expansive Estrin's imagination became, the less likely his scenarios were to find embodiment.) Still, as an instance of a script inspired by revolutionary theater—the Living Theatre's wildest visions of contagious revolution coming true—the piece is representative of infiltrative theater's viral possibilities. Its drama is ongoing and ever-mutating (rather than temporally bounded), leaving open the possibilities for how the new family might influence its new community, and the time it might take to do so. The spectators, unidentified as such, determine the drama's outcome through their responses to the new neighbors, while the unmarked performers never leave their "stage," living out their dramatic fiction as if it were daily reality—which, very quickly, it would become. By remaining invisible, by infiltrating neighborhoods like guerrillas, Estrin's "new family" would infect their surroundings for an unbounded time to come.

Liberating the Spectator: Boal's Invisible Theater

In a brief section of his autobiography, *Hamlet and the Baker's Son*, the Brazilian playwright, director, and theorist Augusto Boal remembered an experience he had as a spectator when he was traveling in Europe, and went to see a politically radical theater troupe on tour from the United States. One scene from this radical work of theater stayed with him afterward: a section in which the company clearly intended to infectiously inspire the audience to action, but which struck Boal as artistically and politically dishonest. He wrote:

> I remember a North American group in Europe, doing an anarchist play in which every night the actors tore up their passports and incited the spectators to do the same. Clearly the US Consulate did not furnish them with new passports every morning to be torn up that night: false prop passports incited the spectators to tear up their own real passports.[38]

Though he does not cite them by name, it is highly likely that Boal is referring to the Living Theatre (which also toured his home country of Brazil in 1970 and 1971).[39] Like Estrin, Boal found the Living Theatre's infectious dramaturgies inspiring and provocative, and as he developed the collection of theatrical techniques for which he would become famous—known collectively as the "Theater of the Oppressed"—ideas about how spectators could be mobilized to action remained central to Boal's thinking. In artistic contrast with Estrin (and the Living Theatre), though, Boal sought immediacy in the communication between performers and spectators. There would be no "Rite of Guerilla Theatre," sacrificing thoughtful conversation for emotional affect; there would be no surprising infiltration for perplexed spectators to unravel, no attempt to provoke skepticism by means of the confusing or strange. Rather, the actions of both performers and spectators would be, as much as possible, the same; spectators would be inspired to reconsider everyday actions during the process of performing them.

Boal's commitment to this tactic was inspired by a series of revelations about performance and reality, including his response to *Paradise Now*, as well as an earlier and much-recounted incident in which his acting company from the Arena theater was touring an agitprop play in Brazil's northeast provinces, advocating peasants' rights against oppressive landholders.[40] After one performance, a farmer from the audience approached Boal, thrilled to have apparently found allies, and offered Boal's company guns to join in the attack on their landlords, which the actors bashfully turned down. "We were ashamed at having to decline this new invitation—an invitation to really fight rather than just talk about fighting," Boal remembers. "We told him we were genuine *artists* and not genuine *peasant farmers*."[41] He concluded: "That episode made me comprehend the falsity of the 'messenger' form of political theatre. We have no right to incite anyone to do something we are not prepared to do ourselves."[42]

In rejecting his own attempt to preach revolution without practicing it, Boal also condemned the Living Theatre's ethics, as they destroyed false passports while suggesting that spectators destroy real ones. And yet the forms Boal called forum theater, invisible theater, and legislative theater—as well as his well-known idea of the spect-actor, a viewer who enters a performance and alters its outcome—all share political and artistic concerns, and theatrical strategies, with the Living Theatre (and with Artaud before them). Likewise, though he advocated reasoned dialogue over artistic ambush, his dramaturgies overlapped with those of Estrin; and overlapped, too, with the audience choreographies of General Idea, though his tone was less satirical, his direction of spectators less formal, than theirs.

Boal worked in many artistic modes, from drama to musical theater to the array of performance practices that he labeled the "Theater of the Oppressed." But I focus here on a single strand of his work: the theory and practice of "invisible theater," first envisioned in the early 1970s. Invisible theater, most clearly among Boal's projects, employed a viral dramaturgy, instigating the communicable spread of ideas and actions through audiences and wider publics. In invisible performances, Boal most explicitly envisioned choreographing his spectators. Invisible theater, too, of all Boal's innovations, offers the most ambitious conception of how performance can fuse with ordinary life. I single out this mode and place it in the context of viral performance as a means of illuminating the artistic, ontological, and political assumptions that underlie Boal's theatrical thinking more broadly. Locating invisible theater within the category of viral performance also helps to distinguish it from the street theater and guerrilla performances with which it has often been grouped, to uncover other, less obvious affinities with avant-garde performance forms.

If Estrin's infiltrative strategies flirted with legal boundaries, and the Living Theatre weathered frequent encounters with police, invisible theater operated below the public radar out of legal and political necessity. Boal and his collaborators conceived this performance mode in the mid-1970s, under a violently repressive dictatorship in Argentina, during one of Boal's many stops in a long, itinerant exile from Brazil's own authoritarian regime.

With a group of Argentine collaborators, he planned a public performance celebrating a much-admired Buenos Aires ordinance which mandated that restaurants provide free meals to the poor. After friends warned Boal of the collaborations among exiled Nazis, Argentine secret police, and the CIA, he realized that attending his own performance would be dangerous and that he risked not only capture but assassination.[43] Rather than cancel the performance, his cast suggested remounting the play in the form of "invisible theater." It would no longer be performed onstage, but in a real restaurant, with the real waiters and restaurant managers replacing the actors who had played those roles. Boal would watch the show from another table:[44]

> From my table on the other side of the room, I was able to observe this extraordinary thing: the interpenetration of fiction and reality. The superimposition of two levels of the real: the reality of the quotidian and the reality of the rehearsed fiction.[45]

Boal concluded that the invisible performance, because it was apparently real, could harness a power to motivate spectators that explicit stage fictions lacked. As with infiltrative theater, invisible theater would address dispersed publics, one newly conscious spectator at a time. Rather than pressuring new recruits through a display of massive numbers, it would "infect" them by prompting the reconsideration of seemingly unalterable conditions. Rather than seeking to overwhelm the existing social order through the frenzy of a charged crowd, these performance modes would permeate society and, Boal hoped, reproduce themselves through considered conversation.

In Joanne Pottlitzer's forthcoming book *Symbols of Resistance: The Legacy of Artists under Pinochet (1973–1990)*, the Chilean actor and activist Mónica Echeverría recalls that, after hearing Boal speak in 1988, she planned an "invisible theater" performance to protest economic conditions under the Pinochet regime. Posing as a wealthy customer in a middle-class supermarket, she filled a grocery cart with caviar and other luxury purchases; a fellow actress, traversing the same supermarket with a young child, selected inexpensive necessities—rice, beans, and bread. When they reached the checkout counter, the "lower-income" performer began railing against the price of food and against the regime, and Echeverría confronted her publicly:

> I started yelling at her with a bourgeois voice, "Shut your mouth! What do you want to do? Go back to the times of Allende? How can you even think about it? We have everything we ever wanted with Pinochet . . ."[46]

While the performance lasted, the gathered spectators believed what they saw. They begged the two actresses to quiet down, bringing whiskey for Echeverría and water for her fellow performer.

To Boal, each unwitting participant in a scenario like Echeverría's would become a spect-actor, an audience member whose actions steer the performance toward its unrehearsed conclusion. "All these experiments of a people's theater have the same objective," he wrote, "the liberation of the spectator, on whom the theater has imposed finished visions of the world."[47] But although liberation of the spectator was often at least temporarily successful—in the sense of provoking sincere participation—the infectious reactions invisible theater inspired were not always the kind Boal intended, or even imagined.

In a 1990 *TDR* article, Boal describes an experience of twelve years earlier, when he visited Belgium in 1978 to conduct an invisible theater workshop with European theater artists. After three days of training in Brussels, Boal's company and their Belgian companions visited the city of Liège, where they planned and staged an invisible theater performance similar to Echeverría's. The piece took place in a supermarket, where its protagonist, an actor named Francois, filled his cart with food, then informed the checkout clerk that he was unemployed and could not pay for the goods. Instead, he proposed, he would work for the supermarket until the value of his labor equaled the value of the food in his shopping cart. The confused supermarket clerk anxiously summoned her manager, who in turn summoned the Belgian police. The police were initially reluctant to arrest Francois, since he hadn't stolen any of the goods—in fact, in the meantime, real customers in the supermarket had raised the necessary funds for him to purchase the food—but they took him to a local station for interrogation.

In the meantime, the performers had inspired a wide-ranging conversation among the supermarket's customers on the subjects of unemployment, Belgian politics, and the relationships between competing Belgian communities: precisely the form of dialogue that Boal's company had hoped to provoke.[48] Though the invisible theater piece culminated in the arrest of one of the company, it spurred its spectators to engage in consciousness-raising conversation and debate. Believing that Francois was one of 600,000 Belgians unemployed at the time, they accepted his predicament as a real one and leapt with little prompting into unscripted conversation about the problems of unemployment in their country.[49] (In fact, the police were also initially sympathetic to his plight—although after learning that Francois was a performer, was not unemployed, and had been following a partially prearranged scenario, they angrily filed charges against him for inciting disorder and for presenting a public performance without permission.)[50]

Boal's 1978 experiment in Liège, and Echeverría's Chilean supermarket performance—as well as, for that matter, Boal's very first invisible theater performance, the restaurant scenario of 1971—featured similar casts of characters and thrust their spectators into similar debates. Boal, like Estrin with his visions of placing tiny reminders of exploitation among the fruits and vegetables on supermarket shelves, wanted performance to challenge capitalism's permeation of everyday life. Each transformed ordinary items—a dollar, a loaf of bread—into theatrical props, throwing into relief the constant, active exchange and circulation of monetary value and material objects. In the Liège performance, Boal's actors reminded the supermarket clerk of the direct correlation between her hourly wages and the goods on the supermarket shelves, telling her:

> You Miss, for instance, what do you do? You work at this cash register 8 hours a day and by the end of the week, after having worked for 40 or 45 hours, are paid. Then, with the same money, you do your own shopping in this same supermarket.[51]

This theatrical strategy echoes the observations put forward by McLuhan (and Canetti before him) that money, crowds, and numbers are intimately linked, that all three demand accumulation, that all ultimately point to the circulation of meaning among and between people. "As a vast social metaphor, bridge, or translator," writes McLuhan, "money—like writing—speeds up exchange and tightens the bonds of interdependence in any community."[52] It is no accident that Boal's invisible performances frequently focused on places where money is directly exchanged; such actions paralleled the communication, circulation, and exchange of ideas and actions that invisible theater hoped to inspire among its audiences.

But, crucially, Boal hoped to provoke such circulations among his audience members without revealing to them that they were audience members in the first place—and here is where his dramaturgy of invisibility and his dramaturgy of provocation come into fascinating tension with each other. In her discussion of embedded performance, Levin takes care to distinguish Boal's invisibility from guerrilla forms like the work of artist-activist-pranksters Sacha Baron Cohen and the Yes Men. "While the term 'invisible theatre' is useful for thinking about unexpected performance actions in public space," she writes, "'guerrilla theatre' might be more accurate, as the chameleons that follow use camouflage tactics that resemble those of the military: acts of concealment that precede an ambush."[53] For the artists Levin describes, "guerrilla" suggests a dramaturgy of concealment and surprise, infiltration and revelation. This term, too, applies to Estrin, who also claimed "guerrilla" as an accurate descriptor of his work. But for Boal (and for General Idea, in a very different way), revelation and surprise—climax and denouement—are precisely what destroy the performance's powers of circulation. Invisible theater, for Boal, should never be revealed as a performance fiction; such a revelation would prevent the continued spread of actions that it inspires.

Boal's insistence on keeping performances covert led to a revealing dispute, during the same 1978 visit to Liège, over the politics and ontology of invisible theater. His supermarket performance inspired an artistic response, a second invisible piece that was not created by Boal and that challenged the theatrical structures his company had attempted to introduce. Several days after his troupe performed, Boal was scheduled to lead a public forum on various topics affecting Belgian communities—racism, unemployment, women's rights. Before he could begin, though, the workshop was interrupted by a group of policemen with a dog, who demanded that he show them identification and insisted he accompany them to the police station. Boal's Belgian collaborators were infuriated, and the crowd chased the police out of the theater; they left, threatening to return with reinforcements.

These police did not return, though. Boal's friends called various branches of the Belgian law enforcement system, only to find that none had ordered the arrest. Boal remembered that the police dog had appeared terrified of him—unlike the behavior of a trained police dog—and that the police had never shown identification. Soon, the group realized that the "arrest" was most likely an act of theater that had employed the same strategies as Boal's own. As Boal wondered aloud whether a right-wing group had staged the arrest in protest of his public appearance, one of the theater artists attending his forum abruptly confessed that her own troupe, the Belgian company Cirque Divers, had orchestrated the false arrest as an invisible theater experiment. The members of Cirque Divers offered a nihilistic explanation of their motives, telling Boal that they'd intended to perform an act of straightforward disruption, one that had no cause or explanation: "We don't believe in people any longer," they told Boal.[54] (Friends of Boal offered another interpretation, recalling that Cirque Divers had initially asked him to conduct his Belgian workshop with their company, and that Boal had chosen other primary collaborators instead. Perhaps the rejected company was jealous and had staged a coup simply to attract attention or prevent Boal from working too closely with their rivals.)

Boal never learned the exact motivations of the artists who so successfully upended his plans, but his response to them offers several insights about the dramaturgy and the politics underlying his vision for invisible theater. Reflecting on the events, he distinguished the actions of Cirque Divers from his own dramaturgy, arguing that even if the Belgian company's provocation seemed to take the shape of invisible theater, it did not qualify as an example of the form because its intentions and concerns were different. "THE INVISIBLE THEATRE never places itself in an illegal position because it does not intend to violate the law," he wrote. "It intends to question the legitimacy of the law, which is a very different matter altogether."[55] More than this, Boal posited that, in the theater, "pure technique does not exist in the same sense that pure mathematics does. Two plus two is four, regardless of the question. But theatre does not struggle against curved lines, angles, numbers, or figures; theatre struggles with the unexpected one wishes to know and it struggles with people."[56] (And yet, to remember McLuhan, numbers can be a matter of touch and feel, and performance's affective spread can be a question of mathematical accumulation.)

Invisible theater, to Boal, was only invisible theater when its tactics and modes were used to the ends he intended for them: questioning legal, social, and political systems, and systematically throwing light on the forces of economic oppression. Yet, as the Cirque Divers performance suggested, the dramaturgy of invisible theater does provide a "pure form" of a sort, a format for surreptitious theatrical provocation. Always political, sometimes provocatively so, it is—like viral dramaturgies more broadly—available and attractive to both forces of revolution and agents of political or economic oppression, equally appealing as a strategy for undermining the routines of consumerism and as a means of marketing new products to routine-dulled consumers. The "arrest" staged by members of Cirque Divers did meet the initial criteria Boal had established for his first invisible theater performance. It was not staged in a theater (or at least, did not use the theater in any conventional sense), did not announce itself as a performance, and gave the spectators no hint that they were witnessing a planned spectacle. It successfully provoked its audience into an infuriated dialogue with the "policemen" who had appeared to arrest Boal, and later into a conversation about the legality of Boal's travel in Belgium and of various forms of identification. Just as Boal's supermarket staging, days earlier, had forced unwitting spectators to decide quickly whether they would assist Francois or ignore him, Cirque Divers's invisible performance prompted its audience to either stand with Boal or to abandon him on the spot.

In his article describing these events, Boal offered a single, central reason that the actions of Cirque Divers did not qualify as invisible theater: the Belgian company's provocation was not only thematically unrelated to invisible theater's concerns, but also, in practical terms, failed to challenge systems of oppression. "The theatre of the oppressed techniques are meant to help the oppressed," continued Boal. "They are actually their weapons of liberation . . . the Cirque Divers actors, apart from doubling the already existing oppression, committed an illegal act by wearing police uniforms which made them subject to a new charge, the fourth one in this crazy story."[57] Here, Boal surpassed his previous suggestion that invisible theater needed to be oriented thematically toward liberation to argue, further, that invisible theater actually needed to put liberating actions into effect. In other words, to have the infectious results he sought, invisible performances must inspire not only critical contemplation but also action on the part of its audiences. Brecht's coolly intelligent spectator, smoking and appraising the stage action, would not suffice here, nor would Rancière's emancipated spectator.[58] The only kind of spectator who could fulfill Boal's goals for invisible theater was the spect-actor, spontaneously reaching into his or her pocket and pulling out real money to pay for Francois's supermarket cart full of real necessities.

And yet: Francois, the protagonist of the supermarket scenario, was an actor, he was not unemployed, and he did not need the groceries these unwitting participants were purchasing for him—at least not as desperately as he claimed to. The impromptu audience members had taken real action, but they had done so in response to a fictive scenario, one that reflected realities but was not literally true. Boal acknowledged this seeming contradiction in writing about the incident, insisting that

> we had not lied at Liège, in spite of having been accused by the police after they discovered that Francois had a good job and was not unemployed or hungry. It was not true that the actor was the character but it was true that they both existed! And their problems were indeed real problems . . . consequently everything was true.[59]

Boal here employed the same theatrical logic for which he had critiqued *Paradise Now*; the same logic that *TDR* reader Martin Trueblood objected to in Estrin's infiltrative performances. Like these other works, Boal's supermarket scenario had attempted to embody large-scale social problems allegorically, symbolically, and in so infectious a way that spectators could not resist participating, whether or not the embodiments were literally real. Infectiousness here transcended the literal truth, just as it did for Estrin, General Idea, and the Living Theatre before them. Contagion demanded performance fiction—even when the performance aimed to become inextricable from the real.

Another of Boal's invisible theater performances, also from 1978, contains a similar approach to spectatorship and contagion, aligning suggestively with the embeddedness of Estrin's guerrilla performances as well as with the technological choreographies of General Idea. During a visit to Bari, Italy, Boal's troupe staged a piece in which a young Brazilian actor sat on a park bench alone, with a tape recorder in hand. As the park filled with passersby, the performer began to make darkly emotional statements aloud, capturing and then replaying each on the recorder as he did. "I am by myself," he announced. "I don't have any friends. Nobody wants to talk to me because I am a foreigner and in this country and in this city there is discrimination."[60] The actor continued, his pronouncements growing more desperate and increasingly demanding intervention. "I am unemployed," he declared. "I tried to kill myself yesterday . . . Maybe today I'll do it."[61] As he presented these confessions to passing strangers, the recorder played his own taped voice back at him, reiterating his words for all to hear.

As Boal remembers, strangers passing through the park did attempt to intervene, approaching the forlorn-looking actor to offer support, sympathy, and company. "It was a scene of rare tenderness, almost an intimate scene despite its public setting with crowds, cars, and noise," wrote Boal.[62] Afterward, though, the members of his own theater company were confused. Hadn't they deceived the public, they wondered, given that the performer in question was not an immigrant living in Italy, and was not unemployed, alone, or suffering from depression? As with the Belgian performance, Boal quelled these doubts by asserting the performance's broad underlying truths, regardless of its literal accuracy:

> The truth was that the Brazilian actor was not suffering any of the tortures that he was describing. But it was true that those tortures existed. If it wasn't true that he himself had attempted suicide, it was certainly true that another émigré a few months earlier had actually killed himself. So although the Brazilian actor's story wasn't strictly true, it was truth.[63]

Again, the desire to provoke audience response transcended, for Boal, the imperative toward factual fidelity. In his description, Boal made no mention of whether the presence of the performer's tape recorder changed his impromptu audience's response—whether it attracted more listeners by amplifying the actor's voice, whether it suggested to observers that the actor was anyone other than a dissatisfied immigrant giving expression to his despair. And yet such a device could have hardly helped but create a rupture in the performance fiction, a hint that what Boal was embedding in the park was not a spontaneously occurring event. As the tape played alongside the live performance, the recording and reiteration of the event would have been concurrent with—and an amplification of—the event itself, just as recording and repetition were, as I will demonstrate shortly, an essential element for the kinds of audience responses General Idea sought to inspire. Recording technology amplified the live event, increased its powers of circulation, and formally reiterated the pattern of events and ideas that Boal's actor performed.

Looked at in this way, Boal's invisible theater, and the orientation toward spectatorship that it implies, begins to take on some of the formal qualities of other types of viral performance—even though Boal himself was careful to distinguish his work from guerrilla theater and related modes of embeddedness. In an essay describing the "Poetics of the Oppressed," Boal argued, "it is necessary to emphasize that the invisible theater is not the same thing as a 'happening' or the so-called 'guerrilla theater.' In the latter we are clearly talking about 'theater,' and therefore the wall that separates actors from spectators immediately arises, reducing the spectator to impotence: a spectator is always less than a man!"[64] Such an assertion lies at the core of Boal's approach to the Theater of the Oppressed as a whole, and underpins his objections to both Aristotelian and Brechtian dramaturgy. Aristotle, Boal asserted, wanted spectators to delegate the powers of both thinking and acting to performers; Brecht changed the equation by insisting that spectators think on their own, but still expected them to delegate the action to characters onstage.[65]

Boal's invisible performances were intended to be infectious in two ways: first, in the moment, when bystanders step up to help the stranger in distress, argue with each other, and debate the conditions that caused the distress; and second, when those bystanders go on to discuss the same events with their friends, families, or coworkers, thus spreading the debate to a wider, dispersed field of contemplative spectators. This second mode of contagiousness is the one that Boal aspired to: the rational, thoughtful series of discussions that can take place after an unexpected incident has sparked thought in those who witnessed it. But the first mode is the one that more clearly constitutes an immediate, tangible form of action—the action of spectators helping to solve the supposedly starving person's problems, by raising funds on the spot, arguing with checkout people in supermarkets, attempting to intervene. Crucially, these spectators give money, or take other action, in order to alleviate an immediate crisis, not as a means to a long-term solution to problems of unemployment or hunger, and they do so in response to witnessing an emotional outburst, not in response to a reasoned analysis of social or political problems.

My aim here is not to critique the ethics of Boal's approach to spectatorship, but rather to illuminate Boal's formal approach to audience participation, an approach that trafficked in more complex forms of affective transmission, and a more complicated politics of audience control, than is often recognized. Like the work of Estrin and General Idea, Boal's invisible theater mobilized audiences not as performers, but as communicative spectators. Like Estrin, Boal removed the visible markers of stage fiction from his invisible performances, and like General Idea, he viewed his performances as parts of a longer, socially transformative process. The performances did not contain shocking "ambushes"—or dramatic climaxes or revelations—because they were not intended to have dramatic endings. Instead, they were intended to circulate continuously, in the absence of visible performance, employing their spectators' bodies and wider social networks.

Image Is Virus: General Idea's Methods of Invasion

"Image is virus," wrote General Idea, in a 1973 special issue of *FILE Megazine*, a periodical the group had recently founded as both a parody of mainstream media and a voice of the Canadian underground arts scene.[66] AA Bronson, Jorge Zontal, and Felix Partz viewed the virus as a model for artistic creation and dissemination, and the concept inflected much of the trio's work from the late 1960s onwards. The aphorism "image is virus" comes from William S. Burroughs's *Nova Express*, a novel rife with viral imagery that, along with other Burroughs works, provided an important source of inspiration to General Idea. Burroughs's significance, for the trio, began with his status as an iconic outsider, a writer who did not identify with any reigning literary establishment, and in whose works images and ideas circulated outside of established communications channels. Virus figures as a powerful image in novels like *Naked Lunch*, *The Soft Machine*, *Nova Express*, and *The Ticket That Exploded*, standing in for a host of subversive and threatening forces: invasions from other planets; the transformative powers of mind-altering substances; and the paralyzing constrictions of modern society, among others. In Burroughs's writing, viral imagery appears in tandem with forces of technology and mechanization, a connection that proved foundationally inspirational for General Idea, as it has been for many other artists and writers.[67]

Bronson, Partz, and Zontal, like Burroughs, viewed images and ideas as viral invaders. Like him, they envisioned their visual, performance, and literary work functioning parasitically and virally within the larger art world and within mainstream culture. Virus was a form of art, a means of making art, and, above all, a description of the relationship between General Idea's art and its dissemination. "Our familiar, *LIFE*-like format belied its viral content," Bronson wrote of *FILE* in a retrospective essay.[68] Using viral imagery frequently and flexibly, General Idea drew on the history of the concept as an emblem of outsider literary and artistic creation, while reimagining the virus not only as an insidious alien force, but also as a route to new artistic methods and forms.[69] The group members shaped their artistic identities around a viral model of cultural transmission: "We knew that in order to be glamourous," they wrote, "we had to become plagiarists, intellectual parasites."[70] Positioning themselves as viral artists two decades before the AIDS epidemic changed the cultural connotations of the word "virus"—and more than three decades before anything "went viral"—General Idea's body of work stands as one of the twentieth century's most pathbreaking expressions of the viral in art.

In this section, I trace the contours of General Idea's viral artistic identity. I argue that conceptions of viral art apply potently and revealingly to the collective's theater and performance practice, a body of work that has not been analyzed in depth as viral—and, moreover, has rarely been systematically analyzed at all. I thus aim to provide a useful counterpoint to existing narratives of the collective's work. While General Idea's visual, editorial, and conceptual practice has been documented in recent art-historical scholarship (for instance, Philip Monk's 2012 *Glamour Is Theft: A User's Guide to General Idea*, and the 2011 anthology *General Idea: Haute Culture: A Retrospective 1969–1994*), the group's performance pieces have been analyzed in less detail, and linked less closely to the artists' viral thinking.

Sometimes, theater has also been deliberately diminished in the collective's narrative, even where theatrical contexts play a vital role. In *Glamour Is Theft*, for instance, Monk enters a discussion of the Miss General Idea Pageants, a series of performances staged between 1970 and 1978, by arguing that the first iteration of the pageant should not be considered alongside later versions because its theatrical setting was inappropriate for understanding General Idea's larger project. He writes:

> That first pageant was framed by the wrong context, reflective of General Idea's experimental theatre interests, and performed in a Festival of Underground Theatre. It was not until the next year, at the Art Gallery of Ontario in Toronto, that General Idea inhabited the right framework by appropriating the format of an art gallery in turn.[71]

There is no doubt that the world of galleries and museums, star painters and celebrity sculptors, constituted an essential point of reference and an ongoing object of satire for General Idea across their body of work. And yet to dismiss performance—and even conventional theatrical form—as irrelevant or as the "wrong" context for General Idea's practice is to miss layers of meaning in their early projects, and to underestimate the significance of live art to their broader theories, particularly the theory of the viral. Theatrical performance was a significant medium for General Idea's work from the late 1960s through the late 1970s, and their pieces involving live audiences should be understood as a key to their theory of viral media and art.

In the late summer of 1970, the artists comprising General Idea—who, at the time, had not yet adopted their pseudonyms and were operating under the names Ron Gabe, George (or Jorge) Saia, and Michael Tims—participated in the Festival of Underground Theatre at the St. Lawrence Centre in Toronto, Ontario. The St. Lawrence Centre had been built earlier that year, and the festival, the first of its kind in Toronto, proved important for interdisciplinary artistic collaborations and the founding of artists' spaces. Even artists who were not primarily theater-makers found the festival inspirational. In a catalog of "artist-initiated activity in Canada, 1939–1987," coedited by Bronson, the 1970 festival's entry noted:

> At this point in Toronto's history the underground theatre scene was attracting all the talent of a new generation. Many of the visual artists circulating in and around that scene came to use the model of the underground theatre as a beginning for thinking about their own work. The festival, inspired by the Bread and Puppet Theatre, Fluxus and street theatre more generally, seemed to offer a new model for both production of and audience for contemporary art, soon to be tested further in Toronto.[72]

General Idea had already been involved in Toronto's underground theater scene for several years. During the late 1960s, Bronson collaborated frequently with artists at the local Theatre Passe Muraille,[73] and in 1969 Bronson, Partz, and Zontal designed the stage set and posters for a production there, entitled *An Evening with the Maids*, based on Jean Genet's *The Maids*.[74] The group also created live performance works of their own devising, including *Laundromat Special #1*, also staged at Theatre Passe Muraille and involving a massive, oversized laundry bag, boxes of detergent stacked in an imposing pyramid shape, and a cast of at least six; as well as *Match My Strike*, a Happening-like performance staged at the Poor Alex Theatre. The latter piece consisted of five independent sections, including a "meat ceremony," a recitation of poetry, and a paper ceiling that collapsed on the audience.[75]

General Idea made two contributions to the 1970 St. Lawrence Centre festival: a staging of Gertrude Stein's early play *What Happened* and the first Miss General Idea Beauty Pageant, which became the inspiration for the larger pageant series and the conceptual project that surrounded it. The performance of *What Happened*, as described in the group's unpublished documentation, was deeply informed by General Idea's interest in media transmission—and, in fact, by Stein's own preoccupation with the circulation and transformation of words and images. Prior to the performance, General Idea acquired a telex machine from the telecom company CN Telecommunications, which they preprogrammed to type out act 1 of Stein's play. Once the performance began, the artists employed the telex to send the Stein text, in real performance time, to numerous recipients including the Toronto Stock Exchange, the library at Simon Fraser University, and Canada Packers, a large meatpacking corporation.

This was one of many ways General Idea toyed with the transmission of Stein's text. A performer inscribed lines from the play on the theater walls in chalk; a local radio station sent Stein's words out over the airwaves; and the performers used rubber stamps reading "Gertrude Stein" to label spectators' arms and legs. As Michael Tims described the piece in his playful press release (which he wrote under the name Eleanor Glass), "The play is taped, typed, telexed, radioed, videoed, written, read, printed, photographed, stamped and telephoned."[76]

After the performance, General Idea conducted a playful interview with a St. Lawrence Centre staff member, who summarily dismissed their work. "I think it's a practical joke and a waste of money and somebody's putting us on," declared the unnamed interviewee. And yet descriptions of the piece suggest that the group's performance strategies were deeply in sympathy with Stein's interest in the transmission, dissemination, and reception of words, gestures, and images—a preoccupation that Stein cited as one of her central motivations for writing plays (and specifically *What Happened*, her first). Stein was famously fascinated by the relationship between spectator and performer, describing the anxiety-inducing situation of live performance as one in which "the emotion of the one seeing and the emotion of the thing seen do not progress together."[77] She envisioned her plays as theatrical landscapes where such frustratingly syncopated transmission could be circumvented by simultaneity and multiplicity. Communications technology, too, was an important influence for Stein, who was exposed at an early age to performances that employed the telegraph onstage, especially William Gillette's Civil War drama *Secret Service*, which, she wrote, offered a new theatrical technique involving "silence stillness and quick movement," at the heart of which were climactic scenes featuring the transmission of text by telegraph.[78]

The telex network, of which General Idea made abundant use in their 1970 staging, was a direct technological descendant of the telegraph.

When she began writing plays, Stein explained, she "concluded that anything that was not a story could be a play and I even made plays in letters and advertisements."[79] The concept that plays were meant to be transmitted, to travel invisibly from stage to audience, and that they could take the form of correspondence and even advertising—a mode of communication particularly intent on inspiring direct action—underscores the central role that concepts of transmission played in Stein's work. General Idea's production drew on Stein's fascination with technologies of transmission and dissemination, and with the mutation of words and gestures as they spread. On a telex printout from the August 19, 1970, performance of *What Happened*, a note beneath the text of Stein's play reads "HI THERE MOME AND BEST WISHES ON YOUR FOURTIETH WEDDING ANNIVERSARY" [*sic*]—a non sequitur that reinforces the importance that these transmissions find recipients.[80]

Beyond an expansion on Stein's ideas about the circulation of images and words, I view General Idea's staging of *What Happened* as an homage to McLuhan, whose *Understanding Media* had a profound influence on Zontal, Partz, and Bronson. McLuhan's observations about the formal and structural qualities of media technologies converge in General Idea's staging. "The 'content' of any medium is always another medium," wrote McLuhan. "The content of writing is speech, just as the written word is the content of print, and print is the content of the telegraph."[81] Technologies of transmission are not neutral containers for "pure" ideas; they are the ideas (a familiar concept now, but a radical one then). McLuhan thought that the telegraph, with its transmission of code across electrical networks, had a particularly democratizing effect on modes of communication. "The separation of functions, and the division of stages, spaces, and tasks are characteristic of literate and visual society and of the Western world," he wrote. "These divisions tend to dissolve through the action of the instant and organic interrelations of electricity."[82] General Idea, by systematically passing Stein's text through telex, video, and radio, tested and retested just such propositions.

For the artists, communications technologies invited the leveling of one long accepted, seemingly obvious hierarchy in particular: the division between spectators who were present in the theater and those who gained even partial access to the performance through technological circulation. Dismantling this distinction is essential for creating the kinds of transmission that viral performance, in general, aspires to. In descriptions of *What Happened*, General Idea asserted:

> The event and the recording of it are interchangeable. During intermissions, all the data gathered during the previous act is played back or displayed (the tapes, photographs, video tapes, verbal descriptions, sketches, documents, etc.).[83]

In context, this statement is strikingly significant, predicting the artistic modes in which General Idea would work for years to come. The idea that a performance event could be "interchangeable" with the documentation of that event—whether in the form of text, image, or video—seems to defy theatrical logic, to deny the ephemeral quality of live performance expressed most famously by (but not limited to) Peggy Phelan's much-disputed dictum that "performance's only life is in the present."[84] Always, the live event stands in close, if vexed, relationship with its documentation; but just as certainly, the live event, it is commonly assumed, is not synonymous, and certainly not "interchangeable," with its recorded form.

Yet General Idea asserts that it is. Such a radical stance can only hold true if the artists, as General Idea did, make transmission and circulation—not a singular live event—the primary action of their performances. This was not only the trio's approach to *What Happened*, but also the way they increasingly staged performances, as they began to conceive theatrical events as "rehearsals of the audience" for the elusive 1984 Miss General Idea Pageant, and to lead their audiences in rehearsed choreographies of spectatorship akin to those envisioned in the trio's manifesto "Target Audience": applause, standing ovations, yawning, falling asleep. If recording is conceived not as the static fixing of the live event on paper or videotape, but rather as a means of transmission, itself unfolding in time and space, then the performance and its documentation do begin to look like equals. Likewise, the repetition of theatrical gesture on video begins to look similar in form and function to spectators' choreographed repetition of archetypal gestures, as in the Miss General Idea series. For the artists, recording a live event was not a way of preserving it, but of spreading it. The Living Theatre used concepts of contagion to collapse the distinction between performer and spectator; General Idea used concepts of contagion to collapse the distinction between a live performance and its many-times-mediated repetition.

Then, too, General Idea began to practice a form of embeddedness—not, as in the case of Estrin or Boal, by creating performances that vanished into everyday life, but rather by creating performances that inhabited the structures of outdated mainstream cultural forms. In addition to performing *What Happened* at the 1970 St. Lawrence Centre festival, General Idea also staged the first Miss General Idea Pageant, which would eventually take shape as a series of projects in many media forms, and lead to the development of the myth of "Miss General Idea" as a central part of the group's artistic persona. The first pageant, performed live, featured a contestant named Miss Honey, who competed with a dozen "bears" (performers dressed in large, slightly dilapidated full-body bear suits) for the crown of Miss General Idea. Décor mimicked the style of a mainstream beauty pageant; one photo shows Jorge Zontal kneeling amid oversized vases of flowers, apparently acquired from a local funeral home.[85] Among other elements, the event featured a talent competition in which Miss Honey emerged victorious at least partially on the basis of her fluency on the telex machine.[86]

This first live pageant marked the beginning of a series of Miss General Idea–themed works: performances, but also essays, architectural drawings, and fashion designs. As the pageants evolved, General Idea began to transform the series (and in fact, the phantom figure of "Miss General Idea" herself) from a succession of timebound events into an ever-circulating myth. They also increasingly intertwined it with the concept of the viral. The 1971 Miss General Idea Pageant took the first step in this direction when, rather than holding a pageant competition, the artists staged a live awards ceremony as the culmination of a contest conducted entirely through the mail. Potential competitors (friends, collaborators, acquaintances within General Idea's artistic network) were sent entry kits containing their very own "Miss General Idea Gown"—which they were instructed to wear in a series of glamour shots—and information about how to send back their complete bids for the coveted title. The accompanying instructions declare that holding a competition entirely based on written and photographic materials serves the purpose of eliminating "those embarrassing bathing-beauty line-ups, those annoying talent demonstrations."[87]

But the significance of this choice went much deeper. The collective was closely connected to artists and groups who were participating in what was then called "mail art," the sending and receiving of artworks through the mail, turning the postal service into a conduit for a performative underground network of countercultural artistic exchange. Closely connected to General Idea's larger artistic community was the network known as the New York Correspondence School, or NYCS ("Correspondence" was also often spelled "Correspondance," the portmanteau suggesting that postal dissemination constituted a form of playful choreography), founded by the artist Ray Johnson, which had its first major showing at the Whitney Museum of American Art in 1970.[88] In his 2009 study *Cruising Utopia*, José Esteban Muñoz describes the NYCS's work in explicitly theatrical terms, arguing that Johnson's collages, mailed to friends and fellow artists, were "performing objects insofar as they danced across the runways and stages provided by the world postal system. They were performative art objects that flowed like queer mercury throughout the channels of majoritarian communication and information."[89] This approach to subverting mainstream modes of transmission finds parallel in General Idea's use of information technologies, their founding of *FILE Megazine*, and explicitly in the establishment of the Image Bank, a Canadian artistic exchange that served as a counterpoint to the NYCS. In addition to working with mail artists like Ray Johnson, General Idea published an "Image Bank Request List" in each issue of *FILE*, listing calls for mail art from artists and community members. The slogan, printed across the top of each edition of the Image Bank, was "Image *is* Virus."[90]

V.B. Gowns on Parade in *Going Thru the Motions*, 1975. Photography by General Idea. Image courtesy of Esther Schipper, Berlin, used with permission of AA Bronson.

The 1971 pageant, then, involved not only a clever evasion of the live competition, but also the transformation of a singular live performance into an extended act of artistic circulation through the mail. That year's pageant did feature a live awards ceremony, held at the Art Gallery of Ontario on October 1. The festivities featured a panel of three judges, who decided which mail-order beauty queen should take the prize, as well as awarding a second, unspecified title of Miss Generality. A band played in the background as Miss Honey and the two previous Miss General Ideas 1968 and 1969 made speeches (their titles having been conferred belatedly, despite there having been no pageants in those years, as a way of including more of General Idea's frequent collaborators in the project). A male contestant performing under the pseudonym Marcel Idea was named the winner.

After the 1971 Miss General Idea contest, the offstage shadow of Miss General Idea grew. Rather than plan a 1972 Miss General Idea pageant, the group decided to reconceive the pageant series as an imaginary, exaggerated, near-apocalyptic progression toward a perpetually deferred final event. There would not be a new Miss General Idea contest the following year, nor the year after that. Instead, the group announced that they were postponing the next pageant until the prophetically meaningful year of 1984 (there is at least a glancing reference to Orwell here). But this did not mean that General Idea stopped creating live performances about the pageant series; to the contrary, after deciding not to hold the competition anymore, the group's Miss General Idea–themed performances became richer, more fascinating, more focused. They began staging a series of events that they conceived of as rehearsals for the audience—rehearsals in which spectators would "learn" how to be the fantasy audience that the fantasy 1984 pageant would require. In pieces such as *Blocking* (1974), *Going Thru the Motions* (1975), *Hot Property* (1977), and *Towards an Audience Vocabulary* (1978), General Idea began placing the physical and emotional responses of the audience at the center of the artistic event and turning the transmission of gesture into the most important theatrical action. Those attending General Idea's performances became the kind of fantasy spectators described in "Target Audience," obsessively and enthusiastically rehearsing the paradigmatic poses of spectatorship. They laughed, they applauded, they gasped, and they dozed off, all carefully orchestrated at the artists' behest.

Before staging these pieces, though, General Idea's members did something else: they published a series of meditations on their own artistic identities, beginning in the 1973 double issue of *FILE*, in which they articulated how and why artists and artistic works could be viral. The double issue offered a comprehensive analysis of the changing landscape of media culture; the role of artists, consumers, and spectators within it; and the ways myth and metaphor could serve subversive artistic ends. In the article entitled "Pablum for the Pablum Eaters: A Method of Invasion," the collective laid out a programmatic description of how subversive artists, in this case the participants in Image Bank, could work within mainstream media culture. Image Bank, General Idea wrote, was "concerned with establishing a culture that relates to official culture as a virus does to an organism."[91] This viral metaphor, articulated in relation to Image Bank, applies equally to General Idea's larger self-image as artists. They understood themselves as subversive, parasitic operatives within the larger artistic and media world, and as they continued to publish *FILE*, they expanded on these guiding artistic principles. "We are obsessed with available form," they wrote, in the 1975 "Glamour" issue. "We maneuver hungrily, conquering the uncontested territory of culture's forgotten shells—beauty pageants, pavilions, picture magazines, and other contemporary corpses. Like parasites we animate these dead bodies and speak in alien tongues."[92] Echoes of Burroughs's viral alien invaders abounded in these texts.

Scholars have frequently agreed that the "bodies" which General Idea animated were "dead" ones: they were, as the artists wrote, "culture's forgotten shells," "contemporary corpses" such as the format of the beauty pageant. This is part of the picture. But what such narratives miss is that the bodies General Idea animated were first and foremost those of their audience members: living, active bodies, performing gesture and action under the artists' direction. Looked at in this way, the group's obsessive choreography of spectatorship comes into focus not only as the centerpiece of a playful campaign to inhabit celebrity identities without the necessity of achieving fame, but also as part of a lineage of participatory performance that includes many more overtly political works. Although the playful beauty pageants did not constitute the same kind of directly political intervention that Estrin and Boal created, they functioned, playfully, as obliquely political acts. The beauty pageant offered a form ripe for subversion: partially for its strict dramaturgy of contest and results, partially for its association with hokey mainstream ideas of power, and partially because beauty pageants were at the epicenter of new thinking about gender at the time. The famed Miss America pageant protests in Atlantic City had happened only two years before, in August 1968. Inhabiting the beauty pageant, for General Idea, was a means of subverting from within, infiltrating and redirecting the aims of a product of mainstream culture, rendering an avatar of normativity delightfully queer. Muñoz, explicating the NYCS's work as a kind of performance, had described the U.S. Postal Service as a "runway": an image that, likewise, gestures to beauty pageants and fashion shows, their formats ripe for adoption and subversion.

Bronson gestured to the group's radical politics in a retrospective essay entitled "Myth as Parasite/Image as Virus," reflecting on projects created between 1969 and 1975. Citing General Idea's disillusionment in the late 1960s and early 1970s, following the disappointments of the Paris uprising and international situationism, he wrote:

> We had abandoned . . . any shred of belief that we could change the world by activism, by demonstration, by any of the methods we had tried in the 1960s—they had all failed . . . Now we turned to the queer outsider methods of William Burroughs, for example, whose invented universe of sex-mad, body-snatcher espionage archetypes provided the ironic myth-making model we required . . . We abandoned bona fide cultural terrorism, then, and replaced it with viral methods . . . utilizing the distribution and communication forms of mass media and specifically of the cultural world, we could infect the mainstream with our mutations, and stretch that social fabric.[93]

In my view, audience choreography constituted one of the most explicitly political dimensions of these "mutations." Though the Miss General Idea pageants were not riots, protest actions, demonstrations, or be-ins, they participated in an ethos of collective action. The revolutionary riot is submerged in the carefully choreographed ovation—but not so deeply submerged as to be undetectable.

The significance of the viral for General Idea's overall artistic work—especially their visual practice and the philosophical and poetic texts printed in *FILE*—has been noted by other scholars, most clearly, to date, by Monk

Suzette as the "Spirit of Miss General Idea" in *Going Thru the Motions*, 1975. Photography by General Idea. Image courtesy of Esther Schipper, Berlin, used with permission of AA Bronson.

in *Glamour Is Theft*. There, he observes the connections between virus and concepts such as repetition ("mimicry was viral," he writes)[94] and nostalgia. What has been less clearly articulated in scholarship about General Idea is that, for Zontal, Partz, and Bronson, viral mimicry was not only something that took place conceptually or in the visual arena. Viruses were not only theoretical, and they were not only performative in an abstract sense. Rather, the Miss General Idea series demonstrated that viral mimicry was actually constituted from performance. (This is, of course, the art form most directly at the heart of "mimicry.") Burroughs conjured strange worlds of alien body snatchers on the page. General Idea—commandeering their audiences—actually snatched bodies.

Between 1974 and 1978, with the specter of the 1984 Miss General Idea Pageant ever before them, the artists created a series of performance pieces aimed at, as they viewed it, training their audience members in the proper modes of spectatorship for the ultimate (and imagined) pageant to be staged years hence. Although, according to the notes in General Idea's archival files, *Target Audience* was never performed, draft text for the piece testifies to spectators' centrality to the company's performance work. From the beginning,

General Idea conceived of their audience members as consumers, something that speaks not only to their understanding of the art world as a marketplace, but also to the simpler idea that the audience would physically engage with and even internalize the performance work. "We tried to visualize an audience that represented today's spiraling cultural market," they wrote, "an audience well-versed in cultural inversions."[95]

The artists described their observations about audience response, which they viewed in terms of circulating gestures, choreographed and rehearsed:

> We soon woke up to the fact that audiences in general have a repertoire of stock reactions which they perform when correctly stimulated. We catalogued these responses as they surfaced in rehearsal. The Miss General Idea Pageant was an archetypal format containing archetypal scenes requiring an archetypal audience performing archetypal responses.[96]

The artists noted and codified these ritualized responses—laughter, applause, absorption, boredom, and shock—and subsequently employed them as central actions in pieces such as *Blocking*, *Hot Property*, *Going Thru the Motions*, and *Towards an Audience Vocabulary*, all of which were advertised as various forms of staged "rehearsal" for the 1984 Miss General Idea beauty pageant. In these performances, General Idea constructed pageant-like events, with speeches from contestants, judges, and former winners, descriptions of prizes, and Miss General Idea–related fashion items (the Miss GI Shoe; trademark "V.B. Gowns"; the "hand of the spirit"). Miss General Idea figured, in these performance events, as an avatar for the artists' imaginations, a character who was ubiquitous because she was nowhere, who represented the fame and glamour to which General Idea ironically aspired.

Central to these performances were carefully scripted sequences in which General Idea's audience took center stage. In *Going Thru the Motions*, performed at the Art Gallery of Ontario on September 18, 1975, for instance, a climactic scene starring the spectators follows the entrances of Marcel Dot (Miss General Idea 1971), and a performer playing the role of the "Spirit of Miss General Idea." Stage directions in the manuscript text read:

> *The DIRECTOR now rehearses the audience in their reaction to the opening of the envelope. The reaction of the audience is threefold: in sequence—a gasp of shock/surprised laughter/standing ovation.*
>
> *A great deal of attention is lavished on the audience at this part as they are rehearsed in this triple reaction in quick sequence.*[97]

In other words, spectators at *Going Thru the Motions* were not simply asked to respond, or to participate in a singular gesture. They were a central part of what was described as "the climax of the evening."[98] The gestures to be performed were, as the artists themselves had observed in *Target Audience*, stock reactions, entirely recognizable spectatorial responses, organized in sequence and practiced until virtuosically smooth. The gestures, in General Idea's performance, physically took up residence in the audience's bodies, inhabited them, moved through them in carefully rehearsed unison. The gestures spread—from performers to spectators, from one iteration to the next—and as they did, became every bit as much the model of a virus as the Living Theatre's careful staging of the plague.

This approach to choreographing the audience reappeared in several of General Idea's later pieces, of which two notable examples—*Hot Property* (1977) and *Towards an Audience Vocabulary* (1978)—combined the staging of audience responses with the revelatory unveiling of the 1984 Miss General Idea Pavillion's devastating and premature destruction. In *Hot Property*, performed at the Winnipeg Art Gallery in October 1977,[99] the artists staged a ceremonial event including speeches from Zontal, Partz, and Bronson, as well as from Mimi Paige (retroactively crowned Miss General Idea 1968); a series of musical numbers; and multiple opportunities for the audience to "practice" a wide range of spectatorial responses including applause, standing ovations, and sleeping.[100]

The video of the piece, edited together with additional footage after the performance, begins with a fascinating image. The camera pans over a wide expanse of land with a ziggurat-shaped territory marked out, the area inside the borders obscured by clouds of smoke and ash. This, we are informed by a voice-over announcer, is the remains of what would have been the architectural pavilion designed to host the 1984 Miss General Idea Pageant. (According to archival documentation, the artists created this spectacle by tracing the ziggurat shape into the ground on the ruins of an abandoned factory in Kingston, Ontario, when they visited St. Lawrence College to stage an exhibition there in November 1977. By dropping smoke bombs onto the ziggurat-shaped ground plan and videoing the event from above, they conjured the effects of the smoldering pavilion.)[101]

And yet, just as the 1984 pavilion was demolished before the fact, this video footage was added after the fact. The live audience at *Hot Property* did not witness the destruction of the Miss General Idea pavilion. Instead, they acted it out. At the end of the performance—as seen on video—the audience waits with bated breath for the announcement of the lucky 1984 Miss General Idea (they are, after all, pretending it is 1984, and that they are attending the valedictory pageant to be held that year). Paige and Bronson ceremoniously walk onstage and ask for the official envelope containing the winner's name. At that moment, an unseen voice calls out "Fire!" Gleefully, the audience members rise from their seats and stampede out of the theater, straining to reach the exits. They are the protagonists of this performance, swarming out of their seats as if a real evacuation were taking place. The full destruction of the pavilion—the live emergency, the filmed clouds of smoke—is available only through the transmedial combination of event and video. No matter that the 1984 Miss General Idea Pageant never happened. It was more viral because it didn't: because it lived only in the bodies of its prospective spectators. Only when the audience itself becomes the cast can the performance, the recording, and the transmission become "interchangeable."

In *Towards an Audience Vocabulary*, staged at Toronto's Masonic Hall in 1978, General Idea confounded its spectators by confronting them with a "fake" audience, onstage, of "thirty local Toronto celebrities . . . performing the various audience responses: . . . 'laughing,' 'gasping,' 'booing,' 'sleeping,' 'clapping' and 'standing ovations.' "[102] Audience response became performance: perhaps one of the most direct artistic embodiments possible of McLuhan's famous decree that "the medium is the message."

In its choreography of gathered spectators, General Idea's theater thus lies directly adjacent to the history of audience-driven, participatory political performance. If these works don't fit the model of interventionist practice represented by Estrin or Boal, or by other artistic fellow travelers from the era—the Living Theatre, the Performance Group—they nonetheless echo those more overtly radical performances in surprising ways. For General Idea, choreographing their audiences was not an attempt to control spectators; it was an effort to place spectators' action center stage. Viral performance was an alternative to all-consuming social change; not a substitute for it, but a way of sustaining queer presence in a world not likely to succumb to revolution anytime soon. In their viral performances, General Idea reminded us that beneath the surface of every audience—every applauding, sleeping, bored, confused audience—is a riotous crowd, waiting to collectively take things into their own hands.

Much later, in the late 1980s, General Idea created a work of visual art that became truly famous—a viral work that bears discussion as a descendant of the group's 1970s-era performances. *Imagevirus*, like many of General Idea's pieces, originated as a visual riff on an earlier iconic work, in this case the Pop artist Robert Indiana's famous "LOVE" logo. Indiana had arranged the word's four letters into a square, the "O" tipping diagonally to the right, the other three block letters solidly upright, blazing crimson against a background of placid blue and green. He first created the "LOVE" logo in 1964, as a Christmas card commissioned by the Museum of Modern Art, but soon it was everywhere, re-created by the artist in paintings and sculptures, copied by others, and reproduced on a 1973 postage stamp.

Seizing upon the simplicity and cultural ubiquity of Indiana's logo, Zontal, Partz, and Bronson imitated it, replacing the word "LOVE" with the acronym "AIDS"—likewise set in solid red letters, the "D" listing rightwards in an echo of Indiana's "O." The first version of General Idea's "AIDS" logo was a single, six-foot-square painting, which they exhibited in an art show benefiting the Foundation for AIDS Research. As Gregg Bordowitz reports in his book on the project, though, the three artists quickly decided that the piece was incomplete, concluding that it did not have enough impact as an individual work. Rather, Bordowitz explains, "it required repetition."[103] The trio reimagined the piece as a "campaign,"[104] and, between 1987 and 1994, they reprinted the logo on posters, stamps, and fabric; sculpted it in steel; inserted it into fake advertisements; and posted it in city streets.

Eventually, General Idea's "AIDS" logo confronted passersby from an electronic billboard in Times Square, a giant outdoor canvas in San Francisco, on New York City subway cars and the walls of Toronto train stations, and in art galleries in Frankfurt, Barcelona, and Montreal. The group changed their original red lettering for rich purples and yellows, and the background colors mutated accordingly: red, orange, aquamarine. The three artists fashioned the image into a giant metal sculpture that was displayed around the world, collecting graffiti wherever it went. They created a series of photos that mimicked "Absolut Vodka" ads, depicting the logo plastered to walls and doors, with the caption "Imagevirus." printed in white across the bottom. Echoing the circulation of an epidemic, commenting on public silence about AIDS, and anticipating the parlance of the internet age, *Imagevirus* "went viral."

But General Idea had been viral since the early 1970s: long before the physical devastations of AIDS inflected viral conceptions of art, and long before "going viral" signaled digital dissemination. General Idea's work was viral not only in its use of the postal system, not only in the artists' self-presentation through *FILE Megazine*, but also, and maybe most importantly, through their physical choreography of audience members. Viral images, after all, require host bodies. In my next chapter, "Germ Theater," I investigate the work of artists who began practicing during the years when General Idea was making *Imagevirus*—a time when the digital connotations of "viral" began to emerge, and artists began to align investigations of parasite, plague, disease, and radiation with viral and contagious modes of creating performance.

Chapter 3

Germ Theater

Critical Art Ensemble, Eva and Franco Mattes, and Christoph Schlingensief

In 1994, Douglas Rushkoff giddily traced the contours of a new phenomenon he called the "media virus." Seeing the potential for democratic social change in countercultural zines, burgeoning niche-interest cable television networks, and the rudimentary beginnings of the internet, Rushkoff employed the vocabulary of infectious disease to describe a proliferating set of cultural practices. He wrote:

> Media viruses spread through the datasphere the same way biological ones spread through the body or a community. But instead of traveling along an organic circulatory system, a media virus travels through the networks of the mediaspace . . . Once attached, the virus injects its more hidden agendas into the datastream in the form of *ideological code*—not genes, but a conceptual equivalent we now call "memes."[1]

His study, also entitled *Media Virus!*, was among the first to use the term "virus" in describing the contagious circulation of images, ideas, and performances in an age of rapidly evolving media technology. Although some media viruses spread through mainstream channels, the ones that most fascinated Rushkoff—and that made him hopeful about the advent of a new, radically egalitarian media ecology—resisted the dominance of government and corporate structures. These ranged, in Rushkoff's descriptions, from the AIDS protest group ACT UP's distribution of highly replicable images and slogans ("Silence = Death")[2] to graffiti artists tagging buildings in underserved neighborhoods, and activists interrupting television stations' signals to broadcast subversive messages.[3]

Though the field of memetics dates back at least to Richard Dawkins's work of the mid-1970s, Rushkoff's refashioning of the "meme" for the early 1990s media landscape signaled a seismic shift in the cultural and political significance of the viral. This was a moment when media was becoming viral, and when the concept of the viral was perceptibly identified with media. Contagion was emerging as a prevalent concept for understanding a dizzying variety of abstract forces: corporate and capitalist structures, the spread of digital information and misinformation, and the proliferation of new kinds of epidemics. Viral terminology permeated the public imagination, and the cultural anxieties of the moment included a spectrum of uncontrollable contagions, physical and metaphorical.

Meanwhile, a growing number of writers and artist-activists were imagining new methods of performative public intervention in viral terms. Five years after Rushkoff published *Media Virus!*, Kalle Lasn—cofounder of the anticorporate environmentalist magazine *Adbusters*—advocated "meme warfare" as a strategy for breaking corporations' power over consumer identity and economic inequality. "The next revolution—World War III—will be, as Marshall McLuhan predicted, a 'guerilla information war' fought . . . in newspapers and magazines, on the radio, on TV and in cyberspace," Lasn wrote, in his influential book *Culture Jam* (which also featured a chapter titled "Media Virus," though with no overt reference to Rushkoff).[4] Artists developed new tactics for infiltrating public space and consciousness, echoing infiltrative strategies developed by artists of previous generations, such as Boal or Estrin, but reshaping them for the dawning digital age. A set of viral dramaturgies began to cohere. Artist-activists reveled in the presentation of fictional events in public spaces, framed as if they were facts. Performances and conceptual works of this era often combined viral structures and tactics with thematic explorations of contagion, epidemic, and contamination.

Beginning in the late 1980s and continuing into the early twenty-first century, these practices emerged in the work of anonymous collectives like Rtmark and gleefully political impostors like the Yes Men, as well as a constellation of groups following the leadership of *Adbusters*. And they emerged, particularly, in the work of the three artists and collaborative groups I discuss at length in this chapter—the American collective Critical Art Ensemble; the Italian-American duo Eva and Franco Mattes; and the German film and theater director Christoph Schlingensief. I single these artists out from political and aesthetic fellow travelers because they began working at the dawn of the digital age, and because their projects—which I trace through the first decade of the twenty-first century—offer particularly rich insight into the shifting stakes of the viral between 1990 and 2016. I conclude the chapter with a brief discussion of recent work by artists Shu Lea Cheang and Anicka Yi, both of whom explore the gendered and sexualized body as a contagious force. Yi's and Cheang's practices register the continued significance of the viral as overlapping social metaphor and biological fact, linked to new technologies and the circulation of contagious affect.

In *Media Virus!* Rushkoff drew an intimate connection between emerging media and the contagious spread of images, ideas, and actions. Preceding YouTube, Twitter, Facebook, and other contemporary sites of viral dissemination by roughly a decade, his insights have proven central to understanding the virtual proliferation of memes in contemporary internet culture. Since the publication of *Media Virus!* the term "viral" has become ubiquitous, commonly referring to ideas, images, videos, and information that spread rapidly, increasing in significance as they gain viewers, participants, and co-creators. YouTube created the viral video; Twitter created viral hashtags; Facebook, Instagram, and Tumblr created viral images and spread them around the world. Each of these platforms rewards contributions that "go viral" in precisely the sense Rushkoff described, and by the end of the twenty-first century's first decade, the term "viral" had come to refer, first and foremost, to the infectious properties of digital media and technology. As Tony D. Sampson noted in 2012, the newfound prevalence of the viral metaphor soon shaped it into a primary term for understanding all digital-age dissemination. "It is via these various contagion models," he wrote, "that financial crisis, social influence, innovations, fashions and fads, and even human emotion are understood to spread universally like viruses across networks."[5]

Sampson's last example—"even human emotion"—is perhaps the most significant for performance. Though, following Sara Ahmed, I do not consider the spread of emotion to be "universal," its circulation in shifting form lay at the center of the emerging cultural relationship to contagion in this period. And emotional contagion did not apply equally to all feelings. In the cultural imagination of the dawning twenty-first century, the most virulently viral emotions included anxiety, paranoia, and terror. "Fear is an object that is omnipresent and transmitted," Schlingensief said. "Politics only needs fear to be able to say, 'Don't worry, we'll look after it.' "[6] Contagious anxiety was the result, or perceived result, of the increasingly viral structures governing a wide range of social, biological, and technological systems, and, as Schlingensief observed, frequently worked to the advantage of repressive political structures, encouraging apathy and disengagement. In response, artists began performing the politics of viral fear.

While Rushkoff was diagnosing the media virus as the harbinger of a new radical politics, philosophers such as Jean Baudrillard were exploring the metaphorical convergences among biological, scientific, and digital viruses. "The high degree to which AIDS, terrorism, crack cocaine or computer viruses mobilize the popular imagination should tell us that they are more than anecdotal occurrences in an irrational world," Baudrillard argued in 1990. "The fact is that they contain within them the whole logic of our system: these events are merely the spectacular expression of that system."[7] In his later work *Cool Memories II*, he again linked epidemiological structure with digital information transfer:

> As integration increases, we are becoming like primitive societies once again, with all their vulnerability to the slightest germ . . . On computer networks, the negative effect of viruses travels even more quickly than

> the positive effect of information. But the virus is itself information. If it gets through better than the other information, this is because, biologically speaking, it is both the medium and the message. It achieves that ultra-modern form of communication McLuhan spoke of, in which information is not distinct from the medium which bears it.[8]

For both Rushkoff and Baudrillard—writing in an era when the HIV/AIDS crisis had recently reached its epidemic height—biological contagion frequently haunts the edges of discourse about viral media or information. It's no accident that Rushkoff cites the AIDS advocacy group ACT-UP as an early maker of memes.

Yet, as both writers observe, viral media also strains against the biological analogy. Even Rushkoff's vocabulary of "datastreams" and ideological code, imagery summoned to reinforce the analogy, proved less durable than the concept of the virus itself, which circulated in media and artistic discourse alongside a constellation of related terms: infection, contamination. The viral performances described in this chapter test, and revel in, such contradictions. They diverge from the shapes and behaviors of biological viruses, but also hold dialogue with them, employing viral artistic structures to explore themes of affective, virtual, or biological contagion. Likewise, they interrogate and often veer away from the viral's relatively narrow set of immediate associations with instant popularity, modeling transmission and dissemination in richer and more complex ways.

These performances also hold explicit dialogue with the viral terminology that, during this era, was increasingly employed in describing the controlling structures of corporations, globalized economies, mass media, and government bodies. Only five years after publishing *Media Virus!* Rushkoff released *Coercion: Why We Listen to What "They" Say*, which reported on the shifting marketing strategies employed by large corporations, who had begun calling upon Rushkoff himself for advice on how to manufacture viral success. "Ironically, perhaps, it was my faith in the liberating powers of cyberspace that made me one of the last people to take such efforts seriously, and to reckon with the Internet's coercive potential," he wrote with dismay.[9] This viral marketing vogue both responded to and inspired viral political intervention. In a 2003 essay heralding the advent of viral activism, Dennis W. Allen argued it was, among other things, the structure of the rapidly globalizing economy that shaped the viral modes of resistance practiced by collectives like Rtmark. "Rtmark's view," he wrote, "is that [corporate] power is 'viral,' by which they mean to suggest both the way that it proceeds through a vast multiplicity of small actions and the fact that it 'reacts to attack by mutation.'"[10] Like Rtmark, Critical Art Ensemble, Eva and Franco Mattes, and Christoph Schlingensief enacted such "sabotage" in public places, testing media's subversive potential and its susceptibility to capitalist forces, merging viral form and viral subject matter.

These artists' works are heirs to many of the radical performance projects described in the first two chapters of this book, explicitly changing the terms of engagement from the radical riots of the Living Theatre, or the overt audience choreography of General Idea, to immerse spectators in provocative public fictions. Critical Art Ensemble (CAE) stages scientifically accurate experiments that mock and undermine myths spread by corporations and governments: anxieties about dirty bombs, fears of terrorist infiltration. Eva and Franco Mattes use the channels of mainstream press and public opinion to spread provocative rumors, which they later dramatically expose. The film and theater artist Christoph Schlingensief made a career of staging politically subversive multimedia events that challenged audiences to rethink habitual relationships to media and politics.

Also like the cultural activists Rushkoff described in *Media Virus!*, many of the projects explored in this chapter take the form of large-scale public *détournements* in the tradition of the French situationists. These artists borrow and reshape the actions and images of other artists or of the institutions under critique. They often work under pseudonyms, and impersonate real or fictional figures from the systems of control into which they intervene. These artists employ different names to describe such practices: for Critical Art Ensemble, they might be called "critical realism."[11] For Eva and Franco Mattes, strategic borrowing—from "cloning" to "plagiarism"—constitutes a core artistic strategy,[12] while the Yes Men refer to their strategic impersonation of corporate or governmental figures as "identity correction."[13] Copying—or copying with a difference—emerged as a significant element of viral dramaturgy in this era, echoing the radical strategies employed by situationists half a century before. "Plagiarism is necessary," Debord had written. "Progress implies it."[14]

The dramaturgy of publicly performed fiction—spectacular stories, unbounded by theatrical stages—also locates these artists within art historian Carrie Lambert-Beatty's useful category of "parafiction": artistic works that are presented to the public as "plausible" reality, and often experienced by spectators as reality, before being unveiled as fictional. Lambert-Beatty argues:

> In parafiction real and/or imaginary personages and stories intersect with the world as it is being lived. Post-simulacral, parafictional strategies are oriented less toward the disappearance of the real than toward the pragmatics of trust. Simply put, with various degrees of success, for various durations, and for various purposes, these fictions are experienced as fact.[15]

Parafiction and the viral make natural allies in the work of the artists described here. Both invoke the dramaturgy of provocation and surprise, and take shape in public space. Both make frequent use of digital media's contagious properties: "Parafiction's natural home is the blog, the discussion board, or the wiki, where information is both malleable in form and material in effect," writes Lambert-Beatty.[16] I employ Lambert-Beatty's term in describing the work of Critical Art Ensemble, Christoph Schlingensief, and (as she herself has done) Eva and Franco Mattes, even as the destination of my argument diverges from hers. While Lambert-Beatty employs parafiction as a means of exploring the contested nature of truth and knowledge, I examine parafictional works as experiments in the contagious properties of performance and media. These artists use parafictional techniques to test the boundaries of live performance, revealing overlaps among viral theme and viral structure: the affective circulation of fear, the physical circulation of viral weapons, or the accumulation of clicks on a provocative page in virtual space.

Molecular Invasions: Critical Art Ensemble

Critical Art Ensemble—collective creators of performance, video, visual art, and theory—has employed viral imagery, and explored themes of contagion, since their founding in the late 1980s. These themes emerged explicitly in an early video project, a two-minute collage entitled "Ideological Virus," which presents an overt parallel between physical contagion and the dissemination of affect and ideology. In the video, familiar Nazi-era film footage plays over a swirling soundtrack of static, snatches of songs, and bits of news broadcasts. A parade of trucks bearing swastika flags fades into shots of a crowd tossing books onto a blazing fire. Slides declare "Symptoms Onset: Censorship" and "Advanced Symptoms: Military Fetishism." We see a human body with badly blistered skin, Nazi rallies, and warplanes assembling into formations in the sky. As the video unfolds, the "Advanced Symptoms" are revealed to include not only fascism, but also consumer capitalism and American politics. A woman's voice advises us about a money-back guarantee, and a newscaster describes a protest by AIDS-awareness activists.[17] The vocabulary of viral transmission links capitalism, genocidal warfare, and the lack of government response to the AIDS crisis.

Though their performances frequently employ new types of communications technology, CAE finds inspiration in the work of earlier practitioners and forerunners of viral performance, including the situationists, the Living Theatre, and Boal. Often, the collective creates "invisible" performances staged outside of theaters, in which they pose as educators or activists, disseminating information about corporations' efforts to genetically modify crops, or about the politics of paranoia in an age of terrorism. In an interview, cofounder Steve Kurtz described his inspirations, positioning CAE as an heir to political experimenters of decades past:

> Groups like the Situationists and the Diggers realized that cultural participation and production is a significant political act, and that

> no successful political campaign or movement can survive without a cultural wing. I think anyone who is interested in using culture as a political force will share cultural DNA with such groups. So we certainly looked back to the Diggers, the Situationists, the Feminist Art Movement, and to the Living Theatre for a lot of our dramaturgical models. The way that they conceived of reality in the theater, their ontology, was what was really interesting to us.[18]

CAE's affinities with the Living Theatre and Boal run particularly deep. The Living Theatre's approach to staging "reality," Kurtz explained, inspired CAE to stage performances outside the bounds of conventional theaters, drawing political power from the relationships between fictive theatrical action and real-world intervention. Kurtz argued:

> The Living Theatre seemed to understand the implosion of the real, and to be able to move around in fictional theatrical space, back into real situations, and then back into theatrical space again. It was such an expansion of the theater, and of how the real and the unreal or the imaginative could be used together with a political purpose, and in their case, a biopolitical purpose. CAE sees them as being very out in front, in terms of what would come in the late seventies, and in the eighties particularly, when all the discourse around simulation began. They already had a battle plan.[19]

In *Paradise Now*, mythic historical narratives and realistic acting blended with blueprints for real social change. In CAE's projects, fictive scenarios and characters—often, performers posing as members of nonexistent organizations—frame the delivery of scientifically or statistically accurate information on subjects such as genetically modified crops, germ warfare, and economic inequality.[20]

Like Boal, Kurtz views carefully constructed fictive scenarios—scenes played out in the real world, unmarked as performance—as a means of profoundly affecting a few audience members at once. In fact, Kurtz explains, reaching vast numbers of potential allies is less important to CAE than creating lasting effects in a few minds. He distinguished CAE's work from conventional ideas of the "viral":

> CAE believes that there is a continuum between the qualitative and the quantitative within which cultural activists position themselves in relation to the audience. We do not believe that any one position is more valuable than another. All points should be occupied and explored. At one end of the spectrum would be a group like the Yes Men. For them, the success of an action can be measured by how

> much viral attention it gets, in conjunction with the amount of secondary representation. So if a million people hear about an action and hundreds write about it, or publish photos, they are doing well. They are banking on power through numbers, mass visibility, and reproducibility. CAE is at the other end of the spectrum, in that we don't really care about quantity. Our concern is with the qualitative experience of the person who sees or participates in one of our actions. We are interested in direct experience and not secondary representation. We want our projects to be fully embodied. We want to capture people's attention for a while. We want them to be thoughtful and reflective. We design our theaters so that people have an actual stake in the performance. So let's say we have information about transgenic bacteria. Who really wants to know about transgenic bacteria? But, if people are walking by and you tell them, "We are about to release some transgenic bacteria here," then they want to understand what is about to happen, and what it means in an existential sense. They have a stake in what is about to happen, and once in that state, we can put all kinds of fairly complicated information into their minds. Complexity and viral information tend not to go well together, but both have necessary functions.[21]

Kurtz's comparison with the work of the Yes Men is an apt one. Famous for, among other projects, their 2004 impersonation of Dow Chemical representatives, calling attention to the company's responsibility for the 1984 industrial disaster in Bhopal, India, the Yes Men stage parafictional performances that employ the most recognizable of twenty-first-century viral structures. The two collaborators, who work under the pseudonyms Andy Bichlbaum and Mike Bonnano, impersonate figures from major corporations or government entities as a means of playfully revealing vast, structural hypocrisies and crimes, primarily focusing on the ravages of globalization and the inequalities fostered by megacorporations and the government entities that aid them. They have posed as representatives of the World Trade Organization, Dow Chemical, and Exxon, and routinely accompany their projects with fake corporate websites, mimicking the aesthetic and tone of the real pages so convincingly that reporters sometimes contact Bonnano and Bichlbaum for interviews or comments.[22]

In comparing the Yes Men with CAE, Kurtz aptly distinguishes between "quality" and "quantity." CAE's performances are not "viral" in quite the way the Yes Men's are. And yet viral performance has never been solely a matter of proliferating secondary representations, but instead has always modeled the relationship between individuality and scale. Viral performance links the viral unit to the expanding viral structure, the isolated gesture with its act of "becoming-number,"[23] and the local performance with its global proliferation, onstage or online. This power to connect local and global manifests in Artaud's vision for plague, erupting in Marseilles and spreading as the infected disperse to other countries; in the Living Theatre's dramaturgy of local revolution with global ambition; and especially directly in the networked performances described in chapter 4. As I see it, in viral performance, quantity manifests its own form of quality—the Yes Men's affinity for secondary representation inevitably shaping the dramaturgy of their live actions—while performances pitched toward quality, evincing little interest in mass dissemination, hold other, equally profound relationships with numerical scale.

CAE articulates its relationship to transmission and dissemination in its manifestos and theoretical texts, available for free download on its website. In its earliest books, *The Electronic Disturbance* (1994) and *Electronic Civil Disobedience* (1996), CAE outlines a theoretical blueprint for what the collaborators term "cultural resistance," invoking the strategies of 1960s-era political theater groups in order to create a proposal for updating those artists' methods for a digital age. "Postering, pamphleteering, street theater, public art—all were useful in the past. But as mentioned above, where is the 'public'; who is on the street? Judging from the number of hours that the average person watches television, it seems that the public is electronically engaged," writes the group in *The Electronic Disturbance*.[24] Power, they argue, now resides in the "bunker":[25] the network of data shaping identity, comprising citizenship information, banking and medical records, and credit scores. This shift renders earlier modes of radical performance ineffective and demands new forms of artistic resistance:

> The aim of The Living Theater to break the boundaries of its traditional architecture was successful . . . The problem is that effective resistance will not come from the theater of everyday life alone. Like the stage, the subelectronic—in this case the street, in its traditional architectural and sociological form—will have no effect on the privileged virtual stage.[26]

The writers describe an imagined performance of digital-age revolt, played out live before an audience, in which the sole "actor" is a technology expert who infiltrates official databases in order to break the shackles of his or her own electronic imprisonment. The result would be viral in a digital sense—disseminating chaos via computer code—and in a wider social sense, as the hacker's actions ripple outward. "Such an action spirals through the performative network, nomadically interlocking the theater of everyday life, traditional theater, and virtual theater," they write.[27] For Critical Art Ensemble, the publication of freely available digital books constitutes one strand of a diverse set of strategies for public intervention, all of them deeply engaged with questions of speed, dissemination, and affective spread.

CAE's performances stage put these questions to the test in public, often for unsuspecting audiences. In *Marching Plague* (2005), inspired by the Bush administration's post-9/11 resurrection of an offensive germ warfare program, the group combined biological infectiousness with themes of contagious political paranoia. Kurtz and his collaborators researched the fraught twentieth-century origins of biological weapons programs, discovering a history of errors and anxieties surrounding germ warfare, and then re-created a heavily flawed British Navy experiment from the post–World War II era. CAE's performance simultaneously protested the germ warfare programs (their enormous consumption of resources, their inability to function as effective deterrents to conflict) as well as the dangers in dabbling with bacterial agents whose true properties are unknown. As a reenactment of a British Navy project, *Marching Plague* functioned as a large-scale *détournement*—as an attempt to spread skepticism about germ warfare, using the physical components of germ warfare themselves.

Few audience members witnessed a live performance of *Marching Plague*. Its central action took place on the North Sea, off the Scottish coast. A video on CAE's website provides a detailed look at the performance and its process, framing the experiment within a larger historical narrative about biological weapons. The video begins by linking post-9/11 fears with World War II–era anxieties about germ warfare. In 1950s America, fears about new kinds of weapons, particularly biological ones, mingled with political preoccupations about Communist infiltration and information warfare. Meanwhile, scientific advances made possible a more detailed understanding of viruses themselves. Priscilla Wald documents this convergence of viral imagery in *Contagious: Cultures, Carriers, and the Outbreak Narrative*, a study of postwar conceptions of infectiousness in film and pop culture, noting that "as viruses became increasingly sinister and wily, sneaking into cells and assuming control of their mechanisms, external agents, such as Communists, became viral, threatening to corrupt the dissemination of information as they infiltrated the nerve center of the state."[28] Viral imagery was flexible, adapting to the fears of the historical moment. Early twenty-first-century America, for CAE, simmered with the same interlocking fears of germ warfare, infiltration by terrorist cells, and the transformative possibilities of information technology.

The video opens in black and white, with a familiar domestic setting: a kitchen counter, a period-appropriate radio, patterned wallpaper, a plate of fruit. A housewife whisks ingredients in a mixing bowl as her husband looks on contentedly. As a young girl enters, smiling, wearing a white pinafore and grasping a blonde doll, the ominous voice of a radio announcer—shades of "War of the Worlds"—reports that new evidence suggests that a biological attack on the United States is underway. The video then shifts to a mid-twentieth-century history of germ warfare, describing weapons developed in

1930s Japan and in the postwar United Kingdom and United States, many of them ineffective or incomplete. The British experiment "Operation Cauldron," of particular interest to CAE, was an effort to use plague bacteria as a naval weapon, to be sprayed from British Navy ships in the direction of enemy vessels. The Navy's first tests used what CAE refers to as a "harmless plague substitute," while the final ones dispersed real plague particles. These experiments, performed near the Isle of Lewis off the coast of Scotland, employed live guinea pigs as their test targets, positioning the animals on a pontoon floating near the ship. Like the Japanese efforts to produce biological weapons, this British attempt to create a method of distributing plague was never proven effective or deployed against an enemy.

Operation Cauldron appealed to CAE both because of its ostensible danger and because of its high-stakes ineffectiveness. The group decided to re-create the British experiment, failure and all. At this point, the video shifts to documentary footage of CAE members from 2005. They have traveled to the Isle of Lewis, bringing test tubes of *Bacillus subtilis*, the same "plague substitute" the British deployed—as well as a raft of guinea pigs and a guinea pig "wrangler." Steve Kurtz, speaking to the camera, explains the layout of the new experiment: the location of their own guinea pigs, the vantage point from which CAE will spray them with bacteria, the direction of the breeze. "We're expecting, just like there is right now, to have a light breeze off the Atlantic, so we're hoping that's going to carry our atomized matter toward the guinea pigs, and that, unlike the British military, we shall be successful," he says, clenching his fist in an ironic gesture of victory.[29]

The camera walks us through the steps of CAE's studious scientific re-creation. Members of the group sit around a table, piping tiny amounts of liquid into test tubes. "We're inoculating broth that we will grow in the incubator," says Kurtz, "and hopefully by tomorrow we'll have all the bacteria we could ever imagine."[30] Outside on the water, Kurtz and his team of scientist-performers work through the stages of "Operation Cauldron," testing the wind direction, aligning their ship with the floating raft of guinea pigs, and spraying whitish fumes in the guinea pigs' direction. Finally, the scientists test the animals for evidence of *Bacillus subtilis*. Kurtz runs cotton swabs down the guinea pigs' backs, then smears the samples into Petri dishes. In the end, only one guinea pig, and its human wrangler, show signs of *B. subtilis*. This, the video captions explain, "indicates the *infection* rate," if real plague bacteria had been used, "would also be poor or zero."[31] As Kurtz explains, the bacteria's non-infectiousness was always part of CAE's attraction to the project. "*Marching Plague* was inspired by the Bush administration's plan to relaunch the U.S. germ warfare program," says Kurtz. "We wanted to remind everyone of how foolish this initiative was the first time, and to show the kind of absurd activities that would be supported by public funds."[32] *Marching Plague* was designed to fail.

CAE's accompanying book, also called *Marching Plague*, overtly linked the specter of epidemic to media hype and mass hysteria:

> Mass body invasion by germs is always one of the potential threats to which the index may refer. This fearsome possibility can then be reinforced by the news fictionalists that are presented to the public as expert consultants. As if this is not enough, mass spectacles of under-preparedness are simulated in cities around the United States in conjunction with the federal government. Coverage of these media circuses circulates on the airwaves and in newspapers nation-wide.[33]

In their live experiment, CAE presumed the presence of a contagiousness beyond biological weapons at work in the public imagination: the proliferation of anxious rumor, disseminated by a news industry inseparable from the larger economic forces that American biological weapons programs are designed to protect.

Yet *Marching Plague* diverges from the model of straightforward political intervention in important ways. The piece unites questions of contagious weaponry and contagious affect, but does so by placing the entire experiment in a quarantine of sorts, far from frenzied crowds and the frantic news media. Most witnesses could only watch it unfold in the form of a video filled with information from CAE's contextual research, and therefore without the possibility of ever being fully absorbed in the action. The backdrop of dangerously infectious paranoia is visible, in *Marching Plague*, only in photonegative form, in CAE's efforts to remove spectators' media-inspired paranoia. The piece functioned most importantly as a *détournement*, a quotation of an action performed by an organization representing power (in this case, the postwar British military) which CAE faithfully replicated,[34] isolating the action from any potential audience reaction in order to examine it on its own terms: to glimpse the virus itself, rather than simply its viral spread. Through hermetically sealed solitude, CAE countered the problems of incessant interconnectedness.

Other variations on *Marching Plague* (some performed, others planned but never executed) altered this formula, calling for more human witnesses and toying deliberately with the possibility of public panic. In a version entitled *Target Deception*, for instance, filmed in Leipzig, Germany, in 2007, CAE artist Steve Barnes sprays *Bacillus subtilis* from the top of a downtown building. A cast of "human guinea pigs"—outfitted with T-shirts bearing the label "human guinea pig corps" alongside biohazard symbols—parades up and down the street below, accompanied by the sounds of a marching band. After Barnes finishes spraying, Kurtz tests the volunteers for signs of *Bacillus subtilis* (as in the naval version, the infection rate is effectively zero).[35]

In 2010 CAE produced a new project, *Radiation Burn*, using a similar model: a seemingly dangerous activity, intentionally slated for failure,

Critical Art Ensemble's *Radiation Burn*, in Halle, Germany, 2010. Photo by Frank Motz, used with permission of Steve Kurtz/Critical Art Ensemble.

followed by a sincere investigation of the fear it inspired. This time, Kurtz explains, the group decided to challenge publicly circulating anxieties about the possibility of terrorists setting off a "dirty bomb":

> In much of Europe and certainly here in the U.S., the threat of a "dirty bomb" has been the big scary bogeyman, and it's been a cornerstone of propaganda aimed at convincing people to give up their rights for reasons of personal safety and national security. We wanted to shatter that cornerstone. CAE also wanted to talk about why, in history, a dirty bomb has never been used.[36]

Radiation Burn took place in a park in Halle, Germany, where members of CAE set off a fake "dirty bomb": a real explosive, whose blast radius was intended to achieve the same geographical reach as a dirty bomb, but without radioactive material inside. A few of the spectators who witnessed *Radiation Burn* were forewarned about the event, but most members of the piece's small, impromptu audience arrived at the scene when they saw the billows of whitish smoke, and as the park authorities, police, and bomb squad hastily assembled and began testing the area for radiation.[37] As a crowd gathered, local public safety officials tracked the scope and shape of the cloud, treating the harmless mist as if it were really lethal.

Meanwhile, Ulrich Wolf, a German medical physicist and radiation expert recruited by CAE for the occasion, stepped up to a lectern near the fake explosive's "ground zero" and began calmly delivering a lecture on radioactive weapons. He mused on the extreme unlikelihood that a terrorist group could successfully secure the necessary materials or expertise to construct and deploy a dirty bomb. He described, for the assembled public, different types of radioactivity and their uses and effects, pointing out, for instance, that people encounter radiation every day the sun is shining and every time they use cell phones. "The biggest problem with these radiological weapons," he argued, "is not so much their immediate effects on human health, but rather the fact that they will trigger panic among the population."[38] The immediate danger posed by a dirty bomb is less the threat of infectious radiation and more the threat of infectious fear.

A photo of the piece succinctly conveys the disjuncture between the two responses to the explosion: Wolf's coolly rational speech, and the terror-inducing sight of officials wearing hazmat suits. Wolf, clad in jeans and a black jacket, stands at a grey podium in the center of a grassy field, speaking into a microphone. Meanwhile, two emergency responders wearing bright yellow hazmat suits, their faces hidden behind plastic hoods, spool out reams of caution tape to delineate the danger zone all around him. ("A nuclear physicist remarks on the triumph of the spectacle of radioactivity over the scientific understanding of radiation," reads the photo caption on CAE's website.)[39]

While he recalls with pleasure that the project surprised some visitors to the park,[40] Kurtz believes *Radiation Burn* was successful in swaying spectators away from unthinking panic. He and other CAE members walked through the crowd as spectators listened to Wolf and watched the emergency responders test the air for radiation, distributing "dosimeter stickers" so that individual audience members could check whether they had been irradiated. These measures, along with Wolf's speech, he believes, managed to preempt spectators' contagious fear:

> After the explosion, we had the voice of reason (a nuclear physicist), standing at ground zero, explaining why this would never happen. In contrast, we also had the full spectacle of emergency, complete with roped-off areas populated with people in hazmat suits, police and fire trucks—everything that tends to scare people so badly, in order to see how our audience would balance out the two events. I do think at the end of it that reason actually won out.[41]

As with *Marching Plague*, CAE appropriated an aggressive militant action in order to demonstrate its unlikelihood and ineffectiveness. The spread of "radioactive" explosive material and the affective spread of fear were measured side by side. The bomb itself was part fact, part fiction—it really exploded, but was not really radioactive—and the emergency responders' behavior was a true-to-life rehearsal for disaster, just as the information in Wolf's speech was drawn from scientific research. The scenario was hypothetical and imaginative, and more importantly, CAE proposed, so are public assumptions about dirty bombs. Like a latter-day, self-conscious echo of "War of the Worlds," *Radiation Burn* drew on the vertiginous terror inspired by technology to stage a performance about viral fear.

Détournement and Plague: Eva and Franco Mattes

In 1994, the year Rushkoff published *Media Virus!*, the pair of artists known pseudonymously as Eva and Franco Mattes began collaborating on a body of playful, provocative works traversing the boundaries of visual art, performance, and digital media. If media and public anxieties provide the context for Critical Art Ensemble's *détournements*, the Matteses' work frequently concerns the "spectacle" itself: representation and spectatorship in a contemporary digital landscape. The two artists were among the earliest and boldest practitioners of Net Art during the early days of the internet, and their works are prime examples of parafictional performances (Lambert-Beatty features their project *Nike Ground* in her article on the subject). Like CAE, the Matteses—who also work under the title of their website, 0100101110101101.org, often shortened to 01.org—view computer networks as crucial sites of social and political control, and as an important arena for resistance and intervention.

Their mode of working, across live performance, visual media, and digital spaces, has been viral from the beginning. In an interview, Franco Mattes described the duo's approach to performance and spectatorship:

> Probably figuring out the viral thing was our only option for spreading something quickly. I never believed in the artist closed off in the studio, painting alone. The kind of art I like usually is the kind that tries to get out there as fast as possible, as loud as possible. I'm especially fascinated when this process comes from the bottom, when it's not top-down.[42]

Mattes not only affirms that viral modes of dissemination are practical, and that they are aesthetically central to his approach to live art, but also that they are ideologically subversive, a means of disseminating ideas, information, and culture that can function outside of mainstream media or power structures. Viral modes of dissemination imply resistance. Meanwhile, large-scale public fictions, spread through mainstream communications networks and then exposed by the artists themselves, present, Mattes explains, an optimal format for viral art. "My ideal piece of art would involve audience in a strong way," he says.[43]

These lines of inquiry led the Matteses to a project that linked the viral metaphor with new technology and live performance, and that offers a model for understanding and staging twenty-first-century viral performance. Invited to present their work at the 49th Venice Biennale in 2001, the duo, in collaboration with another digital art collective suggestively titled "Epidemic," decided to create a computer virus, which they would unleash from the exhibit hall on the exhibition's opening day and send coursing through computer networks around the world. The result, entitled *biennale.py*, was a computer virus with aspirations beyond cyberspace, designed to provoke and examine media-fueled public anxiety.

Spectators viewed *biennale.py* in a variety of formats. The official exhibit at the Slovenian Pavilion, entitled "Contagious Paranoia," included two large computers, placed back-to-back on pedestals, both infected with the virus, their screens displaying streams of code and rogue files, and a large wall hanging on which the computer code that comprised the virus had been printed in large type. The artists also printed the virus code on T-shirts, sold it on CD-ROMs priced at $1,500 (at least three of which were purchased by collectors), and made the code available for download on their website.[44] The international press began anxiously purveying apocalyptic predictions about the virus's effects on important institutional networks, and gleefully inflating the drama that *biennale.py* incited, even as they questioned the virus's status as a work of art. "At 7PM the Slovenian Pavilion officially opens its doors," wrote a journalist named Alessandra C. in *La Stampa*. "The chaos breaks out. Journalists with recorders, televisions with microphones. Everybody hunting the virus."[45]

These journalistic constructions of the project inflated the virus's threatening public image, helping to spread the Matteses' "contagious paranoia." "The organization [the Venice Biennale] got into a panic when it started to reproduce itself endlessly," wrote Rafael Cippolini.[46] Pike van Kemenade called *biennale.py* "the most aggressive self-replicating piece of art I've ever seen."[47] Recalling the sequence of events, Franco Mattes mused, "The virus spread way faster in the media than on the computers. It was basically pure media hysteria."[48]

From computer code, the Matteses thus created a suspense narrative for the twenty-first century, starring the virus as shadowy villain, lurking in virtual networks and waiting for corrupted floppy disks to convey its infectious codes to fresh machines. Antivirus companies like McAfee and Symantec (whom the Matteses warned about the virus, providing information about how to disable it) were cast as representatives of a stodgy status quo, lurching about in the light-footed virus's wake, and dispatching complaints to the

Matteses that computer viruses did not constitute art.[49] The artists, mysterious originators of the virus, became dashingly amoral commandos, seizing new forms of power for the digital age. Observers, including those who watched the virus devouring the computers on display at the Biennale, as well as those who followed its trail in newspaper headlines, were recruited as a new, dispersed audience—or, to use Nicholas Abercrombie and Brian Longhurst's term, a diffused audience[50]—and were asked to see computer networks as the stage for a drama without defined geographical or chronological limits. "A virus is about losing control," Mattes pointed out. "You know where you start and when you release it, but you don't know where it's going to lead you or where it's going to spread."[51]

The project's aim, the Matteses asserted, was to change public perceptions of the dangers computer viruses posed. Echoing CAE's views on the possibility for viral performance to serve as public "inoculation," the artists told reporter Reena Jana of Wired.com, "The only goal of a virus is to reproduce. Our goal is to familiarize people with what a computer virus is so they're not so paranoid or hysterical when the next one strikes."[52] But the formal implications of *biennale.py* are richer and more complex still, and are as deeply engaged with the virus's aesthetic lure as with public education. Speculating on the artists' attraction to the virus as both form and subject, critic Domenico Quaranta mused on *biennale.py*'s larger cultural implications:

> Viruses attracted 0100101110101101.ORG for various reasons. It was probably the only metaphor arising with the advent of the Net that had entered the collective imagination. Another thing they liked about the idea was the psychological effect that viruses have on people, the media-driven paranoia they generate and which in many cases is their only real consequence.[53]

Realizing Baudrillard's vision of information as virus, and literalizing Rushkoff's vision of contagious "memes," Eva and Franco Mattes materialized a tension that lies at the heart of the viral itself: between virus as information, and virus as destroyer of information.

This double identity has attended viral concepts and structures since the early days of computer technology. Long before *Media Virus!*, long before internet memes, when Norbert Weiner was founding the field he called cybernetics, viruses were already understood to be both information and a threat to the systems that allowed information to spread. As Wald notes:

> The thinking that would eventually lead to an understanding of viruses as "among the most primitive means of *information transfer*" was consistent with that technical meaning, but more mainstream representations of viral information produced the image of the body

> as a communication system that viruses could hijack, corrupting the information crucial to its healthy functioning.[54]

For Baudrillard, the virus is "both the medium and the message"; for Derrida, a virus "introduces disorder into communication."[55] Indeed, the history of viral theory is the history of such double identities: viruses are information and misinformation, identity and otherness, language and its disruption.

The Matteses told this story not only through the public events surrounding *biennale.py*'s release, but also within the source code itself. Examining the code comprising *biennale.py*—attending to the text's surface meanings, rather than the commands it contains—reveals playful gestures to the computer virus's namesake (medical disease) and to the social circulations that the encoded virus mimics. Among strings of abbreviated commands, the untrained eye locates recognizable words, tauntingly arranged as if to suggest a narrative: "if find (body, '[epidemiC]')," reads one line; "soul = open (guest, 'w')," reads the next. Another section begins with the line "def chat (party, guest)," and closes with "fornicate (party + guest)"—wryly hinting at the project's social implications, evoking the informal physical networks by which rumors, public fears, and even real human viruses are spread. (Only at the end of its text does the virus offer a definitive statement of its own identity, a line that reads, "This file was contaminated by biennale.py, the world's slowest virus.")[56] Though the string of code is ultimately legible only to the computer "bodies" it is designed to infect, the virus's text, conjuring images of the body and the soul, parties and chatting guests, registers the associative dimensions of the virus: disease; affective transmission; the dramaturgy of contagious transfer within the body politic.

In his 2007 essay "The Virtual Artaud," Jason Farman reads *biennale.py* as deeply Artaudian. I agree, and build on his analysis here: Artaud helps to illuminate the significance of spectatorship for the creators of *biennale.py*, while *biennale.py* contributes to a broader history of Artaud's influence on viral performance. Farman points out, for instance, that the "plague" Artaud envisioned would take the form of "a battle of symbols."[57] The Matteses' piece, Farman argues, offers a suggestive realization of this vision, employing a series of "symbols"—the marks and commands of computer code—to infiltrate the machines' interiors. The virus's effects, meanwhile, are made visible to the user, onscreen, as (to use Artaud's term) forms. Farman also views *biennale.py* as a figure for the global spread of the HIV/AIDS epidemic. While carefully distinguishing the effects of the computer virus from the ravages of a real disease, he argues (and I agree) that *biennale.py* constitutes an electronic analogy for an epidemic whose rapid international spread could only have happened in a globalized era, an age of rapid transit for information and human travelers alike.

I view *biennale.py* as Artaudian not only in its use of signs and symbols, and its epidemic spread, but also in the terms under which it engaged spectators. In "The Theater and the Plague," Artaud details the power of epidemics to create, in Michael Warner's terms, new publics, wreaking havoc on social and political structures and leaving profoundly altered societies in their wake. "Once the plague is established in a city, the regular forms collapse," Artaud writes. "There is no maintenance of roads and sewers, no army, no police, no municipal administration . . . Entire streets are blocked by the piles of dead."[58] As social forms disintegrate, a crowd of spectators gathers to watch, becoming a new public forged by the plague.

These events, for Artaud, are a direct analogy for theater's effects on audience members:

> Just as it is not impossible that the unavailing despair of the lunatic screaming in an asylum can cause the plague by a sort of reversibility of feelings and images, one can similarly admit that the external events, political conflicts, natural cataclysms, the order of revolution and the disorder of war, by occurring in the context of the theater, discharge themselves into the sensibility of an audience with all the force of an epidemic.[59]

Art here distills the violence of the outside world, impressing it on the spectator's senses in condensed, electrified form. *Biennale.py* channeled anxieties about the unknowable corners of the digital landscape—the viruses lurking there, the hackers discharging them—and, framing such dangers as art, presented them to a public that assembled, live and virtually, for the occasion. Artaud's plague, by destroying social structures, also revealed them, illuminating lines of communication and institutional networks as they crumbled. Likewise, *biennale.py* made visible networks of global media and connections among organizations, corporations, communities of spectators, and—across digital networks—computers themselves.

More than fifteen years later, few statistics register the virus's geographical footprint: infecting only Python operating systems, it never made the list of high-priority viral threats. But anecdotal evidence suggests that *biennale.py* did spread beyond the Matteses' control and expectations, infecting machines and provoking publics around the world. Franco Mattes recalls receiving numerous angry email messages from people whose computers were corrupted. According to Mattes, *biennale.py* made its way onto a commercial religious-education CD-ROM, and customers began to complain after discovering, to their surprise, that they'd installed more than a digital Bible on their computers. (The artists even heard from some whose computers were not affected at all: the virus inspired a kind of digital hypochondria, he says.)[60]

Records of *biennale.py*'s existence can also still be found in the databases of major antivirus corporations. Most antivirus companies rename viruses as they detect them, and it lives on, in the Symantec Corporation's alphabetized list of "Threats and Risks," under the title "Python.Bien."[61] Its profile, with the heading "Python/Bien," also lingers in McAfee's virus database (its risk assessment is listed as "low," its origins "unknown").[62] Under the name "Python/Biennale," it has a page on Microsoft's Malware Protection Center website.[63] According to Franco Mattes, there are others: the antivirus Kaspersky Lab named it "Python.Bien.a," while the RAV company called it "Python/Biennale*."[64]

Biennale.py shares with Critical Art Ensemble's projects an element of what Steve Kurtz refers to as "critical realism."[65] Just as CAE, in *Marching Plague*, attempted to spread (harmless) bacteria in a re-creation of germ warfare techniques, and, in *Radiation Burn*, to detonate a "real" dirty bomb (without the radiation), the Matteses' piece was an actual computer virus, a composition of code that infected other computers, rather than simply the representation of that code. Like CAE, the Matteses used technology to create a viral performance piece whose potency, both technologically and in the public imagination, was predicated on its being real. The virus was, to take up Lambert-Beatty's concept of "parafiction," plausible: plausibly destructive, plausibly contagious, inserting itself between fiction and reality as it spread through computer networks and in the public imagination.

One of the Matteses' following projects tested the plausibility principle even more theatrically. In 2003, the pair was invited to create a new project to be exhibited in the historic Viennese square of Karlsplatz. A friend had loaned the artists a sleek glass-and-metal container, roughly the size of a small room, and the pair took inspiration from the container's form, conceiving a project that might be considered a twenty-first-century paradigm for the "media virus" Rushkoff had outlined nearly ten years before. Covering the booth's walls with "Nike" logos and slogans, the Matteses turned the structure into a fake "Nike" headquarters and began to circulate fictive announcements that Karlsplatz had been purchased by the sportswear corporation. Soon, their press releases declared, the plaza would be renamed Nikeplatz, and would feature a giant statue of Nike's iconic "swoosh" logo in its center. "Nikeplatz (formerly Karlsplatz)" was stenciled on the box's glass window, with a statement below reading: "This square will soon be called Nikeplatz/Come inside to find out more." A large "swoosh" rested on top of this legend, as if to mark the company's new territory.[66]

The booth's glossy modern stenciling and sharp angles stood in stark contrast to the square's ornately old-fashioned architecture. Inside the booth, a detailed architectural sketch displayed the square's new "look," with the giant red swoosh as centerpiece. Visitors were invited to contemplate the Matteses' custom-designed "Nikeplatz" sneakers, carefully angled as if alighting gracefully on their concrete pedestal, and decorated with horizontal stripes crossing their toes and white-edged swooshes displayed prominently on their outer sides. Two "Nike representatives" inside the Infobox answered the questions of curious passersby, proudly announcing that Nike would be planning corporate takeovers of many historic city squares in the future, renaming Europe's cultural landmarks, variously, "Nikesquare, Nikestreet, Plazzanike, Plazanike, or Nikestrasse."[67]

In the "NikeGround" video on 01.org's website—which documents the project, while maintaining its fictive premise—a caption informs the viewer that "these days, the Nike Infobox travels from city to city announcing the places that have been chosen to wear the new Nike name." Like *biennale.py*, *Nike Ground* drew its potency not only from its local incarnation, but also from its threatened spread—from the viral leap between local and global, quality and quantity, individual and crowd. "You want to wear it, why shouldn't cities wear it too?" flashes on the screen, as peppy music plays and the "Infobox" zooms in and out of focus.[68]

According to the Matteses' initial press release from October 10, 2003, Vienna's residents began writing angry letters to the editors of local newspapers almost immediately, protesting their municipal government's apparently crass profit-seeking behavior. The Matteses' video contains person-on-the-street interviews with local Viennese, who display varying levels of disgust and resignation over what has been presented to them as a fait accompli, the multinational corporation's latest dismayingly predictable power-seeking move. "It's a disaster!" says a young woman, smiling shyly. "Karlsplatz is historically rooted," says a man, looking mildly concerned. "To convert it into something commercial like Nike is a doubtful decision." "That sucks," declares a younger, long-haired man glumly. "They have all these little children manufacturing their shoes, and now they want to present themselves in such a spectacular way?" Other interview subjects laugh, unsurprised by Nike's newest conquest.[69]

Meanwhile, on October 6, Nike itself had distributed a press release declaring the "Nikeplatz" publicity a fake, and requesting that Vienna residents remain calm until the perpetrators could be identified. Eight days later, the corporation demanded that the Matteses cease all activities related to copyrighted Nike material, and threatened to sue the pranksters for 78,000 euros in damages if they did not comply. 01.org replied with a series of playful press releases of its own. "Where is the Nike spirit?" inquired Franco Mattes in one of these. "I expected to deal with sporting people, not a bunch of boring lawyers!" Eva Mattes, meanwhile, pointed to the history of modern artists' mimicry of corporate brands. "Think of Andy Warhol's soup cans," she wrote. "Nike invades our lives with products and ads but then forbids us to use them creatively."[70]

The mimetic impulse behind *Nike Ground* drew on the dramaturgy of the Matteses' earlier projects and paralleled CAE's wry pranks, but here, rather than replicating real phenomena (a dirty bomb, a computer virus), the artists shifted the fictional stakes, creating a fictive cosmos, a "plausible parafiction." In *Marching Plague*, it is the possibility for successful infection that's fictive, while *biennale.py* amplified the virus's destructive power for performative effect: the viruses were real, their spread imagined. But *Nike Ground* slid further into the fictive, creating a form of viral theater that was, like Boal's invisible performances, grounded in realities but not itself real. In "claiming responsibility" for the performance, Eva Mattes explicated the artists' motives and theatrical vision for the piece: "We wanted to use the entire city as a stage for a huge urban performance, a sort of theatre show for an unaware audience/cast," she explained. "We wanted to produce a collective hallucination capable of altering people's perception of the city in this total, immersive way."[71]

This précis contains many elements in common with earlier ideas of the "media virus," even obliquely echoing the discourse that followed "War of the Worlds," which likewise produced a contagious "collective hallucination" using the formal principles of new media. As embedded performance, to use Levin's term, the piece brought unnoticed urban backgrounds into sharp focus. And as viral performance, the piece not only employed the viral properties of media and rumor; it evoked the viral nature of capitalism, the capacity for one Nikeplatz to rapidly transform into numberless plazas, streets, and squares.

Invoking Warhol, Eva Mattes placed *Nike Ground* in a long tradition of *détournement*, and indeed the situationist legacy is palpable in the Matteses' intervention. Bruce Sterling compares *Nike Ground*, in its brevity and audacity, to "a wheat-pasted Situationist poster during May '68,"[72] but the affinities also run deeper than this. Situationists aimed to reveal the possibilities buried beneath the smooth exterior of buildings and public spaces, to reexamine urban geography as a means of locating escape hatches from utilitarian routine. *Nike Ground* acted in reverse, asking spectators to see the power structures embedded in everyday public space. In doing so, the project offers critical commentary not only on *détournement*, but also on situationism's approach to "recuperation," a concept usefully articulated by Tom McDonough: "the idea that avant-garde innovations might be recovered for use by the reigning social order, that revolutionary negativity might be recouped to strengthen bourgeois affirmation."[73] This concept, McDonough argues, testifies to a significant anxiety attending situationist thought: the possibility that their interventions simply reproduced, in photonegative, the actions of bourgeois capital. He concludes that "the bourgeoisie was as adept at *détournement* as the situationists themselves, that, in fact, recuperation and *détournement* were one and the same, a shared cultural strategy."[74] *Nike Ground* corroborates this conclusion. The megacorporation had already appropriated the language and ethos of freedom and revolt, leaving the artists to *détourne* its *détournement*.

The video documenting *Nike Ground* eventually shifts its focus from the opening "act"—the Matteses' promulgation of their fiction—to the climax and denouement, a revelatory press-conference style announcement of the artists' theories and intentions. "Our life is sponsored," says a masked figure, addressing the camera. "It's here that we make publicity for free with our bodies every time we wear branded clothes. It's more than natural that now we have the desire to manipulate these symbols that we see every day."[75] Like *biennale.py*, and in a distant echo of Artaud's theatrical metaphysics, *Nike Ground* thus staged a confrontation between symbols, the historic Viennese architecture staring down the new marker of global capital, the ever-present "swoosh," an image of motion and speed.

Nike Ground drew on a form of affective transmission that has been described in especially eloquent terms by Maurya Wickstrom in her 2006 study *Performing Consumers*. Wickstrom explores the efforts of several large corporations, "lifestyle brands" such as Disney, Ralph Lauren, and American Girl, to permeate and script the daily lives, self-perceptions, and social attitudes of their consumers. These companies embody what Wickstrom, citing journalist Otto Riewoldt, refers to as "brandscapes."[76] By entering these stores and participating in their rituals—coveting the lifestyle they promise, purchasing and transporting their merchandise into the wider world—customers are seduced into serving as actors in a drama of capitalist world-making, ultimately at the cost of older, less consumerist modes of self-identification.

Perhaps not coincidentally, one of the early stops on Wickstrom's survey of mega-brands is Niketown, the company's flagship store in midtown Manhattan. Wickstrom details the sensory overload induced by the store's hyper-mediated surroundings, the inspirational cant of slogans celebrating physical achievement and record-breaking feats of athletic ability, bolstered by surround-sound video and scientific-looking diagrams of human bodies mastering superhuman tasks. "There I stand, vibrating with the pulverizing, contagious experience of the swoosh, alive with a sense of how I might be changed," she muses.[77] Like the Matteses, Wickstrom views the "swoosh" logo as a potent symbol for movement. In her analysis, the logo is a visual analogue for bodily acceleration; in *Nike Ground*'s appropriation, the "swoosh" looks more like a checkmark registering one stop on a vast agenda of corporate takeover.

The Niketown environment, Wickstrom writes, manufactures a form of contagious affect, drawing her into a performance of identity that the company scripts, while encouraging her to believe she is unique and free:

> Calling out from us our mimetic tendencies as a productive capacity allows the designers of these environments to release the self from its boundaries, and to give us the sensation that our identity is escaping foreclosure (even as the script of the play reencloses us, giddy with our felt escape, into the corporate agenda). Without knowing, and here is the first hint of what my labor produces, I begin to rehearse and produce as a quality of my own subjectivity the continual, restless movement of capital.[78]

Even as she assesses Niketown's sensually overwhelming scenography, Wickstrom observes that Nike is a particularly self-aware corporation, noting that it was one of the earliest large "lifestyle" companies to employ irony in its self-presentation. Sterling, describing *Nike Ground*, likewise draws this distinction between Nike and older, less self-aware mega-brands, suggesting that if the Matteses had staged the same performance just a couple of years later, the company might have been in a position to strategically respond, not with litigation but with glee at the unanticipated publicity. "If some lesser artists than our invisible pair pulled off some similar effort today, Nike would leap all over it as 'viral marketing' and grass-roots 'urban experience design,' " he suggests.[79]

Yet *Nike Ground* also offered its spectators a contrasting mode of participation, one at odds with the comprehensive immersion for which Niketown strives. First, rather than surrounding spectators with sights, sounds, and slogans, the Matteses offered them only an idea: an imagined corporate takeover, rather than a real one, present in diagrams and on slides, superimposed over Karlsplatz in bystanders' minds. Imagining themselves as participants in an urban drama in which new forms of capital confront established architecture, the people on Karlsplatz's streets became self-aware spectators, rather than overwhelmed ones. The artists' video interviews with passersby also reveal a spectrum of opinion about the dangers of corporations taking over urban space. While some interview subjects reject the hypothetical "Nikeplatz," or display scorn for the new project, others accept the news as an unsurprising development in a world where money makes power. One woman asks, laughing, what anyone would do without money; others point out that corporate takeover is an unfortunate but expected contemporary phenomenon. "Nike to me is shoes, and that's it," states an older woman in a long overcoat dismissively.[80]

Allowing for a range of opinion, confronting Nike with its own image, and puncturing habitual relationships to public space, *Nike Ground* functioned as a kind of inversion of the Niketown store. There, as Wickstrom described, Nike's aspirational aesthetic is contagious; in the Matteses' stunt, an even greater act of public imagination inspires rumor to spread virally, the contagious fiction prompting reexamination of everyday facts. Franco Mattes, in his interview, connected *Nike Ground* to the pair's larger dramaturgical strategy, their effort to leverage dramatic public fictions into wider public skepticism about the media:

> My hope is that once you realize that that Nike campaign was not real . . . that you start thinking that maybe other things that you read in the newspaper that day, or saw on TV, could be fake, constructed: maybe what the priest told you, on Sunday during church, may not be 100% accurate.[81]

Like Critical Art Ensemble's experiments, in which imitating the most frightening types of contagious warfare aims to inoculate publics against fear, *Nike*

Ground sought to train its spectators—both live and dispersed—in skepticism toward digital-age media.

In 2010, Eva and Franco Mattes embarked on another experiment with social contagion and public space. This one asked more literal questions about contamination and fear, in what might be seen as a companion piece to CAE's *Radiation Burn*. *Plan C*, first presented at the Abandon Normal Devices festival in Manchester, England, explored the many forms of fallout caused by the 1986 Chernobyl nuclear reactor meltdown. The piece was conceived in collaboration with other artists including the photographer Tod Seelie, New York-based event organizer Jeff Stark, Oakland-based artists Steve Valdez and Ryan C. Doyle, and filmmaker Todd Chandler. As Franco Mattes explained to me, *Plan C* was partially motivated by personal history: Eva Mattes suffers from an illness that many European doctors attribute to the nuclear meltdown's aftermath, when radioactive clouds trailed over the couple's native northeast Italy. The piece was also inspired by Andrei Tarkovsky's 1979 film *Stalker*, in which a group of men follow a mysterious guide (known as the "Stalker") to an eerily abandoned region euphemistically described as "The Zone." This stretch of silent, overgrown fields and crumbling, long-forsaken buildings has been, the "Stalker" explains, mythologized as an area that is potentially deadly to visitors, but also capable of making their deepest wishes come true. Filmed several years before the Chernobyl disaster, *Stalker*'s treatment of the blighted region appears to anticipate the irradiated area created by the nuclear catastrophe (the "Stalker" tells his charges that "The Zone" may be the site of a meteor's fall to earth, but that no one is sure).

In the first stage of preparing *Plan C*, the Matteses and their collaborators traveled to the radioactive zone surrounding Pripyat, an abandoned Ukrainian workers' city that has stood vacant since its hasty evacuation in 1986. Pripyat, one of the Soviet "Atom Towns," built in the 1970s to house entire communities of power plant workers, has long served as a particularly poignant image for the devastation wrought by Chernobyl. As Franco Mattes recounted to me, the town was hastily evacuated three days after the power plant exploded in April 1986, its approximately 50,000 residents crowded onto buses and assured they'd be returning in a matter of days. As a result, Mattes observed, the fleeing community left most of its possessions behind, turning Pripyat into an eerily intact ghost town.[82] An amusement park, meant for the town's children, had been under construction the same year, and was slated to open for the Easter holidays at the beginning of May, only to be abandoned when the town was emptied in late April. In photographs, the Ferris wheel, with its festive yellow-and-orange seats, rises from cracked pavement among the vacant buildings.

After obtaining legal permits to enter the "alienation zone" around Chernobyl, the Matteses and their collaborators arrived in Pripyat, dressed in hazmat suits and holding Geiger counters, which would alert them if they stepped into "hot spots," where radiation levels are still lethally high. There, they began

Eva and Franco Mattes and Ryan C. Doyle creating *Plan C*, public intervention in Chernobyl and Manchester, 2010. Photo by Tod Seelie, used with permission of Franco Mattes.

scavenging scrap metal and building materials from the empty town. Franco Mattes described the otherworldly feeling of walking through Pripyat:

> You have this crazy city, a utopian city created by the Soviets, totally taken over by nature and highly radioactive, where people left one day, without carrying anything. So when you go there, you feel like you're in a science fiction movie, or a horror film, depending on your perspective.[83]

The *Plan C* team transported their finds from Pripyat to a public park in Manchester, where they reassembled the metal scraps into a gawky, makeshift amusement park "ride." Half public plaything and half eerie sculpture, the piece evokes the rusted Soviet-era architecture that still stands, untouched, in the long-desolate disaster zone. Red industrial-looking poles, supported by weathered wooden struts, lean in to brace a central column, from which branches jut out at odd angles. One is pyramid-shaped, like a tiny oil well; others are no more than narrow beams. From these extremities hang a group of mismatched passenger chairs: a wooden bench, a few repurposed car seats. Signs with Cyrillic lettering, one bearing a red star and a yellow lightning bolt, adorn the top of the Matteses' refashioned amusement park ride, and in photographs, park visitors perch gleefully on the seats, smiling as the ride's spinning arms whirl them, slightly shakily, off the ground.

Stark and Doyle created a short film about the project, which documents the making of the irradiated carnival ride and its opening for British audiences in Manchester. At the festival, a line of eager participants waits outside a fenced-in area as the Matteses, dressed in white protective hazmat suits, swing a gate open and allow them to file inside. The artists assist spectators in strapping themselves into the ride's idiosyncratic seats, which range from chairs to a pogo stick-like contraption, which the carnival-goer grasps tightly with both hands. Then the ride begins, spinning slowly, then more quickly, as riders smile at each other and laugh.[84] (The ride, although ostensibly radioactive, poses little threat to public safety, Mattes noted. The "hot" portions of the contraption—the irradiated metal from Pripyat—were placed well out of carnival-goers' reach, while the seats were constructed from presumably safe materials scavenged at local British junkyards.)[85]

Like *Radiation Burn*, *Plan C* attempted to turn radiation, a deadly, imperceptible tool of warfare and destruction, into something both visible and nonthreatening, to challenge public paranoia by forcing spectators to confront the specter of an irradiated environment all around them. Both staged twenty-first-century collective nightmares: in CAE's case, anxieties over the possibility of a dirty bomb; in the case of *Plan C*, the possibility that meltdown looms everywhere a nuclear power plant is insufficiently protected, and everywhere that nuclear fuel lies unsecured. Both toyed with the potential for mass panic and staged the imperceptible, unpredictable spread of radioactive contamination. *Plan C* materialized a borderless form of dissemination, retraced radiation's spread, and made tangible its dispersal across space and time. Franco Mattes explains that the irradiated zone around the power plant won't become clean for at least 50,000 years, making the project, in his view, as timely in 2010 as it would have been twenty years earlier. (After the March 2011 nuclear accidents at Fukushima, he notes, no one questioned *Plan C*'s contemporary relevance.[86]) As Hardt and Negri argue in *Empire*, permeability marks the borders of the twenty-first-century nation, which are porous both to the movements of global capital and to the spread of mass epidemic. Both *Plan C* and *Radiation Burn* walked spectators through the motions of such a confrontation with contaminants.

Plan C also, subtly, expanded the Matteses' dramaturgical model, the large-scale public fiction. One of the reasons why the Matteses found Pripyat's abandoned amusement park so compelling, Franco Mattes recalls, was its brief, fraught history. The so-called Luna Park, intended to be inaugurated on May 1, 1986, was in fact put to use only once, the day Pripyat was evacuated, when the rides were turned on as a sort of mass distraction. "The story goes," Mattes says, "that they only turned it on one day, during the evacuation, so that it would transmit a sense of normality to the people—you know, so the music of the Ferris wheel, the Luna Park and so on, would calm people down. So it was actually used to entertain them, but in an extremely evil and sad way."[87] In reconstructing a Luna Park of sorts, one whose defining quality was its score on a Geiger counter, the collaborators reversed the ruse, assembling the irradiated materials back into the form of an amusement park ride—a strange, lopsided one, with its history and radioactivity explicit rather than concealed. Chandler, Seelie, and Stark's film about the project is, appropriately, entitled *Let Them Believe*, a direct quotation from Tarkovsky's *Stalker*, but also a broader gesture to the questions of public credulity and deception that run through the story of Pripyat, and of the Matteses' work. (Franco Mattes reports that many of the pair's longtime followers, and even curators seeking to book *Plan C* into galleries and museums, refused to believe that the construction materials were really imported from Pripyat, instead insistently waiting for the artists to reveal the piece as a fiction. "People that know what we have done before are still waiting for us to say that the whole thing was a fake. It's a fake fake.")[88]

If *biennale.py* translated Artaud's ideas about the plague into computer code, creating a twenty-first-century corollary to the philosopher's concept of public communicability, *Plan C*, too, should be seen as an updated version of Artaud's metaphysical contagion. This project addressed another form of communicability, equally hidden from easy public view, equally abetted by porous borders. Examining *Plan C* alongside "The Theater and the Plague" reveals a number of unexpected ways in which the piece realized Artaud's ideas for a theater of contagion, offering new models for understanding the plague as a template for artistic work. *Plan C*'s divergences from Artaud, meanwhile, testify to the shifting stakes of contagion over time, and to the viral's political flexibility. For Artaud, the plague's devastations presaged authoritarian rule, while for the Matteses, the unacknowledged contagions of Chernobyl constituted fallout from an authoritarian regime.

First: the narrative overlaps. Both "The Theater and the Plague" and *Plan C* contain narratives of communicability across borders, and particularly between the exoticized "East," from whence Artaud's plague springs, and the apparently safe West. In Artaud's story, commercial ships hailing from Asia deposit a plague of nightmarish proportions on European shores. The Matteses' story is a post-apocalyptic parable about a group of rogue artists who enter a disaster zone in Eastern Europe and import artifacts from it to the apparently "safe" zone of suburban England. In Artaud's description, the plague that infected Marseilles had two points of origin: it was imported to France, but it was also lurking in French territory already, waiting to be activated. *Plan C* takes up both of these modes of contagion. In describing the project, Franco Mattes explained that growing up in Europe after Chernobyl had meant confronting the disaster's fallout as a persistent presence in the air, the soil, and the bloodstream. Like the ever-present plague of Artaud's essay, radiation remains. It is, as Artaud wrote, a "latent disorder," lingering in Europe the way the plague lingered, unseen, in France. *Plan C* made these invisible dangers available: if not visible, then tangible, contained in a whirling contraption that was both entertainment and threat.

The project also materialized Artaud's description of a plague delivered on a trading ship, the result of the global circulation of people, goods, and, of course, invisible infectious particles. In a contemporary era of globalized trade and easy international mobility, such networks are faster, more comprehensive, more geographically dispersed than ever. Even the theoretically contained disaster zone could not be cordoned off from the rest of the world. Radiation drifted in clouds over Europe, affecting people far from Pripyat. (A blog entry about *Plan C* also noted that, after the disaster, Soviet authorities sold Pripyat's trove of abandoned vehicles to China—suggesting endless possibilities for where the bulk of the town's irradiated detritus might have ended up. Perhaps the seats on the Matteses' ride, scavenged from materials in England, weren't so safe after all.)[89] Like the sailors on Artaud's plague-bearing ship, the remnants of the Chernobyl meltdown circulated, and in transporting building materials from the alienation zone to England, the Matteses made this circulation tangible.

The theatrical plague Artaud envisioned was intended to subsume its spectators entirely, leaving no space for contemplation. And this is where the Matteses part ways with Artaud. While *Plan C*'s spectators experienced the ride physically, their encounter with the ride's meaning was also staged in their minds, in their reflection after the fact. *Plan C* was contagious not only because it spread radiation, but also because it generated headlines, circulating in public discourse as well as in the air. It was, in this sense, a critique of contagious paranoia just as much as a requiem for a destroyed city. As with CAE's *Radiation Burn*, *Plan C* presumed the presence of media-fueled anxieties in its audience and, also like CAE's project, it asked spectators to confront these fears physically and directly, without media to either guide them or to amplify the alarm.

Plan C also diverges from Artaud's vision in a darker way, by evincing a different image of the plague's aftermath. Artaud viewed the theatrical plague as apocalyptically final, a total cleansing from which some new power structure might emerge. And Artaud's vision for a new power structure was explicitly totalitarian: at the essay's conclusion, he wonders whether "there can be found a nucleus of men capable of imposing this superior notion of the theater."[90] Writing during the interwar period in Europe, such a construction makes sense: catastrophe did feel final, and totalitarian powers were on the rise. *Plan C*, by contrast, examines a form of contagion that erupted, and was repressed, by an authoritarian power, whose invisibility was due partially to the public lies that followed in its wake. The project is a meditation on aftermath, evoking a contemporary world in which there is no finality to disaster and in which the media might not accurately report the fallout. This is a world in which the physical, social, and geopolitical remains of nuclear catastrophe linger without disappearing, or float across borders unannounced, in which tense nations are always on the brink of conflict. In the world of *Plan C*, the plague is a permanent condition.

A Bit of Poison: Christoph Schlingensief's *Ausländer Raus—Bitte liebt Österreich*

This chapter's third case study takes up a single project created by the German film and theater director Christoph Schlingensief in the year 2000, a "media virus" in the sense of Rushkoff's vision that manifested both in public space and in the media-fueled public imagination. As with *Marching Plague*, *Radiation Burn*, *biennale.py*, and *Plan C*, the contagious affect under investigation was fear. *Ausländer Raus* confronted a spectrum of anxieties: public preoccupations with immigration into Austria, fueled by the rise of right-wing ideology in the Austrian government; and concurrently, anxiety about that very rise in extremism and its implications for the Austrian public. (Fear would be a recurring subject of Schlingensief's work: his 2003 project, *Church of Fear*, not only interrogated the affective dissemination of fear, but was also arguably viral, expanding internationally to create a global network of participants.)[91]

The Freedom Party of Austria (FPÖ), led by Jorg Haider, a right-wing populist and overt Nazi sympathizer, had made unprecedented gains in the 1999 elections, garnering 27 percent of the national vote.[92] The party espoused an extreme form of xenophobia and employed slogans and imagery deliberately reminiscent of the Nazis (Haider was notorious for a 1991 speech in which he praised Nazi hiring practices).[93] When the party was incorporated into a new, controversial conservative government,[94] several members of the European Union, frightened at what appeared to be a resurgence of policies and public sentiment reminiscent of Nazism, began diplomatic sanctions against Austria.[95]

Schlingensief responded by staging a public performance that was part reality television show, part experimental theater piece, part parafiction, and part political demonstration. In *Ausländer Raus—Bitte liebt Österreich* (*Foreigners Out, or Please Love Austria*), the director confronted the Austrian public with its own anxieties about immigration by gathering a group of international refugees, all seeking asylum in Austria, and offering them temporary housing in a large shipping container situated in one of Austria's historic squares. Video cameras filmed the refugees' daily lives inside the container, reality television-style. Each day, Austrian citizens were offered the opportunity to vote online, registering preferences about which of the asylum-seekers should be allowed to stay and who should be forced to leave the country.

Ausländer Raus was partially inspired by the Dutch (and later, internationally franchised) television show *Big Brother*, which restructured surveillance into entertainment, and emerged as one of the earliest widely popular reality television shows in Europe. *Big Brother* offered viewers a glimpse of its characters' otherwise-hidden "real" lives. Accordingly, Schlingensief's project allowed the public to pore over the daily minutiae of members of one of the most contested groups in Austrian society. Here, though, the television footage available for view occupied a kind of limbo between everyday life and deliberate performance, between the participants' real situations and Schlingensief's scenario. Though their status as refugees was real, the performer-participants wore outlandish disguises—wigs, funny glasses—in order to conceal their identities; and the publicized "biography" of each asylum-seeker, intended to assist members of the public in voting, was also falsified.[96] When walking in front of the cameras, the participants often held newspapers over their faces, heads down, rendering them unrecognizable.

Ausländer Raus was almost instantly notorious in the Austrian media, condemned both by those sympathetic to the FPÖ, whose political stance the piece skewered, and by those anxious about the performer-participants' fates, and their level of agency in the performance. In the years since the container took up temporary residence in Vienna, Schlingensief's deeply political provocation has also become a touchstone for critics exploring questions of digital-age performance, public art, and the avant-garde. Denise Varney views the project as a contemporary instance of Brechtian *gestus*, a "Street Scene" updated for a digital-age audience.[97] Christopher Balme understands the project as a turning point in the relationship between theater and the public sphere, an instance in which digital media fused a theatrical audience with a wider public.[98] Michael Shane Boyle invokes the piece as an instance of twenty-first-century "container aesthetics": works of art and performance housed in shipping containers, which function as metonyms for the increasingly standardized movement of global capital.[99] Claire Bishop's observations, in *Artificial Hells*, are particularly useful to my reading of the piece. She points out that, for the Austrian public, the highly visible presence of an artistic project about deportation proved more provocative than the presence of a real detention center, housing many more refugees, just a few miles away.[100] In the end, Bishop argues, the piece reveals a deep contradiction in the construction of democratic political regimes ("Schlingensief's model of 'undemocratic' behaviour corresponds precisely to 'democracy' as practised in reality," she writes). The project exemplified, she notes, a form of artistic efficacy premised on disruption and provocation rather than advocacy or persuasion.[101]

I view *Ausländer Raus* as deeply viral. Reading the piece in this way illuminates the stakes of spectatorship and links the project's thematic and historical dimensions with its approach to participation. This reading also assists in the larger historical project of tracing the emergence of works that include multiple kinds of viral dramaturgy: Schlingensief's piece unites the Living Theatre's practices of live provocation and affective spread with the infiltrative strategies of Marc Estrin, and the Matteses' digital-age *détournements*. In what follows, I describe the piece in viral terms, sketching out the plot, and attending to the biological metaphors at work in Schlingensief's project—the immunological thinking that both fueled his artistic self-conception and undergirded the fascist history that *Ausländer Raus* invoked.

Filmmaker Paul Poet's documentary *Schlingensief's Container* offers vivid footage of the performance and its spectators' responses.[102] The first time we see Schlingensief's cast members, they are clambering onto a bus, its windows covered with newspaper to preserve their anonymity. Several of them wear sunglasses and wigs: a bright orange pageboy on one performer, a mess of gray curls on another. The bus glides through downtown Vienna, as twilight turns the city's fairy-tale architecture even more picturesque. The camera cuts between shots of the asylum-seekers, riding placidly toward their indefinite voluntary confinement; crowd shots of gathered viewers' expectant faces; and Schlingensief himself, addressing the audience from a perch atop one of the container structures.

Finally, the bus halts in the middle of a crowded square, and Schlingensief leads the performers out, their faces covered, eyes averted from the crowds of spectators pressing in and the banks of television cameras aimed at them. A marching band plays. Men in "security" T-shirts are everywhere. The performers disappear inside their new home: a large white shipping container, its makeshift form standing in contrast to the surrounding stately architecture, which includes the famous Sacher Hotel and the Vienna State Opera House. Soon, the performers reappear on video screens around the square, where they can be glimpsed from above, through the surveillance cameras inside their very public bunker. Perched on top of the container is a large sign proclaiming the project's title: "Ausländer Raus" ("Foreigners Out").

If *Nike Ground* staged the infiltration of public space by faceless capitalist forces, *Ausländer Raus* meditated on a related aspect of globalized, late-capitalist society: increased mobility and population shift, the movements of workers following the movements of capital. (And capital, as Sampson reminds us in *Virality*, is increasingly structured and understood in epidemiological terms.) But Schlingensief's piece also made these concepts concrete: *Ausländer Raus* was not just a parafictional abstraction, a set of symbols meant for media distribution, a live staging oriented toward, as the Yes Men would say, "secondary representation." It was also a real instance of what Austria's right-wing politicians, and their followers, so feared: the daily presence of non-Austrians in Vienna's city square. Indeed, *Ausländer Raus*, more than any other project described in this chapter, made both deliberate and unintentional use of the affective possibilities of live performance. Unlike *Marching Plague*, *biennale.py*, or *Plan C*, Schlingensief's piece consistently drew large, emotionally charged crowds of spectators together, offering a study in affective contagion that was, in certain ways, reminiscent of the Living Theatre's participatory spectacles. *Paradise Now* trapped spectators between the competing emotions of revolutionary rage and affective confusion, and *Ausländer Raus* deliberately placed its audiences in an equally contradictory emotional landscape: it confronted contagious fear, while causing contagious anger.

On the one hand, *Ausländer Raus* thematized the affective spread of FPÖ ideologies: Austria's growing, increasingly contagious paranoia over immigrant populations. At the same time, the spectators who gathered outside the shipping container—with varying amounts of context about the project's status as a performance piece—were outraged by the presence of such unabashedly xenophobic sentiments in public space, as well as by the plight of the refugees inside. And their outrage, a response to the circulation of fear, spread too. Live affective contagion was perhaps most palpable at a moment, partway through the weeklong performance, when a segment of Schlingensief's public became dissatisfied with following the modes of participation he'd set out for them. A group of, according to Schlingensief, more than 3,000 protesters attempted to intervene directly, storming the staging area and freeing the asylum-seekers from their container.[103] This brief scene, recorded in part in Poet's documentary, looks like chaos. One activist leads chants through a megaphone, while two more scramble to the top of the container and, kicking and grabbing at the giant "Ausländer Raus" sign, frantically attempt to dislodge it. The asylum-seekers look on, apparently bemused by the proceedings, from a small window in the container's side. Soon, unable to destroy Schlingensief's billboard, the activists begin spray-painting their own slogans over it. In the end, calling themselves members of the "Anti-Fascistic Front," this group of activists forces the immigrants out of their container home. *Paradise Now* imagined contagious outrage as a revolutionary feeling, meant to propel theatrical action beyond the theater and into the street. Here, contagious outrage was a (deliberately provoked) rebellion against the terms of performance, as the anger of gathered spectators turned inwards to intervene in the staged event itself.

Throughout the six-day proceedings, Schlingensief's willing captives performed skits and cabaret acts, commenting ironically on their own situation. They took part in a German language class, repeating basic German phrases over and over. One performer danced to a German song.[104] The Austrian playwright Elfriede Jelinek, a regular collaborator of Schlingensief's, developed a short puppet play with the asylum-seekers, which they performed on the roof of the shipping container for an audience gathered in the square. The hand puppets, which the performers hoisted over their heads above a plywood "stage," resembled the stock figures populating children's stories: a crocodile, a blonde princess with a tiny crown, a bizarre clown, a devil. The characters acted out a goofy, childlike distillation of the real-life conflict being played out by their puppeteers. A puppet named Gretl mechanically announced her love for Austria, asserting her desire to acquire a work visa and stay there. "Please help me, I love Austria," she exclaimed over and over again, to no avail. Finally, the "Crocodile"—who repeatedly identified itself as Heidemarie Unterreiner, a leading Freedom Party politician—put Gretl out of her misery by abruptly eating her. "We live in Europe with Europeans! Our greatest wish is to become actors. Please help us. Thank you!" announced Crocodile, along with a figure named Kasperl, who self-identified as Federal Chancellor.[105]

In an email interview, Sandra Umathum, a German scholar and a collaborator of Schlingensief's, recalled the puppet performance as a deliberate attempt to skewer the patronizing attitudes encountered by non-German-speaking immigrants to Austria, attitudes displayed even by well-intentioned politicians and activists.[106] Its satire ran deeper than that, too. By speaking the stock phrases and impersonating the stock characters of Austrian culture, the immigrants were, in a sense, assuming the mantle of Viennese culture, inhabiting Viennese identity, just as they were infiltrating Viennese public space. (One might consider this as a reinvention of Marc Estrin's "A New Family Moves In" scenario, intended to introduce families from different cultural contexts to each other through a housing swap—a one-sided reinvention, of course, an infiltration with higher stakes than he might have imagined.) The Austrian characters repeatedly declare their desire to become actors, but, Jelinek suggests, they already are. Temporarily donning the cultural trappings of their new homeland, the puppets, and the bodies operating them, hidden behind plywood walls, gestured to the hollowness of any such essential cultural designation. The asylum-seekers' story became a new Austrian fairy tale, as grisly and dark as any traditional fable. In Poet's video of this unsettling piece of "children's theater," the camera pans back from the performers' puppets to the watching crowd—a large gathering of spectators who gaze with rapt attention at the puppets' childish antics.

Ausländer Raus, like several other projects described in this chapter, created a new public all its own, through its operation in both live and virtual realms. Running parallel to the live performances was the circulation of *Ausländer Raus* on screens, its media presence superimposing the ironies of a reality television show onto the deeper ironies attending the refugees' situation and Austria's larger political context. Schlingensief's website provided "profiles" of the performers, and advertised the voting numbers. Each day, after the latest deportees had been voted out of the country, members of Schlingensief's "Security" team brought them out of the container to a waiting car for their "deportation,"[107] and newspaper headlines regularly announced new developments in the asylum-seekers' plight. *Big Brother* provided a particularly apt template for Schlingensief's project, partially because the television series was itself a model for global mobility and international replication. Developed in the Netherlands, it was so successful that it was quickly reproduced by television networks from Denmark to Italy, Poland, the United Kingdom, and the United States, and eventually Russia, Mexico, Argentina, and Brazil.[108] The show employed a newly popular formula, developed perhaps most famously for MTV's *The Real World*, in which cameras follow a group of housemates through their daily lives, giving spectators the sensation of spying on others' ordinary activities. Unlike *The Real World*, *Big Brother* was also a contest, with participants periodically ejected from the televised "house." Different versions of the show involved the public in varying ways, but in most cases, viewers were allowed to vote, online and by text message, on who should be evicted. This made the series, like Schlingensief's project, a transmedial event, played out across multiple forms of media, including text messages, websites (both official and unofficial), and news headlines that documented the contestants' victories and losses.[109] As Lothar Mikos points out in an essay on the television series, *Big Brother* combined the dramatic elements of a drawn-out competition with the "reality" effects produced by surveillance; the show, he explains, was "a carefully produced drama of authenticity."[110]

By inviting his spectators to participate digitally, casting votes for the least desirable asylum-seeker, Schlingensief not only mocked the reality television format, but also gestured toward the larger questions of participation and agency that viral media implies. Like the work of CAE and the Matteses, *Ausländer Raus* employed a framing device from pop culture—which had in turn adopted its format from government surveillance culture—thus borrowing the format of the institutions under critique. But *Ausländer Raus* also directed spectators' participation, offering them only a single sanctioned way of engaging with the project: by voting asylum-seekers off the show. (Alternatively, they could break Schlingensief's rules and object to the options that the project's frame provided, as the live protesters did.)

In channeling its public toward a particular mode of participation—voting to expel was a given, voting on who to expel next was the only variable—Schlingensief implied a critique of communications modes that aligns, in a deep way, with the critiques suggested by media philosophers like Baudrillard, who viewed communications modes as inherently ideological. In *Requiem for the Media*, the philosopher argued that mass media obviate true response and reciprocity in the same way that a political referendum obviates open dialogue, by implying a single answer to the question it poses, by eliminating the possibility of any response outside of affirmation or denial. Likewise, to Baudrillard, in the case of both consumer goods and mass media, "the consumption of products and messages is the abstract social relation that they establish, the ban raised against all forms of response and reciprocity."[111] Schlingensief's piece provoked spectators into responding, and then, as Baudrillard suggests, channeled their responses into the ideologically constricted format of the television competition. In the gulf between digital voting and live protest, spectators' responses to *Ausländer Raus* raised, once again, questions Brecht had posed nearly a century before: whether communications technologies could function as channels for multidirectional dialogue, whether media could serve democratic ends.

Though viral media and affect were the primary sources of contagion in *Ausländer Raus*, biological metaphors lingered in the background: in Schlingensief's artistic self-conception, and in the Austrian politics attending the piece. The son of a pharmacist, Schlingensief reportedly "used to say that like his father . . . he administered a bit of poison to his audiences in order to cure them of the ills of our time."[112] In this philosophy of performance, tinged with Aristotelian thinking, theater is inoculation, injecting spectators with small doses of disease to prevent them from succumbing to the full force of epidemic. *Ausländer Raus*, in its transmedial complexity, constituted a form of creative inoculation: rather than "contaminating" Viennese public space with radioactive particles or contagious bacteria, Schlingensief brought people into the city square, and infectious, virulent rhetoric to the forefront of public attention.

More than this, by invoking Austria's Nazi past and its neo-Nazi present, *Ausländer Raus* summoned an attendant set of immunological metaphors. As many critics have noted, by housing the refugees—theatrical captives and disenfranchised non-Austrians—in a temporary shipping container, Schlingensief at once orchestrated a confrontation with the FPÖ's xenophobic rhetoric and politics and visually echoed the deportation trains and concentration camps of the Nazi era, invoking Austria's history of collaboration.[113] The piece overtly staged a fable about the invasion of the body politic—a narrative structure that, historically, served as a powerful framing device for Nazi ideology. Nazi rhetoric frequently emphasized, as Jennifer Kapczynski has written, "notions of a healthy *Volk* and its perceived enemies,"[114] and, as Robert Esposito notes, viewed the purgation of Jews and other persecuted groups as a form of homeopathic cure for Germany as a nation.[115]

In his insightful essay about Austrian playwright Thomas Bernhard's viral polemics, Jack Davis observes that to summon the specter of the Nazi era is, inherently, to invoke an immunological metaphor. Davis argues that Bernhard's language not only functioned in a homeopathic register by "incorporating aspects of an oppositional discourse in order to oppose that discourse," but that "this process becomes all the more apparent and important when the oppositional discourse Bernhard appropriates is the rhetoric of fascism."[116] *Ausländer Raus* operated similarly. Invoking an immunological narrative served both as an expression of Schlingensief's personal artistic identity, and as a gesture toward the biological metaphors haunting fascist history. And spectators responded in kind. The philosopher Peter Sloterdijk reportedly argued, in response to debates over whether *Ausländer Raus* participated in avant-garde aesthetics, that "'the epoch in which an avant-garde could work with surprises or with direct attacks on an unprepared nervous system is over . . . [we] are thoroughly immunized.'"[117]

Sexuality and Quarantine: Shu Lea Cheang and Anicka Yi

Critical Art Ensemble, Eva and Franco Mattes, and Christoph Schlingensief began working in viral modes at a moment when convergences of virus as media, virus as performance, and virus as scientific pathogen were fresh. Viral media disseminated contagious anxiety, and artist-activists intervened. Though I view the 1990s and early 2000s as a crucial point of departure for works investigating the overlaps among contagious affect, scientific contagion, and new technologies, such projects, and the converging contagions they registered, continued to evolve. I conclude this chapter with a brief look at two recent projects, conceived and created between 2009 and 2016, that continue to probe the questions brought up by CAE, the Matteses, and Schlingensief, pressing on the prospect of viral anxiety in new ways. Neither project is explicitly parafictional, yet both engage with the viral as a primary structuring principle for understanding biology, systems of information and technology, and affect and emotion. In distinction from the previous works examined in this chapter, both projects explore perceptions of the gendered or sexual body as a contaminant or source of contagion, and align these themes alongside other forms of viral spread. These works suggest that viral technology and viral anxiety continue to emerge in tandem, and that viral sexuality figures as an evolving subject matter for artists working across media forms and exploring the contagious dissemination of emotion and affect.

In 2009, the multimedia artist Shu Lea Cheang began work on a transmedial constellation of projects titled *U.K.I.*—an inversion of the title of her 2000 feature film, *I.K.U.* Comprising video, live performance, and a participatory digital game, *U.K.I.* constructs a futuristic, apocalyptic sci-fi universe that envisions viruses as biological, technological, and affective forces. In the 2000 film, a corporation employs new technology to collect mass data about sexual pleasure, and then to formulate a device able to dispatch "sexual pleasure signals . . . directly to the brain without physical friction"; in other words, achieve orgasm without sex.[118] In *U.K.I.*, the transmedial sequel, sexuality and information have merged, and biological code converges with computer code:

> In post-netcrash UKI, the data deprived I.K.U. coders are dumped on the Etrashscape where coders, twitters, networkers crush and crashed. Exchanging sex for code, code sexing code, UKI as virus emerge while GENOM retreats to BioNet. Taking human body hostage, GENOM reformats blood cells into microcomputing ORGANISMO (organic orgasm). UKI, the virus, enacted to infect a city, propagated, mobilized to infiltrate BIONET, sabotage ORGANISMO and reclaim the lost orgasm data.[119]

Between 2009 and 2016, Cheang staged a series of "UKI Viral Performances" across Europe and in Canada, beginning with a performance in Barcelona that combined the work of computer programmers, noise artists, and "queer/postporn performers." Videos blended imagery of digital code and biological cells, and four tons of "e-trash junk"—heaps of discarded computers, disks, cables, and other fragments of recently obsolete technology—served as set and props. Simultaneously, Cheang developed *U.K.I.* as a participatory game, staged in Norway in 2014 and in Switzerland in 2016, in which players themselves take on the roles of virus, with the goal of infiltrating

Anicka Yi, *You Can Call Me F*, The Kitchen, 2015. Photo by Jason Mandella, courtesy of The Kitchen.

vast biological systems. "Infiltrate the BioNet. Sabotage the Production . . . Your heartbeat, your blood flow, your emotion, your actions are your assets to join the UKI bio-game," read the instructions superimposed onto a video of live players taking part in the game.[120] In the video, human participants interact with projected images of streaming digital code and abstract shapes resembling red blood cells.

In *U.K.I.*'s various forms, Cheang offers a vision of a future world (the narrative ostensibly takes place in 2030) where the distinction between technology and biology has entirely dissolved, and where virus is the defining structure for both. Sexuality has been divorced from individual human behavior and desire, and governmental systems are vulnerable to both biological and technological infection. This narrative, though fictive and apocalyptically tinged, suggests continuity with the work of groups like CAE, which—even from their early video "Ideological Virus"—viewed scientific, informational, and affective contagion as linked and overlapping forces. It reflects Sampson's observations about "contagion models" as the central means of understanding twenty-first-century systems of all kinds. It also suggests gender and sexuality as emerging subjects for viral art, a theme also under investigation in Anicka Yi's 2015 installation piece, *You Can Call Me F*, which was rooted not in the future but in the live interaction between gendered, ideologically charged biological material and human spectators, present in a gallery. These explorations of contagious gender and sexuality would find new form—employing less biological, more structural visions of the viral—in the networked performances I describe in chapter 4.

Between March 5 and April 11, 2015, Yi transformed the upstairs gallery at the New York performance and art space The Kitchen into a site of biological quarantine. At regular intervals along the glossy black floor stood rectangular tents of transparent plastic, dotted with colorful, blocky shapes and patterns, like sets of mod shower curtains. Inside the tents nestled idiosyncratic arrangements of objects: shiny metal bowls, glass decanters, a motorcycle helmet. Each of these prop collections, carefully arranged inside its translucent stall, served as a host environment for Yi's primary object of interest—live bacteria, which Yi had collected from approximately one hundred women's bodies, "mostly friends, or friends of friends," explained an article in *Artforum*.[121] (The Kitchen's website credited the long list of "participants," including several anonymous donors.)[122] *You Can Call Me F* was an exploration of the conceptual and affective links connecting "society's growing paranoia around contagion and hygiene" and "the enduring patriarchal fear of feminism and potency of female networks."[123]

Yi's vision fused commentary about gendered bodies, the politics of the art world, and contemporary discourse about contagion, contamination, and quarantine, both biological and metaphorical. Bacteria swabs from participating women were subjected to a series of scientific interventions, accomplished in collaboration with biologists and a custom scent-development firm called Air Variable. First, Yi and her collaborators followed a scientific process that allowed them to preserve the scent molecules produced by the live bacteria. Next, these molecules—the "scents" of the women's cells—were combined with scent samples taken from the Gagosian Gallery during an exhibition of work by the artist Urs Fischer (a sardonic nod to the rarefied air of the male-dominated art world). Using a process akin to the procedures for creating commercial perfumes, this combination of molecules was then formulated into a synthetic compound, to be sprayed by a scent diffuser into the air in the Kitchen.

The Kitchen's gallery, in Yi's playful conceit, thus smelled both like the art world, and like the combined bodies of one hundred different women. These scents (barely detectable when I visited near the end of the exhibition, but highly distinctive, according to other writers who likely visited earlier)[124] accompanied the clean, carefully arranged installations within each clear plastic tent, which were meant to mimic, Yi explained, the structures of quarantine tents. (The Ebola outbreak of 2014, with its attendant contagion of public anxiety, would have been fresh in collective memory.) Lingering invisibly in the air, these molecules—whether perceptible or not—would have physically entered the spectator's body, circulating in ways that echo Teresa Brennan's description of how an affective "atmosphere" in a social situation "literally gets into the individual."[125] Matter from female bodies was circulated and disseminated, and the piece, according to the statement on The

Kitchen's website, was intended to "cultivate the idea of the female figure as a viral pathogen."[126]

In Yi's vision, both abstract and insistently literal, the "potency of female networks" was subjected to scientific testing, available for affective and metaphorical as well as physical dissemination. Yi's assembled bacteria represented, at once, biological pathogen, inquiry into the logic of public paranoia, and contagious artistic form, unavoidable (even when undetectable) to the spectator passing through. As many viral artworks do, the project challenged the boundaries of liveness, containing real biological matter that grew and changed over time, but corralling it into still installations, without performance's more overt forms of living human presence. As in the work of CAE, the Matteses, and Schlingensief, biological and metaphorical contagions overlapped, merged, and held tension with one another. As in the work of Cheang, biological contagions emanated from the sexualized body. And as in the works described in the following chapter, individual bodies were linked—and linked again—into vast networks, which drew their power from the tensions between local embodiment and geographic dispersal.

Chapter 4

"Everything Is Everywhere"

Viral Performance Networks

In March 2003, the theater-makers Kathryn Blume and Sharron Bower organized approximately one thousand simultaneous readings of Aristophanes's fifth-century B.C. comedy *Lysistrata*. The event, which evolved over two months of development and came to be known as the Lysistrata Project, was conceived as a protest against the impending U.S. invasion of Iraq. Initially, Blume and Bower had no idea how many people would participate: "We didn't ever think we would get up to a thousand," says Blume. "We weren't shooting for all 50 states, or every continent, but after a while, it just started building."[1] Before long, and especially after National Public Radio aired an interview with the pair, the project was inundated with participants. Blume remembers being surprised by "the pace at which we were adding new readings all the time," she says. "And the scope, the number of states, and the number of places in the world, that I hadn't even heard of."[2] Participants in the Lysistrata Project have similar memories of the project's speedy dissemination. Robert Neblett, who coordinated readings of *Lysistrata* in St. Louis and held a reading of his own adaptation of Aristophanes's play, recalls that the network of fellow participants grew exponentially in the weeks leading up to the performances. "Once I became part of the Project, I heard about it everywhere I read—on Playbill.com, in *American Theatre* magazine, on the ATHE listserv. The more I heard about it and its goals, the more I was proud to have jumped on board in the early stages of the appeal for participants."[3]

That same year, from November 2002 to November 2003, the playwright Suzan-Lori Parks had embarked on a marathon project in which she wrote one play each day, all year. The results of Parks's experiment, 365 minidramas (plus three "constants" to be performed alongside them at any time), became a yearlong national festival, in which artists and theaters around the country staged a week each of Parks's plays, from November 2006 to November 2007. About two years later, Caryl Churchill's short play *Seven Jewish Children* ignited political controversy when it premiered at London's Royal Court Theatre, and then became the catalyst for an emerging political

The Lysistrata Project. Reading of *Lysistrata* in Nikko, Japan, 2003. Photo courtesy of Kathryn Blume.

and artistic network when artists and activists began rewriting and restaging the dramatic text, revising it to reflect their own politics and performing it both for live audiences and dispersed spectators in cyberspace.

These three projects—all of which both employed and created performance networks—were not only designed to "go viral." They were, conceptually, viral from the start, representing their creators' desires to make performances that were reiterated and reproduced many times over, available to potentially limitless numbers of artists and spectators. In this chapter, I explore theatrical networks as potent instances of twenty-first-century viral performance, viewing viral dissemination as a fundamental element of these three projects' artistic and political aims. In each case, local productions drew much of their artistic and political charge from performers' and spectators' consciousness of the many other virtually linked performances unfolding simultaneously elsewhere. In each case, too, themes and imagery within the plays aligned with the structures of production and performance. These performance networks were mobilized as forms of political resistance, marshaling performing bodies together as a means of protesting violence and war. Each project, in its own way, pitted the power of geographically dispersed, conceptually connected artistic acts against global networks of military and economic power. Each also, implicitly or explicitly, explored the gendered nature of power and violence; it is no coincidence that all three projects were created or organized by women theater artists.

Viral culture and networked structures of dissemination are, in twenty-first-century media discourse, inherently linked. The nodes and edges that comprise networks are created by, among other forces, the contagious spread of ideas and actions; and those structures, in turn, provide lines of communication through which "viruses" of all kinds flow. In a 2007 article describing the role of "the viral" in a digitally networked society, Jussi Parikka makes this connection explicit, arguing that "the viral can be seen as a mode of action inherently connected to the complex, non-linear order of network society marked by transversal infections and parasitical relationships."[4] Parsing the intimate connection between the conceptual structures of the virus and the network, Parikka builds on Hardt and Negri's well-known statement that "the age of globalization is the age of universal contagion" to argue that "universal contagion" is a flexible concept: neither implying, solely, a network defined by centralized control (as, in his view, Hardt and Negri believed the network society to be), nor one that is inherently democratic in structure. Rather, and significantly for my argument here, he suggests that viral contagion must simply be seen as the essential mode of economic and social connection in the twenty-first century. "The age of universal contagion, then, is not restricted to a negative notion of a vampire or a hostile virus," he writes, "but rests on the notion that viral patterns of movement characterize the turbulent spaces of networks as a very primary logic."[5] Imagining, together, the virus and the network—or the virus in the network—clarifies the social and artistic significance that performance networks held for Parks and for the Lysistrata Project organizers, and the significance of the network that *Seven Jewish Children* created.

Viral dissemination was essential to the formation of each network. Though the image of a "network" can imply a constellation that is already established, its nodes identified and linked to one another, with data coursing seamlessly through it, this is not how any of the projects under discussion evolved. While avenues of communication were shaped by existing relationships, none had emerged as a performance network before the Lysistrata Project, *365 Days/365 Plays*, and *Seven Jewish Children* summoned them into being. To the contrary, each of these projects spread using at least some measure of spontaneous viral expansion. *365/365* gained participants as increasing numbers of theaters learned about the project and expressed interest in taking part. In an essay about her work as coproducer and archivist of the festival, Rebecca Rugg notes that after announcing plans for *365/365*, the producers quickly "began to field interest from outside the United States," to which they responded by creating the festival's international network, 365 Global.[6] Likewise, in a *New York Times* article, Campbell Robertson recounts that although Parks and the producer Bonnie Metzgar initially envisioned seven regional hubs, "after Ms. Metzgar raised the idea at national theater conferences over the summer, the phones started ringing." This resulted in an expansion to fourteen networks around the country.[7] Similarly, the organizers of the Lysistrata Project had no idea how many theaters or political groups would sign on. Caryl Churchill's play went viral largely without planning, as it was not only produced by theater groups and read aloud at demonstrations and town hall meetings, but also inspired artists and activists to write their own versions of the play, to be performed live or posted online.

In this chapter, I propose that embodied networks—those created and inhabited by live, performing bodies, those employed as modes of resistance to other, less easily visible networks of power—contribute significantly to contemporary discourse about the social and political properties of viral networks. Network theorists, both before and after the ubiquitous association of networks with digital culture, have frequently explored the politics of networked structures of communication, and the types of communication such structures imply. Bruno Latour, founding philosopher of actor-network theory, has argued that the era of digital networks inspired a profound shift in the term's meaning. Before the digital era, he wrote, "the word network . . . clearly meant a series of *transformations*—translations, transductions—which could not be captured by any of the traditional terms of social theory."[8] And yet "with the new popularization of the word network," Latour continued, "it now means transport *without* deformation."[9] Such questions about the nature of the network have profound implications for the performance networks described here, which in many ways staked their success on the openness of networks to difference, and on the power of networks to reshape the social structures of the theater world. The critic Benjamin Piekut, whose recent book *Experimentalism Otherwise* employs network theory to describe relationships among experimental music composers in the 1960s, builds on Latour's idea by proposing that "a network, then, describes a formation not simply of connected things (as we might assume in the post–World Wide Web era) but of differences that are mediated by connections that translate these differences into equivalences."[10] Such acts of translation take on added significance when the points of connection are performances: events unfolding in the present tense, necessarily altered through acts of interpretation, embodiment, and spectatorship.

Other scholars have argued that contemporary society as a whole, not simply specific communities or digital subcultures, must be viewed through the lens of network theory. In their 2007 study *The Exploit*, the media theorists Alexander R. Galloway and Eugene Thacker argue that politically and economically powerful forces—governments, media outlets, corporations—rely on various kinds of networks, channels by which information and capital are distributed, to assert and maintain their positions of dominance. Galloway and Thacker use the term "control society" to identify this sociopolitical landscape, understanding contemporary Western society as a civic arena organized and ruled by networks: political, technological, biological, and social.

But networks are not always ordered or centralized, and they do not always serve dominant economic forces. The more thoroughly networked a society becomes, Galloway and Thacker argue, the more quickly and pervasively can its networks be co-opted by subversive forces. Their description of such an interconnected culture is worth quoting at length, since it establishes the centrality of viral modes of communication and dissemination to contemporary networked culture:

> Inside the dense web of distributed networks, it would appear that *everything is everywhere*—the consequence of a worldview that leaves little room between the poles of the global and the local. Biological viruses are transferred via airlines between Guangdong Province and Toronto in a matter of hours, and computer viruses are transferred via data lines from Seattle to Saigon in a matter of seconds. But more important, the solutions to these various maladies are also designed for and deployed over the same networks—online software updates to combat e-mail worms, and medical surveillance networks to combat emerging infectious diseases. The network, it appears, has emerged as a dominant form describing the nature of control today, as well as resistance to it.[11]

The advent of networked technology has also led to highly optimistic interpretations of the possibilities that networked communications or social structures can offer. In his 2004 book *The Laws of Cool*, Alan Liu observes that many theorists of technology have argued that a networked society implicitly invites decentralized power and offers more freedom to marginalized groups of people. Elucidating this "emancipatory" view, he writes, "the decentralization thesis held that networks are innately antihierarchical, empowering to the individual user, and therefore democratic."[12] These ideas have even extended to new visions for the reorganization of labor and power relations in a networked economy. Liu cites the theorist Don Tapscott, who frames his predictions in near-utopian terms, writing that "the crowning achievement of networking human intelligence could be the creation of a true democracy," and adding, "rather than an all-powerful centralized government, arrogating decisions to itself, governments can be based on the networked intelligence of people."[13]

Many of the performance projects I discuss here operate in such a utopian register, particularly *365 Days/365 Plays*, in which "radical inclusion" constituted a central premise and primary production strategy. Rugg describes this concept, as understood by herself, Metzgar, Parks, and the other festival producers:

> Radical inclusion is a notion different from plain, unadorned inclusion. "Inclusion" smacks of liberal good intentions and is related to

> strategies for community building like outreach, which often involves an unexamined notion of center, magnanimously inviting the edge or margin to participate but not to lead, to attend but not to organize . . . Radical inclusion, on the other hand, involves destabilizing the comfortable polarities of center and margin.[14]

Radical inclusion, like utopian visions for technological networks, proposes to level artistic, geographical, and economic hierarchies. The three performance projects discussed in this chapter actively sought to eliminate standard economic factors affecting theatrical production: distributing scripts for free, insisting that no admission be charged, and fostering a performance culture in which low-tech (or no-tech) productions in unconventional performance spaces were celebrated equally with fully produced stagings at major theaters. Digital networks were essential to this mode of production, allowing for the coordination of participating artists across state lines and time zones.

In some cases, the performance projects under discussion in this chapter have not only attempted to foster inclusive, democratic artistic networks, but have also offered direct resistance to other, more powerful networks of political control. Such was the case with the 2003 Lysistrata Project, which launched a linked series of readings of Aristophanes's antiwar comedy in response to the United States's imminent invasion of Iraq—itself, of course, the geopolitical mobilization of a network, a "coalition of the willing," against a perceived network of enemy powers. Others, such as *365 Days/365 Plays*, had less explicit policy aims, but resisted established modes of artistic organization in many ways: the project sought to create a virtually linked artistic community, extending to places where none had existed before, and to reduce the economic pressures affecting new productions and premieres across the country. *Seven Jewish Children* did not operate through an official network of producing organizations, but summoned a network of dispersed activists and artists into being—often blurring the lines between artists and activists—and created a network of plays and productions in dialogue with each other at live performance events and online.

Though Galloway and Thacker do not explicitly theorize performance networks, their description of networked society contains an observation that aptly reflects the power that networked theater holds for its creators. "Perhaps if there is one truism to the study of networks," they write, "it is that networks are only networks when they are 'live,' when they are enacted, embodied, or rendered operational."[15] This idea is particularly suggestive for thinking about theatrical networks, which are literally live (literally enacted, literally operational), making their structures and connections tangible in ways that other media rarely can. These projects are case studies in viral networking that, to borrow Galloway and Thacker's concept, are inherently physical; digitally connected, yet manifestly live. In turn, they suggest a new theatrical form: the viral performance network, in which individual productions make up an enormous, often rapidly expanding constellation of performances. Actors' and spectators' consciousness of simultaneity—of other performances unfolding across geographical space—becomes a central theatrical element in these projects. Numbers and scale become dramaturgical form.

"The First-Ever Worldwide Theatrical Act of Dissent": The Lysistrata Project

Lysistrata, first written and performed at the Lenaia Festival, the Athenian festival of comedy, in the early spring of 411 B.C.,[16] has a long history as a vehicle for protest performances. The play's original production took place at a time when Athens was deeply embroiled in the Peloponnesian War; in fact, only seven years after *Lysistrata* premiered, the Athenians would surrender to Sparta for good, and see their civic life and theatrical culture largely dismantled. By 411 B.C., Athens was already beginning to crumble. Sparta had recently taken control of the city's surrounding farmlands, cutting Athenians off from agricultural supplies and forcing them to retreat within the guarded city walls.[17] Aristophanes's play was urgently topical: his tale, in which an alliance of Athenian and Spartan women bring peace to the warring cities by staging a sex boycott against their husbands, addressed itself to a public that was intensely involved in conflict, and aware of the dangers of ongoing war.

Given the historical circumstances surrounding the writing of *Lysistrata*, scholars have debated the play's intended political effect: Aristophanes's drama could hardly have been clearer about the need for an end to the Peloponnesian War, and the play appears, on its surface, to be a pacifist parable, making the case for Athenian-Spartan collaboration in order to restore domestic bliss to both societies. But, as many have pointed out, Athens was so fully embroiled in war by the time *Lysistrata* was performed that a playwright as politically savvy as Aristophanes could hardly have believed that a plea for cooperation between the city-states would be taken seriously.[18] "If he did," writes H. D. Westlake, one exponent of this view, "he must have been strangely blind to the realities of the situation, which were only too obvious to others, or else unreasonably optimistic."[19] The play's gleeful proposal that sexual subterfuge could convince armies into laying down their weapons, fantastical in its own time, has been equally fantastical since.

It has also been highly appealing to playwrights, directors, and composers over the last three hundred years. Marivaux wrote a version of *Lysistrata*, as did Schubert, and the play was reshaped into an opera repeatedly in the eighteenth and nineteenth centuries. These early adaptations, though still sexually explicit enough to be frequent targets of censorship, were usually less politically topical than the ancient Greek original,[20] but twentieth-century directors were more overt in pitching *Lysistrata* toward political ends. A 1958

Italian version reset the play during the Cold War, with Athens and Sparta reimagined as the United States and the Soviet Union, while in 1960, the State Theatre in Bucharest presented a pacifist *Lysistrata* in which the protagonist is a slave fighting for her own freedom.[21] In 1967, students at Wayne State University protested the Vietnam War in their musical adaptation, entitled *Lysistrata & The War*.[22]

It is fitting, then, that a play that has been summoned up time after time as a parable of dissent became the basis for the viral network created by Kathryn Blume and her collaborators in 2003 to protest the United States's imminent invasion of Iraq. Blume had been considering *Lysistrata*'s possibilities as a protest play for years, and was planning to adapt it for other political ends, turning it into a screenplay designed to protest global warming. "My idea was to write a modern environmental version," she recalls in an article about the creation of the Lysistrata Project, "a sex boycott to save the planet."[23] That screenplay was still unfinished when, one Saturday in early January 2003, Blume received an email from THAW—Theaters Against the War, an alliance of New York-based theater companies organizing protests against the Bush administration's planned invasion of Iraq. THAW was calling for a "national day of action" to take place that March, and asking theater companies to help by placing antiwar materials in their printed programs and on their websites, and by making curtain speeches in protest of the imminent war. Blume, inspired to participate, decided to stage a reading of *Lysistrata*.

By the following morning, Blume was in conversation with a collaborator, Sharron Bower of the Mint Theater, and the two had decided to stage their reading as a benefit, sending all proceeds to the organizations EPIC (Education for Peace in Iraq Center) and MADRE, which works for women's rights around the world. They quickly realized that MADRE's celebrity spokesperson was Susan Sarandon, an actress that Blume had fantasized about casting as Lysistrata in her own unfinished screenplay. This discovery prompted Blume and Bower to begin imagining their staged reading more ambitiously: what if they attempted to recruit celebrities for the cast, and what if they organized not one *Lysistrata*, but many *Lysistrata*s, for THAW's simultaneous day of action?

The resulting project—in which Blume and Bower coordinated hundreds of simultaneous readings of the play on March 3, 2003—constituted not just an outcry against the seemingly inevitable push toward war, but more particularly a viral outcry, one that echoed and subverted the networks of power that were mobilizing the country for conflict. In the play, withheld female sexuality provokes a kind of contagious lust among warring Athenian and Spartan men, forcing them to broker a truce, and the Lysistrata Project's organizers aimed to inspire a similarly contagious response, using virally replicable performances to counter public apathy and fear.

Bower and Blume began by setting up a website with a "How-To" kit for staging readings of *Lysistrata*, including press releases, logos for companies to use on marketing materials, and contact information for anyone interested in finding out more.[24] Then they began sending invitations to participate to everyone they knew. When I spoke with her in September 2012—nearly ten years later—Blume recalled the elation she felt over the initial flood of communications about the project. "The day after we sent the email," she says, "we heard from a woman in Iowa about [participating in the project]. She had received two forwards of the email: one from Delaware, and one from London."[25] *Lysistrata* was already everywhere.

Within a couple of weeks, Blume says, "we knew it was going viral."[26] To her and her co-organizers, no other concept could have adequately described the rate at which news of the Lysistrata Project spread, and the geographical distances it covered. "It was definitely an Internet-era project," says Blume. "There's no way, pre-Internet, that something like this could have happened, start to finish, in two months. The speed was extraordinary and the reach was extraordinary."[27] At the time, Blume says she knew of only one recent project that had sought to create simultaneous linked performances: Eve Ensler's *The Vagina Monologues*, which, after its premiere, had catalyzed a theatrical network, encouraging artists around the world to stage the play on Valentine's Day as a celebration of women's bodies and a protest against gendered violence.

The Vagina Monologues figures as an important predecessor to all of the projects described in this chapter, not only for its networked performance model, but also because, even more explicitly than these examples, it was a gendered event, an embodied network created to address questions of the sexualized body. A documentary-style drama compiled from Ensler's interviews with women about their sexuality, experiences of rape and abuse, and about cultural taboos surrounding female genitalia, *The Vagina Monologues* opened in 1994 for an off-Broadway run. In 1998, inspired by the production's success, Ensler founded V-Day, an international organization dedicated to ending violence against girls and women, primarily through annual networked performances of *The Vagina Monologues* each February.[28] The first V-Day event, a benefit reading of the play in New York's Hammerstein Ballroom featuring celebrity performers, raised $250,000 and allowed Ensler to formally launch the V-Day organization. Following this influx of donated capital, the producers of V-Day—like the artists examined in this chapter—chose to circumvent the conventional economics of theatrical production. The organization allows artists and activists to perform *The Vagina Monologues* free of royalty payments, provided that participants adhere to a few central requirements: that performances occur during February; that participants coordinate their work with other V-Day event organizers; and that the proceeds from ticket sales be donated to local organizations working in opposition to gender-based violence.[29] V-Day has become an annual tradition, and in 2016 the organization reported performances of *The Vagina Monologues* in 767 locations across 48 countries.[30]

Yet even as it promoted conversation about female sexuality and gender-based violence, the discourse surrounding V-Day has been complex. Critiques of the project, as I see it, are significant because they register the multiple meanings that networked performance structures can hold: the democratic potential of networks, as well as the possibilities (even inadvertent) that networks can promote homogenization and centralized control. In a 2007 *Signs* essay, Christine M. Cooper notes that standardization has been important for the distribution of the monologues, pointing out that each organization wishing to stage a V-Day performance must perform the most recent edition of the text (which is updated annually), with no alterations or omissions.[31] More than this, Cooper suggests, as a play originally produced in an era rife with anxiety about the feminist movement's decline, *The Vagina Monologues* served as more of a half-measure than a full-throated defense of women's rights. The play, she writes, advocated a form of easily palatable feminism that homogenized as much as it diversified; that promoted an overly essentialized equivalence among vagina, sexuality, and self; and that, in its monological structure, dampened dialogue and diminished difference. "Collapsing vagina and self, the monologues reify a universal ontology of womanhood," she writes.[32] Likewise, Sealing Cheng's 2009 essay "Questioning Global Vaginahood" critiques what Cheng describes as a "core-periphery relationship" between the V-Day organization and participants worldwide.[33] I note such critiques because they reveal the contradictions inherent to networked structures, and more specifically to embodied networks—the tensions between local difference and geographically dispersed sameness, and between embodied, live performances and virtually dispersed performance structures. And, it is worth noting, such tensions do not play out in inherently binary terms: embodied performances, too, can promote sameness; and virtual networks, as this chapter demonstrates, can create space for difference. Such tensions are significant because they are central to the meanings held by the networks explored in this chapter: as in, for instance, *365 Days/365 Plays*, whose organizers sought to replace a "core-periphery relationship" with "radical inclusion"; or *Seven Jewish Children*, in which virtual circulation created space for individual dissent.

Though it set the model for, in some ways, all of these ventures, V-Day—having begun as a single off-Broadway production, and produced a star-studded benefit before constructing a network—was not viral in quite the same way as the projects that follow. The *Lysistrata* network was conceived differently, Blume explains, because it was intended to be grassroots from the start. Rather than aiming for a high-profile first production, she and her collaborators would consciously attempt to make the barriers to participation as low as possible to begin with. As a result, on March 3, 2003, a little over two weeks before the United States invaded Iraq, community groups and theaters staged a total of 1,029 readings of *Lysistrata*.[34] There was at least one reading in every U.S. state, and some states boasted hundreds, in

The Lysistrata Project. Reading of *Lysistrata* in St. Louis, Missouri, 2003. Photo courtesy of Kathryn Blume.

what Blume and Bower termed "The First-Ever Worldwide Theatrical Act of Dissent."[35] There were readings in China, Greece, and England, and an international reading was orchestrated via simultaneous streaming video.[36] According to the Lysistrata Project's online archive, approximately 300,000 people attended the readings that day. Performances were held in a range of theatrical and nontheatrical locations: in cafés, schools, parks, community centers, and on subway platforms, as well as in conventional theater spaces.[37] Blume and Bower encouraged theaters to collect donations for antiwar organizations and charities—both their chosen beneficiaries and those of local artists' preference—and their archive boasts a total of $125,000 raised for MADRE, EPIC, and other nonprofit groups chosen by individual theaters.[38] The readings thus (if in a small way) constructed an alternative route of economic transmission, channeling antiwar dollars to counter the mechanisms of pro-war capital.

Stagings of *Lysistrata* varied in scale and artistic emphasis. In a video of a performance staged in Mexico City by the Mexican playwright and director Jesusa Rodríguez, large flats displayed life-size drawings of "classical" Greek figures, clothed in togas and arranged in tableaux, with cutouts for live performers' faces and hands to peek through.[39] The effect, with the actors' bodies almost entirely concealed behind two-dimensional line drawings, gives the impression of a contemporary political agenda emerging from behind the veil of a well-known myth. The Messenger Theatre Company, in New York

City, presented puppet versions of *Lysistrata* in Grand Central Station and on the sidewalk across from the United Nations plaza. The female characters wore masks shaped like giant pairs of lips, while the male characters wore masks depicting cannons and guns.[40]

A documentary about the project, *Operation Lysistrata*, contains footage from a selection of the readings that took place around the world on that day. Many of these are similar in their makeshift simplicity: a group gathered in a Seattle public square wore white sheets draped around their shoulders, and gestured flamboyantly as they shouted the play's dialogue amid the noise of passersby, while a group in New South Wales wore black robes and featured a male Lysistrata sporting a pale blue mop on his head. A group of women performing the play outdoors in lower Manhattan wore winter coats, with paper party hats strapped over their chests, creating colorful, exaggeratedly conical breasts. At a performance in San Francisco, the stage was adorned in plastic American flags. A group in Venice, California, was costumed in lingerie and wore exaggerated makeup and wigs in cotton-candy pink. There were topical references (one actor, playing an angry Athenian man, interrupted Aristophanes's dialogue to announce that he was raising the terror alert to "code orange"). And there were celebrity participants (the cast of the soap opera *Guiding Light* held a reading).[41] Viewed together, the similarities among the productions outweigh the differences, and suggest that the makeshift, boisterous, unfussy ethos of the network's organizers permeated, at least a little bit, the network itself. (If any single aesthetic decision ties the many protests together, it is most likely their effort to represent the angry male chorus's erect phalli onstage, something that appears even in many productions that employed no other costumes or props. Phallic balloons and stuffed stockings were popular strategies, and appeared frequently in news coverage of the events. The play's bodily humor thus, in a sense, rendered the project itself more hilariously newsworthy, assisting in its dissemination.)

One of these versions of *Lysistrata*, created by the Montreal-based theater artist Donovan King, suggests that Blume and Bower were not the only participants who saw the project as an overtly viral one. King, after signing on to participate, decided to use the event as an occasion to stage a media stunt that would skewer the Bush administration's War on Terror messaging, and turn his reading of *Lysistrata* into a theatrical infiltration of sorts. King described his approach in detail in a section of his University of Calgary master's thesis, recounting that on the afternoon of March 3, his cast assembled in front of the American Consulate in Montreal, dressed as public officials and FBI agents. (The real consulate staff, upon seeing the performers arrive, locked the doors to the building and watched through the windows, while their security cameras captured every detail of the proceedings.)[42]

Once situated in front of the consulate, King—wearing a cowboy hat and speaking with a George W. Bush twang—began to warn the crowd of a fast-moving epidemic, a series of thousands of performances of the play

Lysistrata, spreading quickly across North America. His speech satirized national security warnings, and cast the project in deliberately viral terms:

> We recently received information about a cell, in New York City, which was using the Internet for their agenda of destruction. Calling themselves "The Lysistrata Project," they are distinctly un-American. And a threat to our security. It started off as one "reading" in early January, set up by Sharron Bower and Kathryn Blume. What started off as an idea to stage some theater, has managed to somehow spread like a virus . . . This dang thing is spreading like a disease; it's not stopping at borders, and attacking the very values that we as Americans hold close to our hearts. Our Intelligence Officials have traced this thing back to FRANCE.[43]

This tongue-in-cheek security warning continued, as King went on to blame the dangerously viral properties of live performance on a French "terrorist" he'd "discovered" named Antonin Artaud, who, King reported, had notoriously compared the theater to the plague.[44] "Now we all know that the Plague is a deadly virus, and we all know that viruses are Biological," King went on to say. "The Lysistrata Project, ladies and gentlemen, is a Biological Weapon of Mass Destruction."[45] Maintaining his George W. Bush persona, King reassured spectators that his team had intercepted the plans of a group of actors intending to stage *Lysistrata* that afternoon, and that the performance had been prevented.

Then King's collaborators took over, staging a mock intervention. A fellow cast member emerged out of the crowd and smashed a pie in King's face, while the "FBI" officers turned on him and began wrapping him in plastic and duct tape. The remaining actors then rushed in from among the audience, and began to perform an abbreviated version of *Lysistrata*.[46] The play, in this iteration, was turned into a performance-within-a-guerrilla-performance, viral in multiple ways—as an act of infiltrative theater, and as part of a worldwide theatrical network.

Even when framed by less overtly self-conscious production strategies, *Lysistrata* was an apt choice for an antiwar performance project, not only for its explicit themes, but also for its interrogation of the nature of networks and their relationships to violence, power, and gender. In the Greek comedy, the female populations of Athens, Sparta, and other war-torn city-states establish an unsanctioned political coalition, intervening in the workings of the official institutions that have sent their husbands to war. They physically occupy the Acropolis, the seat of Athens's democratic power, and lock the treasury, taking control of the powerful city's public finances. Next, and most famously, they make a compact to deny their husbands sex until a truce is concluded. Much of the play consists of an extended standoff between male and female choruses, as the women become more powerful and the men become increasingly physically frustrated. The play pits two very different forms of networks against each other: a militarized male network and a subterranean domestic female network. By enforcing mass abstinence, Lysistrata and her followers render sexuality contagious in its absence: it is not sex acts that are infectious, but rather performances of sexuality, which make women's bodies irresistible through their unavailability. (In one scene, Lysistrata trains the women to make themselves as attractive as possible; the results are particularly evident in the sequence in which the character Myrrhine teases her husband, Kinesias, delaying sex again and again.)[47] In the 2003 readings, artists repeatedly emphasized this humorous bodily drama.

In staging a play that foregrounds bodily needs, the organizers also gestured obliquely to the darker physical confrontation unfolding offstage on the battlefield. Aristophanes invokes images of contagion and contamination repeatedly, to describe both the horrors of war and the angst the women have visited upon their husbands. Lysistrata advocates "cleansing" Athens of its involvement in war, and at one point the women's chorus takes this injunction literally, dousing the men with pitchers of water.[48] Later, Lysistrata declares that the city must be washed clean of "all corruption, offal, and sheepdip."[49] In answer, the male chorus takes up similar imagery, but reverses the alleged source of contamination. They complain that "this trouble may be terminal; it has a loaded odor, an ominous aroma of constitutional rot," and conclude that Spartans must have infiltrated the Athenian women's social networks, creating disorder of epidemic proportions:

> Predictably infected,
> These women straightway acted
> To commandeer the City's cash. They're feverish to freeze
> My be-all,
> My end-all,
> My payroll![50]

The men accuse their wives of forging a subversive network with Athens's enemies, employing the imagery of contagion to describe female interventions in both the democratic institutions of governance and the financial institutions that assure Athenian power. But it is actually the men who are infected: first with the urge to fight, then with desire. As the play's eventual return to the happy status quo suggests, sexuality constitutes a contaminant only when it exceeds or subverts its containment in marriage. The real social infection here is war.

Aristophanes presents a more conservative conclusion to this standoff than is often registered in performances that employ the play as an antiwar vehicle. Although the female network—overtly subversive, and strategically more intelligent than the male—is ostensibly victorious, the women also part ways, dismantling their organization when its antiwar goals have been achieved, and reconfiguring themselves, with their husbands, into conventional domestic pairings. (Also worth noting is Lysistrata's suggestion that Athens and Sparta unite in order to better fight more distant and powerful enemies; this is no paean to pacifism.) Lysistrata herself falls silent in the play's final moments, suggesting that the subversive female network was, in fine comic tradition, a departure from ordinary life that served to reinforce its hierarchies.

Though the original play dramatizes a reversion to the status quo, the Lysistrata Project, in practice, suggested that radical networks can leave legacies, both in the form of new artistic relationships and in the form of new performance models. As with the other pieces to be discussed here, this project is significant not only for its creation of a network, bit by bit, as it went viral over the course of several weeks, but also because it revealed social constellations that already existed. Blume and Bower created a website, sent out an email, and hoped the word would spread. As new participants emerged and the roster of readings grew, the project illuminated lines of communication and political sympathy that had been already in existence, waiting to be made active. This principle applies, too, to *365 Days/365 Plays* and especially to *Seven Jewish Children*: the networks in these projects are latent, waiting for new forms of viral expansion to render them embodied and live.

Then, too, interviews with participants in the project suggest that viral performance networks lend an invisible but palpable power to the individual performances they comprise. Whether or not participants were influenced directly by other artists' interpretive choices (and Blume believes that mostly they were not: rehearsal periods were too short to allow for much consultation),[51] each individual performance within the *Lysistrata* network was, I argue, altered by the sheer potency of its association with the hundreds of other performances taking place on the same day. Performances were received differently by audiences, and imagined differently by creators, because of their awareness of the larger network. Robert Neblett recalls:

> When we began the reading that night in March 2003, knowing that we were doing so alongside famous Broadway actors in New York, film stars in LA, Afghan women in their living rooms, colleges across Europe, and even a second local reading in St. Louis, there was an incredible sense of community that meant we were not the only ones who felt this way about what was going on in the world.[52]

Sheila Cohen Tissot, who organized a French-language reading of *Lysistrata* in Paris that day, echoes Neblett's assessment. "It filled me with hope to know that people all around the world were joining forces at the same moment to express a shared desire for peace," she remembered.[53] Blume remembers a similar feeling; she recalls receiving an email from a woman who played Lysistrata, describing an overwhelming sense of kinship with all the other women who were playing the same role on the same day.[54]

Years after the Lysistrata Project was over, Blume was contacted by an artist who proposed to revive the event: not just to restage a reading of *Lysistrata*, but to reawaken the network itself, to stage a second series of linked performances of the play. The mere suggestion of this possibility (which, to my knowledge, has not yet been realized)[55] registers the change that viral networks have wrought in contemporary conceptions of performance. A play can go viral, a performance can create a network, and that network can become an inextricable element of the performance itself.

The Interconnectedness of All Things: *365 Days/365 Plays*

The *365 Days/365 Plays* festival was partially inspired by producer Bonnie Metzgar's experiences working with the National New Play Network, an organization founded in 1998 with the aim of expanding the circulation of new plays among nonprofit theaters around the country—increasing the chances that a playwright's work would receive multiple productions rather than an isolated premiere.[56] Drawing on this model, Metzgar and Parks conceived a performance strategy for Parks's mini-dramas: they would produce a networked series of premieres across the country over an entire calendar year, promoting an ethos of "radical inclusion." They were, by any measure, successful. More than 800 theater companies produced Parks's plays between November 2006 and November 2007.[57]

The national network was organized around regional hubs, which included the Public Theater in New York, the Center Theater Group in Los Angeles, and an alliance of several institutions including the Goodman and Steppenwolf theaters in Chicago. Each hub was charged with recruiting and coordinating productions among fifty-two "satellite" theaters, one for each week of premieres, in their area. While some of these regional partnerships already existed, others—such as the La Colectiva network based in San Antonio, Texas—were assembled for the purposes of producing *365 Days/365 Plays*. La Colectiva eventually also included theater groups that were founded specifically to participate in the project.[58] In addition to this roster of professional and community theaters, *365/365* boasted a national network of college campus productions, and a network of deaf theaters producing the plays.[59]

The organizers sought to complement geographical inclusivity with economic inclusivity. Parks and Metzgar allowed theaters to purchase production rights for one dollar, and in order to encourage attendance, also mandated that artists forgo charging admission. Parks has described this system as "negative money,"[60] aligning it with the donation-driven economics of the Lysistrata Project and, as I will discuss later, *Seven Jewish Children*. This decision alone—the choice to eliminate, as much as possible, financial barriers to both theatrical producing and theater attendance—suggests how deeply immersed in a utopian idea of network the creators of *365 Days/365 Plays* were. Parks, as a Pulitzer Prize–winning playwright, could have commanded substantial ticket prices, and could have offered her dramas to major theaters for fully realized productions. Instead, whatever might stand in the way of potential audience members' attendance at the hundreds of performances of Parks's plays, it would not be cost. Network theorists might agree with the producers' focus on money: the controlling forces of capitalism constitute, according to Galloway and Thacker, the dominant network in a twenty-first-century control society. Such forces also traditionally govern the creation of theater projects in the United States, where fund-raising, marketing, and box office budgets so frequently circumscribe artistic scope.

In summoning a virtual network of participants into existence, *365 Days/365 Plays* also created an economy of performance, in which Parks's bodily and emotional experiences were dispersed and reimagined by hundreds of artists simultaneously. Individual theaters typically took on a week's worth of plays, and many days during that year, the same play premiered in multiple locations at once. Many critics have noted that this producing paradigm echoes the structures of digital networks. Writing of *365/365* during its first week, Campbell Robertson pointed out that the project created a "sort of theatrical Internet," inspiring artistic exchange among theaters that previously had no relationship with each other or with Parks. The critic Philip Kolin, speculating on *365/365*'s future, proposed that "ultimately, *365* might best be realized as cyberspace, or digital theatre," and described the plays as "analogues to screens in indeterminately linked web sites . . . Each *365* play, or group of plays, might be envisioned as a link connecting readers/audiences to yet another link."[61] What makes the dramas of *365 Days/365 Plays* so significant for a consideration of networked performance is that they were not just networked in their eventual production, or held together by the logic of the calendar year. Instead, these plays are rife with theatrical structures, actions, and images that meditate on the concept of the contagiously proliferating embodied network—and that express ambivalence and doubt about the nature of such structures.

Many of the plays feature riots, crowds, mobs, or assemblies, require infinitely increasing casts of characters, and call for endless variations on each type of person gathered onstage. One of these, a play entitled "Does It Matter What You Do?" calls for a stage full of performers, costumed to represent an eclectic combination of forms of identity. (Parks's suggestions include "Doctor, Lawyer, Indian Monk, Fireman, Ballerina, Wastrel, Mother, Wrestler," and many more.) This crowd, she specifies, should travel downstage, acting their "roles," then tumbling into the orchestra pit. As in many other *365/365* plays, this action is to repeat indefinitely, "even as the curtains go down, and even as the audience and crew and entire world goes home."[62] In another play, from the "Father Comes Home from the Wars" series (more on the series shortly), Parks calls for a uniformed "Soldier Man" to enter. She then adds that he may be dressed as a warrior from any conflict ("the Trojan war, WWI, American Civil, Iran-Iraq, Napoleonic, Spanish Civil, Crimean, Zulu," and more),[63] conjuring an image of vast numbers, endless soldiers fighting endless wars. There are many more examples of Parks's fascination, in *365 Days/365 Plays*, with impossibly enormous casts of performers. In the piece "All Things Being Equal" a queen, decked out in a gold crown, waves proudly to the audience, apparently unique in her royalty, until she is joined by an identical figure, then another, until the stage is crowded with queens, waving and jostling for space.[64] In "A Scene from the Great Opera," two onlookers watch an "endless Line of People," all carrying luggage, as they inch across the stage to a soundtrack of Puccini.[65]

Much has been said, in critical analyses of *365/365*, about the contrast between Parks's brief, lapidary dramas and the visions of vastness they invoke. (Deborah Geis, for instance, writes in her 2008 monograph about Parks that "there is a striking tension between the brevity of the plays and the indication Parks often makes at the end of a piece that it repeats itself or goes on in perpetuity.")[66] My argument builds on such observations, but also departs from them. As I see it, in these examples, Parks is not just summoning images of infinite variety, but also specifically envisioning enormous networks of characters, endless in their variations, linked by the stage directions that collectively call them forth. Such images anticipate the distributed network that eventually produced her plays: in many cases, nodding specifically to the local or regional difference that would become an essential aspect of *365 Days/365 Plays* in production. One play, "Learning English," for instance—a comment on Americans' inhospitality toward immigrant communities—emerges as necessarily different depending on its geographical setting. In this page-long drama, an apparently endless number of students attempt to pronounce English words correctly, and are "secretly" beaten by native "English Speakers" for failure to do so. A group of "watchers" looks on, reminiscing about the lost "Good Old Days," when beatings could take place in public. Some of the students eventually achieve "success" and join the native speakers; others do not. This continues, not, Parks specifies, until all of the students are competently conversing in English, but rather, until "the English language is less desirable to learn."[67] Actors' interpretation of such a play, and audiences' reception of it, would surely vary by location, infusing Parks's parable about difference with specific, local differences in performance.

In addition to dramatizing theatrical networks within individual plays, numerous constellations of mini-dramas loop through the collection as a whole. One of these takes shape in Parks's repeated invocation of her web of artistic influences, a collection of playwrights, novelists, poets, and musicians spanning centuries and forms. Some of these constitute a sort of highlights reel spinning through the Western dramatic canon: the mini-drama "Blackbird (A *Sea Gull* Variation)" pays homage to the first scene of Chekhov's play;

"The Birth of Tragedy" winks at Nietzsche; the numerous "House of Jones" plays suggest the influence of Aeschylus's cycle of wartime tragedies about the House of Atreus; plays written during the month of February include "Project Macbeth" and "Project Tempest." There are many more.[68]

Two of Parks's plays, one written in December 2002, near the beginning of the cycle, and one written in September 2003, near the end, address the networked nature of storytelling itself, providing the audience with explicit images of writers or storytellers at work, and with theatrical hypotheses about how stories and dramas are disseminated. September's play, entitled "(Again) PERFECT," provides an enticing depiction of the collection's contagious genesis. Here, a writer named "Woman" faces off against a mysterious figure called the "Timer." "Whats the question?" says Woman, to which the Timer replies only, "Aaahhh," and then starts a stopwatch and exits. Woman sits, scribbling on her notepad, becoming increasingly frustrated with her own work. She writes, crumples the page and stuffs it into a pocket, writes again, rejects her idea, and crushes the new page, until "her pockets, blouse, shoes, socks are all full of crossed-out, imperfect, balled-up answers. She is reduced to throwing her balled papers onto the floor."[69] To the writer's apparent surprise, the Timer soon returns, lovingly gathers the entire heap of discarded texts, and kisses their creator, declaring them "Perfect."[70]

On its surface, this is a prescriptively optimistic parable about the act of writing: process makes perfect, it seems to say. But "(Again) PERFECT" also offers a revealing image of *365 Days/365 Plays* as an embodied network, in which each page is a scrap of the writer's own imagination, which, crumpled and crammed into her clothing, expands her corporeal presence onstage. As the Timer recovers the discarded drafts, she is, imaginatively, collecting pieces of the writer's own body. We witness the writer creating a contagiously growing collection, as her panic feeds on itself, propelling the generation of a sprawling work of art. The network here is not a controlled channel of communication, but rather a mutating web of texts, which in the end exceeds physical borders: onstage, in the writer's body, and hypothetically, as spectators are invited to imagine them circulating.

Such expansive visions also emerged in performance. Productions were frequently minimalist in conception, and often gestured toward the larger circulation of the plays in the festival as a whole. Out Of the Black Box Theater, based in Greenbelt, Maryland, for instance, staged "(Again) PERFECT" in September 2007. Performed at a local coffee shop called the New Deal Café, the company's presentation was starkly simple, and faithful to Parks's stage directions. In production photos, a Writer, wearing a black dress and colorful shoes, is visible, seated on a folding chair, anxiously scribbling, as a Timer looks on sternly from the side. There are no props onstage aside from the sheets of paper accumulating on the floor, and in the final production photo, the Timer is smiling warmly, collecting the crumpled documents, as the Writer looks down, appearing tired and a little ashamed.[71]

Out Of the Black Box's production was spare, clearly produced on a minimal budget, and staged at a local café. This is characteristic of performances that are part of large networks; it was true of the *Lysistrata* stagings, and of the presentations of Churchill's *Seven Jewish Children*. Throughout the *365 Days/365 Plays* festival, artists performed on the street, in the lobbies of office buildings, and in nursing homes and youth hostels, among other locations.[72] The Los Angeles premiere of the festival took place at an outdoor plaza, with actors performing amid (and interacting with) large public sculptures.[73] When the plays were staged in theaters, they often shared space with other, longer-running productions, as in Hartford, Connecticut, where the regional theater Hartford Stages produced a week's worth of Parks's plays on the set of August Wilson's *Fences*.[74]

To some observers, these constrictions—both Parks's decision to write 365 plays, no matter how limited in scope each one might be, and the festival's emphasis on the quantity of participants rather than the particularity of the performances—meant that *365 Days/365 Plays* produced less than satisfying theater. Commenting on one production in Houston, Texas, for instance, the journalist Everett Evans complained that the festival's format prevented it from creating individual productions that were complex or interesting: "All together, 365 plays is too much: How many theater goers will really see even a significant fraction of them?" he wrote. "But taken singly, each playlet is too little . . . the concept comes up empty."[75]

Viewed another way, though, the simplicity of each individual production was not simply a necessary concession to the festival's larger goals, but integral to the nature of networked performance. Each production can also be seen as deliberately partial, its simplicity and incompleteness a gesture toward the larger festival of which it constituted one small fragment. Viewing the plays in the form of low-budget, unfussy, minimalist performances asked spectators to maintain an awareness that the productions they attended were small nodes in a large web. This awareness, as in all of the viral performance networks I discuss, lent each production its primary artistic power. Elaborate sets and lengthy rehearsal periods would have directed spectators' focus to the individual performances; scrappy, spare productions drew attention to the invisible whole.

Another local production, the California-based Chance Theater's staging, from Week 7 of the festival, imagined the invisible whole in an even more tangible way. The associate artistic director Jocelyn Brown, after deciding to stage the week's plays as a single evening, sought a means of connecting the seven individual dramas, and decided to present them onstage as seven figments of the writer's imagination. The process of writing, as in "(Again) PERFECT," would become the process of staging. Accordingly, Brown decided to seat her audience on her black box theater's stage, along with an actor portraying a "writer," a stand-in for Parks. The seven individual dramas played out among the theater's risers, just above and behind the performer playing

Parks.[76] This staging strategy emphasized the connections among the plays, while also laying bare their disparate narratives and concerns as they spiraled out into imagined landscapes, linked only by the writer's imagination. Like the many other productions that were aesthetically stark, out of budgetary necessity or artistic choice, Chance Theater's version of *365 Days/365 Plays* drew attention to the individual plays' capacity to complete and complement each other, to each play's role as a fragment of a much larger pattern.

One of the plays in Chance Theater's production also directly examined this aspect of the festival by questioning the gaps, the missed connections, the dangers, in the network form itself. Written in late December, about six weeks into the project's creation, and entitled "2 Examples from the Interconnectedness of All Things," the drama takes explicit aim at the image of the network, so prevalent in Parks's dramatic form and subject matter. The play features two griots who tell the audience competing ghost stories, both contemplating the presence of the past in contemporary African American life. In the first, a fable about a narrow escape from slavery, an enslaved family flees a Southern town. As they do, one family member suddenly notices that the ghosts of all of her ancestors have arrived to help her. There are, Parks specifies, "folks the woman recognizes and folks she's never seen." There are "grandparents and then boys wearing baseball caps on backwards and girls listening to shiny metal music boxes—future folks, they come too."[77] Here Parks offers us an image of endless generations, timelessly linked together in their efforts to shepherd their relations to freedom.

The second griot counters this fable, which celebrates oral history, family interconnections, and the benevolent influence of future and past generations, with a different sort of network: the specious rumor. "Martin Luther King is alive and living in Las Vegas," she declares.[78] Going on, she conjures up an image of King as an old man, enjoying himself at the Bellagio casino's buffet. Soon, without obvious provocation, her tale veers into defensive anger: "MOTHERFUCKER, WOULD I LIE TO YOU?!?!?!" she screams, outraged at an unheard objection to her tale. "YOU WOULDNT KNOW THE TRUTH CAUSE YOU WOULDNT WANT TO KNOW THE TRUTH. I SEEN HIM. I SEEN THE KING."[79] Parks characterizes this spiral into rage as a communal one, dragging all black Americans, as Parks notes in stage directions, directly from uplift to chaos: "The race, which up until now, had been doing so well," she writes, "takes 2 steps backward."[80] The play culminates in a scene of violence: police arrive to take this second griot away, and the first griot attempts to defend her only to be violently assaulted too. The cops beat the first griot, "not to death, not enough to cause a riot—but just enough to make us all doubt the interconnectedness of all things,"[81] the stage directions specify.

Which of these stories, which of these examples of networked narrative, defines the other? How could they, together with the scene of violence in which this latter play culminates, cause the audience to "doubt the interconnectedness of all things"? (Did the audience believe in "the interconnectedness of all things" to begin with?) The tales offer two models of storytelling networks, one affirmative—the historical fable, attended by generations of well-wishers—and one highly questionable, the classic rumor. Both forms rely on word of mouth, an inherently viral means of communicating, but the first suggests that conversation and fable-telling are a means of summoning intergenerational solidarity, while the second offers a vision of the dissemination of tempting untruths. The first affirms that an imagined network can be as nourishing as a live, present network. Meanwhile, the second griot's insistence on the accuracy of her report ("I SEEN THE KING") implies the opposite, that conversational networks spread doubt and anger, that as information strays from its source it becomes more and more subject to misinterpretation and more vulnerable to being reshaped by forces of repression.

Buried, then, in the midst of a performance project that appears to explicitly endorse an interconnected view of family, art, society, and community—in the contents of individual plays, in the thematic and formal connections linking the plays, and in the vast festival in which they were staged—is a seed of doubt about whether "all things" are connected, a hint of concern about what that would mean. Are networks benevolent, as in the intergenerational fable, or tempting but misleading, as in the rumor that Martin Luther King is alive and well? Or are they sinister? (In Parks's stage directions, the police are suspiciously close at hand: they must have been lurking right offstage the whole time.) If we, as audience members, question the "interconnectedness of all things," where does that leave the yearlong festival, founded upon interconnectedness, which would have barely begun when this play was staged in December 2006? A further conundrum: Parks's injunction to sow uncertainty is embedded in a stage direction, rendering it imperceptible to audience members unless performers take deliberate steps to make them aware of it. Wouldn't the successful communication of doubt, from actors to spectators, therefore rely on a high level of emotional interconnectedness between the two?

The only reliable witness to this final stage direction, the only person guaranteed to be on the receiving end of Parks's doubt, is not the theatrical spectator but the reader of the published plays, the audience of one who, reading in isolation, might actually be prompted to question the "connectedness" that Parks refers to. This moment of tension—between the play's title, which advertises instances of the "Interconnectedness of All Things," and the concluding stage direction, which silently unravels that philosophy—subtly punctures the potentially naive vision of community that the project might otherwise conjure up. Not everything, Parks suggests here, is as connected as digital-age media leads us to assume. (Brown recalls enjoying the apparent gap between the play's hopeful title and its dark ending, seeing the play as a parable about miscommunication.)[82]

Further, interconnection itself can be as dangerous, as threatening, and as constricting as it is beneficial. Another subset of *365 Days/365 Plays* explicitly critiques networked society's drive toward war. The eleven dramas in the "Father Comes Home from the Wars" series recur pointedly throughout the year, forming a kind of internal network that aligns with the Lysistrata Project's aim of offering an embodied form of dissent to the impending Iraq War. Each of these plays features the return of a father figure from a tour of duty, often to an unsettling homecoming scene. One father must enter and reenter repeatedly; another father, injured in battle, discovers his family posing for a portrait in his absence, using a surrogate "father figure" in his place.[83] These plays are chronologically dispersed; the first occurs in November, on the second day of Parks's project, and a cluster were written in April, following the late March invasion of Iraq. Others are spread out between June and the following fall. When Parks wrote the plays, the American government was struggling to direct public attention away from the human sacrifice that war demands. By the time *365/365* was staged, the war was four years old, and the nightmarish scenes Parks imagined were no longer imaginary.

The scenes in Parks's "Father Comes Home from the Wars" plays are frequently domestic and heavily gendered. The returning fathers in these plays usher in images of blood and violence, contaminating home life by importing echoes of the horrors lurking on battlefields, out of sight. In the first drama of the series, a wife nearly kills her recently arrived husband with a frying pan, the act of senseless domestic angst gesturing to a wider world that has gone off-kilter.[84] Another, a play from April, stages the welcome-home festivities of a father named Joe, who renders the scene grotesque in small ways: squeezing his wife's hand "too hard," hugging her "too hard," insisting on his taste for raw meat.[85] In the next play, written the following day but set many years later, Joe is absent, and his neighbor expresses relief that he "doesn't come home with blood on his clothes anymore."[86]

365 Days/365 Plays is far from the first time that Parks has depicted families in wartime; her first major play, *Imperceptible Mutabilities in the Third Kingdom*, produced in 1989, concluded with a sequence featuring an army family and a father's return from battle. Mr. Sergeant Smith, in this scene, is the family patriarch, and we see him posing in his army uniform, anticipating his homecoming, and then returning to his wife and children. Mrs. Smith and her progeny, Buffy, Muffy, and Duffy, eagerly await Mr. Smith's return, but when he arrives, the scene becomes, as in the later *365/365* plays, distorted and grotesque. Language and chronology mutate; the family's speech becomes choral and impressionistic, and Mr. Smith seems to be both at home with his family and on the battlefield encountering bodies falling from the sky. As in the "Father Comes Home from the Wars" plays, participation in war is a male activity, while the domestic sphere is a female domain (likewise, in *Lysistrata*); and in both cases, Parks draws on such dichotomies to suggest the complicity of global and domestic violence.

The comparison with *Imperceptible Mutabilities* contextualizes Parks's depiction of fathers returning from war (in her book, Geis likewise connects the 1989 play with this series from *365/365*, noting that both drew on Parks's experiences as an army child).[87] But, more importantly for my argument, the differences between *Imperceptible Mutabilities* and the war dramas of *365/365* illustrate how viral performance alters texts, stories, and dramatic form. In *Imperceptible Mutabilities*, the father's return from war occasioned an extended, poetic stage sequence. In *365/365*, these events are repetitive and condensed: fathers return from war, briefly, again and again, the action altered with each reiteration. Like the epic theater of Brecht—to borrow the words of Walter Benjamin, quoted in my introduction—the dramaturgy of *365/365* served to "make gestures quotable."[88] In the "Father Comes Home from the Wars" series, the fathers' returns become contagious. The earlier play's action goes viral.

The final installment in this series, written on November 4, very close to the end of the cycle itself, is entitled "Father Comes Home from the Wars (Part 11: His Eternal Return—A Play for My Father)." This performance consists only of stage directions, and in it Parks calls for a "never-ending loop of action,"[89] the kind of infinite sequence contained in so many of *365/365*'s plays. Here, groups of five soldiers stride onstage at once, heroes returning proudly from an unidentified war. A joyful wife and child rush onstage from the auditorium to greet each soldier, completing a triumphant family tableau, before making room for the next round. "The action," Parks instructs, "repeats eternally."[90] Again, Parks uses the image of an infinitely connected network of soldiers, wives, and children to suggest a darker network just offstage. If soldiers are eternally returning home from war, then they must also be consistently and endlessly heading off to war as well. And if performers are eternally "reuniting" with "audience members," then spectators must be a part of this infinite wartime loop as well. "Part 11" of Parks's "Father Comes Home from the Wars" series is far from the only one of the *365 Days/365 Plays* repertoire to involve crowds of performers leaping out of the audience, but it is the only one of this wartime subseries to do so. This final installment ostensibly features a scene of happy reunion, but it also points in the direction of endless and constant offstage war and violence. Like the eerie scene of police beating the griot in "2 Examples from the Interconnectedness of All Things," Parks stages here a scene of "connectedness"—but not a scene of naive togetherness.

This is where the concept of the network describes *365 Days/365 Plays* in especially precise terms, adding a dimension to the other descriptors—grassroots, democratizing, radically inclusive—that have been employed to characterize the project. Networks, both live and digital, governed the relationships among themes, images, and gestures within and between the plays, and among the theaters that staged the plays. These networks were, for the most part, generative, inclusive, founded on difference and taking pleasure in connection. But the networks depicted onstage were also invasive, militant, and economically exploitative. The Iraq War mobilized a network of politicians, public relations experts, reporters, and of course, soldiers, and this network, too, is implicated in Parks's dramatic project. Networks bring together audiences and artists and communities. But they are also the structural model for wars of insurgency and counterinsurgency, for the surveillance systems of police and intelligence agencies, and for the hyper-repetitive rhetoric of mainstream media.

Writing about *365 Days/365 Plays*, critics have frequently emphasized the festival's utopian elements: the organizers' upending of conventional producing structures, their inclusion of artists not accustomed to producing experimental work, their efforts to encourage a scrappy, egalitarian aesthetic, rather than insisting on expensive productions for a prominent playwright's premiere. Kolin describes the project in terms that echo the most optimistic strands of contemporary network theory:

> Promulgating radical inclusiveness, *365* erases the entire spectrum of theatre—how it is created, coordinated, financed, marketed, staged, and received. Perhaps at its most productively radical, *365* assaults the hegemonies by which theatre has been controlled.[91]

Parks's yearlong festival, he argues, established a "new theatre ideology that empowers the creative spirit of nation."[92] Geis likewise employs optimistic language to describe the project's achievements: "Needless to say," she writes, "no previous playwright has attempted such an ambitious project."[93] A short statement by Metzgar and Parks, included in the published edition of the plays, demonstrates that the creators' ambitions were expansive in similar terms. "Never has a project aspired to include this many artists and audiences across the country," they write. "To all those who proclaim that theater is dead, this Festival shows that theater is alive and kicking up a dust storm from Hendrix College just north of Little Rock to the poetry posse of Universes in the Bronx to Steel City Theatre Company in Pueblo, Colorado."[94] Such statements testify, in revealing ways, to the conceptual apparatus driving the project. Whether it could be possible to prove these statements—that no project has ever attempted to be as inclusive as *365 Days/365 Plays*, that it definitively demonstrates that theater is not "dead," that it manifests an entirely new "theatre ideology"—is, in my view, less significant than the desire, on the part of artists, producers, and critics alike, to describe the project in such terms. These statements register the significance of numbers, the importance of spread. *365/365*'s meaning, in both conception and reception, was predicated on its inclusivity and ability to attract widespread participation: on numbers as dramaturgical form.

The significance of the idea of "going viral" offers a particularly suggestive context here. In its most colloquial twenty-first-century meaning, "going viral" insists on the importance of numbers—enormous numbers—and viral "success" relies on garnering a higher number of viewers, audience members, fans, participants, or clicks than anyone has before. In this vision of the viral, multitude and scale are everything. If Parks's project can be understood not only as a network, but more particularly as a viral network, designed to begin large and expand rapidly, then the stakes of numerical scale become clear.

The dualities inherent to networked structures—the push toward dispersal, the pull of centralization—also attended *365/365*'s producing model, particularly as organizers looked toward the festival's legacy. Participating artists and theaters, upon acceptance into the festival, signed a common participation agreement (one agreement covered professional and community performing arts groups, while a separate one governed the work of college and university participants in the 365 U network). Among the many stipulations that made radical inclusivity possible (minimal or nonexistent participation fees, the careful scheduling of participating artists' groups) was a clause requiring that individual theaters provide photographic documentation of their productions, to which the festival itself would then hold the rights.[95] Individual artists maintained control over the embodied moment—over staging, visual elements, and acting choices—while the festival retained control over the digital archive. Undoubtedly, this requirement limited the circulation of individual *365/365* documentation, precluding the kind of digital afterlife that, say, *Seven Jewish Children* led. The festival could go viral; its digital documentation could not. Just as importantly, to my mind, it registers a desire for a different kind of afterlife, one with artistic and narrative coherence, one in which becoming-number also translates into becoming whole again, where the Timer from "(Again) PERFECT" picks up the writer's scattered scraps of paper and returns them to her, where the writer's body once again takes up residence at the center of the embodied network.

Indeed, even as the project in its entirety gestures toward a nearly abstract vision of numerical scale, the plays themselves insistently bring our attention back to the bodies: to the gendered, raced, particular bodies onstage, to the violence visited on bodies by the war that erupts repeatedly throughout the cycle, lurking offstage in those plays where it is not explicitly invoked. Networks implicate bodies, Parks implies: most directly, in "(Again) PERFECT," where the playwright's own body is envisioned as the ever-circulating source of dramatic text, but obliquely in nearly every play. The more artists who participated in the festival, the more bodies inhabited Parks's network, a network that was not only inclusive and democratic but also reflective of larger, more dangerous networks shaping twenty-first-century society. After all, this is a time when "terrorist networks" fill the airwaves even as "social networks" fill our screens.

Critics discussing the networked nature of *365 Days/365 Plays* frequently acknowledge the presence of war, death, and violence in the plays themselves, but it is tempting to sequester these darker elements from the cheerful community spirit that attended the production of the festival. The discourse that lauds Parks's project as a radically inclusive performance piece suggests that we view the project as networked—but not in the way that war is networked, and not in the way that capitalism is networked. Yet, I argue, viewing both plays and productions as networked performance reveals that these elements can't be separated, that they are part of the same structures of power and communication. Parks's production and the Iraq War are intimately linked; the *365/365* festival was an uncontained, open-ended network of participants and events, but the Iraq War is a far larger, far longer-lived, far less contained network. By mapping the violence of the war onto hundreds of actors' bodies in hundreds of communities around the country, Parks made visible the kinds of networks that we would, mostly, prefer to forget. *365/365* sought to, in Kolin's words, "empower the creative spirit of nation" at the same time that the Bush administration was attempting to subsume Iraq into the network of international democracy, into what Hardt and Negri would call the American empire's network of influence and control. By writing a play in which the reunion of returning soldiers with their families would go on "forever," a play of "eternal return"—one requiring the bodies of spectators to fulfill its stage directions—Parks subtly acknowledged that the war's participants would continue to greatly outnumber the performers onstage, and that the war's network would infinitely outlast her own.

Going Viral: *Seven Jewish Children*

Shortly after *Seven Jewish Children*[96] premiered in London, a company called Rooms Productions staged the play in their Chicago gallery space. In a YouTube video boasting more than 11,000 views,[97] this performance unfolds in a spare white gallery strewn with wooden tables and chairs. An ensemble of actors works furiously, all urgently attempting to relay messages to unseen, offstage recipients. A furrow-browed man murmurs into a black telephone receiver; a couple argues quietly as they scrawl missives on sheets of notebook paper. Panning across the room, the camera finds a wide-eyed woman pecking cheerfully at typewriter keys, and then rests on another pair of performers dictating hopeful phrases into a tape recorder.

Of the many iterations of Churchill's drama to circulate in embodied and digital form since 2009, Rooms Productions's version renders the themes of *Seven Jewish Children* particularly tangible. Onstage, performers deploy communications technologies—attempting to send messages—while the play, writ large, meditates on the dissemination of messages between generations and across historical time. *Seven Jewish Children* comprises a series of sparse scenes, with few stage directions and no character names. The play chronicles seven generations' stuttering attempts to explain the modern Jewish and Israeli experience to their progeny, from the Holocaust to Israel's independence to the 2008–9 Israeli war in Gaza. "Tell her," begins one line; "Don't tell her," rejoins the next. As one scene gives way to another, these words become a transhistorical refrain, marking the inherited ambivalences and fraught semantics surrounding each successive crisis in a violently contested past. In the Chicago production, Churchill's phrases echo from one anonymous voice to the next, building to cacophony: overlapping injunctions transmitted live, by phone, on paper, and in projections on gallery walls.

Just below the video's frame, on the YouTube page that guarantees this staging perpetual preservation in cyberspace, a larger context for the performance comes into view: echoes and distortions of *Seven Jewish Children*'s charged ideologies and its contagious poetry. Pages of comments offer congratulations, historical quibbles, political objections, and vitriolic outrage over Churchill's rendering of the Jewish and Israeli past. Many of these responses spew self-righteous fury at the play—and tellingly, the angriest commenters often mimic the language of the play itself, twisting Churchill's turns of phrase to their own ends. "Don't tell her that over ONE MILLION MUSLIMS live as Israeli citizens," writes one incensed commenter. "TELL HER SHE NEED [*sic*] TO KNOW THE TRUTH," writes another.[98] Repeating and distorting both Churchill's rhetoric and her theatrical form, these comments resemble ever-tinier versions of Churchill's play, rewriting *Seven Jewish Children* in miniature for an expanding international stage.

Alongside the play's controversial London premiere, and subsequent productions in the United States, Israel, and England, *Seven Jewish Children* inspired a flurry of virtual and live responses. Many performances now play on in cyberspace, alongside new playtexts that draw on the original's structure, but revise its rhetoric to reflect their authors' own perspectives. If Churchill's play frames, in microcosm, consecutive generations' efforts to inculcate their descendants with particular historical convictions, its production history offers a twenty-first-century, media-enabled imitation of that act. The play's text chronicles the viral spread of historical ideology; its public presence embodies the viral, audience-driven dissemination of performance itself: dramaturgy that mutates in the internet's endless echo chamber.

Unlike the Lysistrata Project and *365 Days/365 Plays*, *Seven Jewish Children* was not produced as a networked festival. There were no planned simultaneous premieres, and it was not explicitly conceived as an opportunity for local theaters to build community with others around the country or the world. Even so, *Seven Jewish Children* has revealed unexpected artistic and political connections through its international circulation, and as it "went viral" in the most commonly employed sense of the word—it circulated online, becoming the subject of endless internet conversation and giving rise to numerous reiterations and parodies—Churchill's play also became a networked performance. Like *Lysistrata* and like the dramas comprising *365/365*, *Seven Jewish Children* is a theatrical palimpsest, layering networked performance strategies on top of viral dramaturgies. It is a play about networks that became a performance network in production, and the critical discourse surrounding it, as in the case of *365/365*, suggests that its controversy and dramatic potency stemmed from its significance as a networked phenomenon.

The text of *Seven Jewish Children* is a series of conversations about conversations. Each short scene is a meta-discussion without designated speakers, that suggests, in its seesawing contradictions and quick reversals, a dialogue rather than a soliloquy. Through these internecine struggles, Churchill's adult voices decide which facts their absent daughter must remember, which interpretive glosses she must internalize, in order to become a citizen in command of her national and religious heritage. The play's first lines imply a frightened family hiding from the Nazis:

> Tell her it's a game
> Tell her it's serious
> But don't frighten her
> Don't tell her they'll kill her
> Tell her it's important to be quiet[99]

The unseen girl at the center of this (and every) scene, the dialogue suggests, will be irrevocably shaped by what she's told, her understanding of home, family, and her own identity guided by these ostensible authorities. By the middle of the play, Churchill's voices celebrate hard-won Israeli military victories, alluding to the Israeli war of independence and the 1967 Six-Day War. The final scene suggests the aftermath of Israel's 2008–9 war in Gaza, and as time progresses, the adult voices harden: initially sighing with relief at their own survival, then justifying their claims to land and water, and finally spewing hatred at their equally anonymous foes.

Churchill's starkly poetic exchanges model, in microcosm, the loaded dissemination of history, political ideology, and cultural bias from older generations to younger ones. Each equivocating admonition constitutes a new attempt to shore up national myth through painstakingly chosen rhetoric, and to instill in new citizens carefully constructed national identities. ("Tell her we're making new farms in the desert," suggests one voice; "Don't tell her about the olive trees," warns the next.)[100] As the play hurtles through the twentieth century and into the twenty-first, Churchill's text assumes the logic, and stages the mechanisms, of viral dissemination: compact revelations meant to expand exponentially, one whisperer at a time; messages that mutate with each successive speaker.

This model of ideological dissemination relies, crucially, on the overlapping of public and private spheres, on conversations that are held in private, but are meant to infiltrate public consciousness on the broadest scale. Each scene offers a glimpse of the most intimate kind of exchange, the whispered debates and barely voiced anxieties that unfold before a personal conversation even takes place. At first, these appear to be just the opposite of the media cacophony that so frequently buffets public opinion from one prejudice to the next. Here there are no newspaper headlines, no radio broadcasts, no advertising campaigns intruding in the shaping of the anonymous child's views. A few times, we even catch a glimpse of how defiantly Churchill's voices work to displace other media: "Tell her she can't watch the news," they advise in one scene,[101] later warning, "Tell her you can't believe what you see on television."[102]

In passages like these, Churchill narrows her lens to a single medium of transmission, conversation itself. But although these domestic interludes hold the crash of rockets and the roar of protesters at bay, they replicate, in miniature, the collective conversations of the imagined Jewish-Israeli public at large.[103] Examining collective actions and public responsibilities in the privacy of a series of anonymous homes, Churchill frames those interior spaces as the smallest units in a long historical chain and a broad public arena, each sequence portraying one family that is, implicitly, surrounded by millions of others, all holding conversations of political and historical import. Each of Churchill's families constitutes one point in a vast constellation, all of them conscripted into the laborious task of repeating and disseminating a single perspective on Israel's past and its current behavior. Private homes, in this play, are an embodied double of public media outlets. Even when the television is turned off and the newspaper hidden away, families gather around kitchen tables and in living rooms, attempting to voice and repeat the best, truest, most patriotic type of historical tale.

Michael Warner's writings on the nature of public speech prove suggestive in illuminating the urgent anxieties that Churchill maps, and I draw on two of his essays here, "Public and Private" and "Publics and Counterpublics," both collected in his 2002 anthology *Publics and Counterpublics*. In "Public and Private," Warner charts the many historically conditioned distinctions that have been drawn between those two terms, and demonstrates how, despite natural inclinations to view them as a binary, they are frequently overlapping and intertwined. Warner proposes, quoting Hannah Arendt, that while the domestic sphere might appear to be just the opposite of society at large, in fact, compelled by public opinion, "'people suddenly behave as though they were members of one family, each multiplying and prolonging the perspective of his neighbor.'"[104] The family's private life, under such conditions, becomes, not an escape hatch from the pressures of public citizenship, but an extension of them. Churchill's figures strain under the pressures to personally replicate the ideological formations of the public sphere. They displace the swirl of global media, only to scrupulously reproduce its messaging in the safety of home.

Conditioned by this convergence of the communal and the personal, Churchill's fragmentary conversations direct themselves to two types of political and ideological networks at once. Her voices plan addresses to a tiny audience, a single recipient, but they are also shaping the messages that this younger generation will, in turn, transmit to unknowable audiences beyond: cycling through both immediate encounters and secondary representations. This is one of the constitutive elements of public speech that Warner identifies in "Publics and Counterpublics," where he argues that speech becomes public by virtue of its intention to address not only known listeners, but unidentifiable strangers, whose participation in any given public is established in the moment when they decide to pay attention.[105] In the case of *Seven Jewish Children*, the adults' political prescriptions (their admonishment to "Tell her again this is our promised land,"[106] for instance, or the impulse to "tell her it's our water, we have the right")[107] are calibrated so obsessively because the speakers' national legitimacy relies on their children's transmission of their message to future generations.

As the play unfolds, the ghost of a third kind of public emerges tentatively into view, visible mainly by its absence: a public entirely separate from the microcosmic family unit, and from their implied Jewish and Israeli communities around the world. In the opening scene, Churchill's voices are those of the frightened and persecuted, those without the luxury of imagining themselves as any particular kind of national public. But as soon as the voices belong to a group in possession of land and military prowess, they suddenly bear the burden of characterizing their own social polity. In the fourth scene, these voices offer a glimmering recognition of a Palestinian society that exists, although it goes deliberately unrepresented here. "Tell her they're Bedouin, they travel about," suggests one voice, "Tell her about camels in the desert and dates"; "Tell her they live in tents," adds another.[108]

These are fictions, as Churchill makes abundantly clear when one of the voices warns, "Don't tell her Arabs used to sleep in her bedroom."[109] They're strategic lies, told in order to cast Palestinians as a non-group, an entity that does not operate by the same societal rules as they do. Seen through this distorted lens, Churchill's Palestinians are not a "public" in the sense that Israel is attempting to become one, because they do not operate according to the same collective rules. In this Orientalist fantasy, Palestinians live in tents, roam itinerantly, and ride camels; in other words, they do not participate in politics, watch television, read newspapers, or otherwise operate channels of communication within contemporary political networks. Their network of public figures and private debate is less developed than the Israeli equivalents; in fact, their networks do not exist in the same sense that the Israeli ones do. In the imaginations of the Israelis that Churchill depicts, a play centered on Palestinian, rather than Israeli, children could not be written, because they lack such coherent ideological networks. (Of course, precisely that play was written, and many like it; more on this when I discuss *Seven Jewish Children*'s networked production history.)

In this fourth scene's most telling exchange, the voices parse the semantics of the loaded word "home." "Tell her this wasn't their home," offers one of

Churchill's speakers—and the reply rejects even that simple terminology, cautioning, "Don't tell her home, not home."[110] This debate distills the conflict to its most succinct elements, while also reflecting the kinds of real political discourse that have surrounded just such subjects. In 2001, for instance, CNN directed its reporters to stop referring to the Israeli town of Gilo, constructed east of Jerusalem on land conquered in the 1967 war, as a "settlement," and to call it, instead, a "neighborhood."[111] The next year, the Israel Broadcasting Authority attempted to ban news organizations from using the word "settlement" at all.[112] If the voices in Churchill's play can lay sole claim to being the kind of society that lives in "homes," the kind of public that organizes itself into neighborhoods—the kind of public that transmits its own history through conversations—then the other group is not only excluded from the public Churchill depicts, but is excluded from being a public at all.

Churchill's conversations deliberately illuminate her point of view through its opposite: the more imaginary Israeli voices her play includes, the more fully the echo of a Palestinian perspective takes shape. This dynamic emerges most notoriously in the last scene, when the rules of conversation break down altogether, and the discourse swerves away from rhythmic, tempered exchanges, erupting into a furious monologue. As the historical trajectory barrels into the present, one voice forgets to parse political logic into phrases, instead stringing words together into one run-on paragraph:

> Tell her, tell her about the army, tell her to be proud of the army. Tell her about the family of dead girls, tell her their names why not, tell her the whole world knows why shouldn't she know? tell her there's dead babies, did she see babies? tell her she's got nothing to be ashamed of. Tell her they did it to themselves.[113]

Abandoning punctuation, rhetorical poise, and vestiges of compassion all at once, this speech mimics the motion of a military operation spinning out of control. The previous exchanges—ideologically charged, but written in the form of vacillating dialogues—give way to an anti-conversation that tumbles paranoias together into a frenzied wall of text. Ideology bursts the bounds of conversational form.

This image of war—conflict that spirals contagiously out of control, that merges public with private, domestic life with international relations, that seems to leave no one, ultimately, untainted by struggle—has a precedent in Churchill's dramatic vision. Her 2000 play *Far Away* (also first produced at the Royal Court), stages just such a scenario, following a central character, Joan, from a childhood scene in which she witnesses strange and suggestively violent events to adulthood as a guerrilla fighter. Returning from war at the end of the play, Joan tells her aunt of a world that is completely embroiled in conflict, not only among nations, peoples, or armies, but also among every element of the natural world. Light and dark, birds and insects, gravity and water have all joined in battle.[114]

Far Away's depiction of a conflict that begins as a recognizable dispute, but ends as a vertiginously expanding war, with every element of the world conscripted into combat and no clear moral distinction among combatants, is also what Churchill stages in *Seven Jewish Children*, using, of course, real places and histories. The earlier drama thus offers dramatic context for *Seven Jewish Children*, in ways that echo Parks's dramaturgical evolution from *Imperceptible Mutabilities* to *365 Days/365 Plays*. Locating the traces of *Far Away*'s fantastical, proliferating war zone in the historical conflicts of *Seven Jewish Children* clarifies the ways in which Churchill reshaped dramaturgy to make it contagious, and reshaped stage gestures to make them quotable. *Seven Jewish Children* is, like *Far Away*, a depiction of contagious war; but it is a depiction of contagious war that has itself been made contagious: compressed until it is easily replicable, and provocative enough to prompt replication.

Also as in *Far Away*, *Seven Jewish Children* places a young woman—the female child on the receiving end of the adults' admonishments—at the center of its political-historical maelstrom. In fact, the child's gender is the only identifying information Churchill provides; she has no specified name, age, or place of residence, nor is there any indication of whether she has requested to hear about the histories under discussion or whether they are in the process of being foisted upon her. In *Far Away*, relationships between women are central to the network of resistance in which the main character, Joan, participates (she learns about the resistance from her aunt, Harper). In *Seven Jewish Children* it is a female child, in a domestic space, who is tasked with correctly understanding and accurately repeating ideological stories about the past. Such gender specificity would apply, too, to many of the revisions of Churchill's play, which frequently featured male children—in some cases, young Palestinian boys, figures whose bodies would likely be on the line in confrontations with Israeli forces. These works by Churchill address the connections between gender and war more obliquely than did either *Lysistrata* or the Lysistrata Project; but the connections are present, inflecting the plays' visions of the complicity between domestic and public speech, and surfacing in *Seven Jewish Children*'s digital afterlife.

As with the play, so with the production. Churchill wasn't just writing a drama that depicted the highly charged discourse surrounding the Israeli-Palestinian conflict; she was, I argue, deliberately writing a play whose reception would echo and model that discourse itself. The angry comments on Rooms Productions' YouTube page were not incidental to the play's dramaturgy, but an essential aspect of Churchill's viral vision, drawing attention to habitual modes of discussing the conflict by re-creating them in miniature. Discussion within the plays was viral on the smallest possible scale: the brief messages embedded in Churchill's scenes acquire their legitimacy from the intimacy of their transmission, suggesting them as a species of discourse that borrows the mechanisms of gossip to spread ideologies that reach far beyond gossip's usually parochial purview. By telling their children about the past—Churchill's text implies—the parents in these scenes hope to inoculate their offspring from lies and rumors, and to enjoin them to spread agreed-upon histories, person to person, to new generations.

In production, *Seven Jewish Children* rode an international gust of viral media writ large. Its London premiere, on February 6, 2009, was presented free of charge with donations channeled to the organization Medical Aid for Palestinians. These became the terms under which Churchill subsequently offered the rights to the play to any company for production, creating a network of performances that were produced largely independently of conventional economic structures—much like the "negative money" and the ethos of donations that governed, respectively, *365 Days/365 Plays* and the Lysistrata Project. The Royal Court's premiere triggered a burst of media responses: some reviewers praised the play, while many protested what they saw as thinly veiled anti-Semitism, a vicious attempt to erase the distinction between the worldwide Jewish community and the state of Israel, and a dramatic resurrection of all the old stereotypes about Jews. One blogger denounced it as a "ten-minute blood libel" and charged Churchill with writing a modern version of the medieval mystery plays.[115] The Board of Deputies of British Jews objected to the play, and sixty prominent members of the British Jewish community signed an outraged letter and sent it to the *Daily Telegraph*. That same month, the BBC refused an offer to air a broadcast of the play, noting that the network intended to "remain impartial."[116] Not surprisingly, it was the final scene, with its frantic unleashing of vitriol, which drew the greatest anger. Churchill was accused of summoning an "atavistic hatred of the Jews."[117] Jeffrey Goldberg, writing on the *Atlantic Monthly*'s website, declared that "the mainstreaming of the worst anti-Jewish stereotypes—for instance, that Jews glory in the shedding of non-Jewish blood—is upon us."[118] American theaters were soon producing *Seven Jewish Children*: the Rude Guerrilla theater company in Los Angeles and the New York Theatre Workshop in Manhattan, among others, had both staged the play by the end of March. In the same short time, it had become a catalyst for controversy wherever it went.

But as the outrage against Churchill proliferated, versions of the play proliferated as well. The brevity and sparseness of Churchill's text made it easy to copy and disseminate, so the *Guardian* published the full text of the play online and posted a video, made with Churchill's consent, of actress Jennie Stoller performing the entire play herself. The *New York Times* posted a link to the Royal Court's website ("Is a Play about Gaza Anti-Semitic? Read the Script," the headline challenged, inevitably drawing many more readers to the text of Churchill's play).[119] Soon, such readers weren't just perusing Churchill's text; they were rewriting it. The American playwright Deb

Margolin composed a dramatic response called *Seven Palestinian Children*, in which Palestinian adults parse recent history for a young boy. The lines borrow Churchill's phrasing, but change her words to reflect an alternate perspective. "Tell him they moved into our house," reads a representative line. "Tell him the house was full and big with doors large and small and with windows like paintings . . . Show him the key to our house that's still in his father's pocket."[120] The Israeli playwright Robbie Gringas, by contrast, shaped Churchill's play into an ambivalently Zionist response entitled *The Eighth Child*:

> Tell her that it's more complicated than that.
> Tell her that we love Israel.
> Tell her that we hate Israel.
> Tell her that Israel is in our veins, like oxygen, like a virus, like an antibody.
> Tell her that to be Jewish is far more than watching the news and looking for balance, and far more than being a Zionist, and far more than just praying to God.
> Tell her that Zionism isn't a dirty word like racism. Zionism is a complicated word with good intentions and ambiguous results, like idealism.[121]

Both *Seven Palestinian Children* and *The Eighth Child* were read aloud at Washington, D.C.'s Theatre J beside Churchill's original.

On the other end of the political spectrum, the British actor Richard Stirling wrote a theatrical disquisition, dubbed *Seven Other Children*, accusing Palestinian adults of fanning the flames of anti-Semitism among their children. Its scenes take place at different points in the Israeli-Palestinian conflict, from the war of 1948 to the Second Intifada. A long paragraph, for instance, mimics Churchill's violent run-on passage, but addresses itself to a participant in the Palestinian uprising:

> Ask him if he will not join with me in laughing at the body of the hook nose teacher, ask him if I would care if we rubbed them out, took them off the map, the world will thank us, they are ready to thank us, ask him if he can ever do better than this, better in the world's eyes, ask him to look at the body of a child on their side and ask him what he feels? Don't ask him what I feel, ask him to give thanks it is not him.[122]

"Ask him if Hitler had the wrong idea," the piece grimly concludes.[123]

The list of responses to Churchill's play goes on. On March 16, 2009, the day after the BBC refused to air Churchill's play, citing "impartiality" and explaining that "it would be nearly impossible to run a drama that counters

Churchill's point of view,"[124] a blogger boasted that he could "help the BBC out" by composing a version of the play that would be just as theatrically accomplished as Churchill's, and would represent the opposite perspective ("I estimate it will take ten minutes" to compose, he added).[125] This riff, entitled *Seven Arab Children*, depicts a Palestinian community that is calculating, violent, and virulently anti-Semitic. A sample passage reads:

> Tell him that we are "Palestinian"
> Tell him not to say "Jews" in English, only "Zionists"
> Tell him that the Arabs will help us push the Jews into the sea this time[126]

Even two months later, iterations of *Seven Jewish Children* continued to appear online. On May 16, 2009, an angry blogger on a website called "Blue Truth.net" wrote a self-proclaimed "Islamophobic" rendering, which he entitled *Seven Muslim Children*, and which offers a political viewpoint similar to that of *Seven Arab Children*. Here, Palestinian parents coach a young suicide bomber:

> Tell him to put on the bomb belt
> Tell him he will have 72 virgins
> Don't tell him that he must die
> Don't tell him that he must kill children[127]

Some online responses strayed from straightforwardly depicting Palestinians as terrorists, but found other ways to attack Churchill using her form.

One of these, published on April 1, 2009, accused Churchill of furthering a history of theatrical anti-Semitism. The playwright Edward Einhorn's blog, "Theater of Ideas," published an anonymous rewrite of *Seven Jewish Children* called *The More Things Change*, which substituted for Churchill's historical moments seven instances of anti-Semitism in the theater itself, from medieval passion plays to *The Merchant of Venice*. "Tell them Mirror up to Nature: Jewes covet blood," reads a line from the passage representing *The Merchant of Venice*. At the end of the play, *Seven Jewish Children* enters on cue. ("No Jews appear in the play," insist the stage directions, explaining that the anonymous voices here are directors and literary managers—a parody of Churchill's own opening directive, "No children appear in the play.")[128]

Through this process of distribution, replication, and revision, *Seven Jewish Children* went viral. Just as each of the play's scenes offers a model for disseminating ideology, these response plays also disseminate and distort, replicating Churchill's dramaturgy onstage and online. But the media-enabled proliferation of *Seven Jewish Children* also alters and contradicts the types of ideological dissemination modeled within the play. In Churchill's whispered histories, mass media and public understandings are shaped by private interpretations, by hearsay. But the rush of theatrical responses was

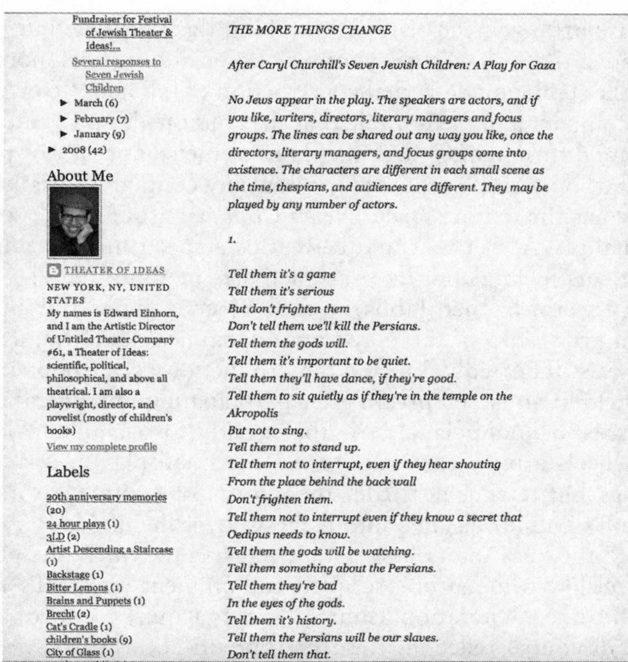

Fundraiser for Festival of Jewish Theater & Ideas!...
Several responses to Seven Jewish Children
► March (6)
► February (7)
► January (9)
► 2008 (42)

About Me

THEATER OF IDEAS
NEW YORK, NY, UNITED STATES
My names is Edward Einhorn, and I am the Artistic Director of Untitled Theater Company #61, a Theater of Ideas: scientific, political, philosophical, and above all theatrical. I am also a playwright, director, and novelist (mostly of children's books)
View my complete profile

Labels

20th anniversary memories (20)
24 hour plays (1)
3LD (2)
Artist Descending a Staircase (1)
Backstage (1)
Bitter Lemons (1)
Brains and Puppets (1)
Brecht (2)
Cat's Cradle (1)
children's books (9)
City of Glass (1)

THE MORE THINGS CHANGE

After Caryl Churchill's Seven Jewish Children: A Play for Gaza

No Jews appear in the play. The speakers are actors, and if you like, writers, directors, literary managers and focus groups. The lines can be shared out any way you like, once the directors, literary managers, and focus groups come into existence. The characters are different in each small scene as the time, thespians, and audiences are different. They may be played by any number of actors.

1.

Tell them it's a game
Tell them it's serious
But don't frighten them
Don't tell them we'll kill the Persians.
Tell them the gods will.
Tell them it's important to be quiet.
Tell them they'll have dance, if they're good.
Tell them to sit quietly as if they're in the temple on the Akropolis
But not to sing.
Tell them not to stand up.
Tell them not to interrupt, even if they hear shouting
From the place behind the back wall
Don't frighten them.
Tell them not to interrupt even if they know a secret that Oedipus needs to know.
Tell them the gods will be watching.
Tell them something about the Persians.
Tell them they're bad
In the eyes of the gods.
Tell them it's history.
Tell them the Persians will be our slaves.
Don't tell them that.

The More Things Change. Screen capture from Edward Einhorn's "Theater of Ideas" blog, 2009. Used with permission of Edward Einhorn.

communal and public, unfolding on blogs and YouTube videos, as well as in public venues such as town halls and conference centers. No longer were spectators secondary recipients of one-way messages, eavesdroppers on the play's private conversations. Instead, audience members were participants in an endlessly mutating international conversation, with their own dramas and ideologies imitating, revising, and circulating Churchill's play in live and mediated form.

Just as Churchill framed her dialogue as the conversation of fictive Israeli voices, each of the response plays—some poetic, others manic or furious—puts words into the mouths of its imagined foes, revising not only the original text but also its imagined public. In Margolin's *Seven Palestinian Children*, adult voices debate the relative merits of literally summoning the words to participate in the Israeli public's conversation. "Tell him to smile and say *shalom*," says one of Margolin's voices. Two lines later, the same speaker (or another: the voices are anonymous) thinks better of it, concluding, "Don't make him say *shalom*."[129] If the original ostensibly portrayed Israelis speaking to Israelis, illuminating, through its absence, a Palestinian point of view, the responses depict deliberately skewed Palestinian and Muslim perspectives. And as they do so, each of the response plays carefully mimics Churchill's elegant, spare arrangement of text, inscribing their outrage into brief lines, and assembling those as minute synopses of crucial historical moments. Each one retains her emblematic verbal construction ("Tell her," "Don't tell her"): phrases so compact and memorable that they aid the drama's endless reiteration. The viral diffusion of Churchill's play was fueled not only by provocative politics, but also by easily replicated, irresistibly contagious dramatic form.

Not only has the text of *Seven Jewish Children* proliferated; so, too, have the performances. A visit to YouTube reveals a spectrum of production videos: by students in England, by peace activists in Santa Fe. The first Israeli staging, by director Samieh Jabbarin, took place in June 2009 in a Tel Aviv square (in a grim echo of the play's own dynamics, Jabbarin, a Palestinian citizen of Israel, reportedly directed the production by telephone because he was being held in an Israeli prison after participating in political demonstrations against Israeli politicians).[130] In this version, also available on YouTube, a woman wheels a baby carriage around the small playing space, a pile of garbage bags buttressing her from the chorus of commentators, who call out Churchill's lines, translated into Hebrew, over the divide.[131] As passersby drift through the busy intersection, some pausing to watch, the performance begins to feel like a miniature, scripted embodiment of Israel's contentious public debate. In each iteration, Churchill's text acquires some of the tenor of local public discourse, reflecting the artistic predilections of its ever-increasing roster of performers.

Seven Jewish Children was not conceived as a networked performance event, but when it began to be performed, an implied network around the world took shape: a collection of participants, a set of theaters, theater companies, and activists employing Churchill's script as a means of embodying their own local public debate. Like many of the dramas comprising *365 Days/365 Plays*, *Seven Jewish Children* deliberately invites amateur production. Its simplicity of form and sparse dialogue tailor it for non-actors, non-directors, and unlikely performance spaces. There are no requirements for cast size, age, or gender, no specified settings, no theatrical effects not compressed into Churchill's charged poetic text. This text is, thus, written to go viral: a phenomenon that relies on the transformation of audiences into amateur performers, the mutation of private viewers into public participants. Churchill, like Parks, could have elected a well-publicized tour of the large nonprofit theaters that were already planning to stage the play, and where her works often premiere: the Royal Court, the New York Theatre Workshop. The play's politics would likely have inspired public discussion in reviews and audience responses, and she could have retained control over actors' performances and the productions' visual landscapes. Instead, like Parks, she pitched her playwriting toward a viral premiere. Here, though, rather than an effort toward "becoming-number," *Seven Jewish Children* functioned as a kind of virus in the network, exposing connections and antagonisms, revealing amateur playwrights and activist-performers. Participants produced the play in small and scrappy ways; disagreements found local forums everywhere. Rather than a single controversy centered on a single large theater,[132] Churchill provoked a geographically dispersed, viral controversy, a network of small scandals.

More than this, *Seven Jewish Children* created an opportunity to use this sudden new network to confront a larger, more difficult network, that of pro-Israel support in the United States, which takes the form of a highly particular set of alliances—religious Jews, Evangelical Christians, and conservative political leaders. In one particularly telling YouTube video, filmed in Washington, D.C., in May 2009, members of the American antiwar organization "Code Pink" prepare to present *Seven Jewish Children* to the delegates at the annual conference of the American Israel Public Affairs Committee (AIPAC). What we see on video is their rehearsal: like the play itself, this filming captures the conversations before the conversations. Standing by a busy street, the Code Pinkers are arrayed in a row for the camera, bundled against the cold in parkas and scarves and hats, one of them swathed in the red-and-white kaffiyeh so often used to signal solidarity with Palestinians.[133] They read from Churchill's play, cycling through the lines one by one. Occasionally, one of them inflects a line with a particular attitude; from time to time, someone loses the thread and needs to be reoriented. Mostly, though, these activists aren't acting. Mostly, they're performing public acts of reading. The play here becomes the script for their confrontation with the powerful network of organizations that has gathered at the AIPAC conference.

For a moment in 2009, Churchill's play didn't just circulate virally, or make visible a network. It achieved an element of the most emancipatory type of network, by temporarily eliminating artistic hierarchies as well. When Theatre J in Washington, D.C., produced *Seven Jewish Children*, they staged Margolin's *Seven Palestinian Children* beside it, an equal with the original. When angry bloggers and pro-Israel activists wrote their own versions of the play, they crossed an artistic boundary, becoming not just commentators, but also playwrights. In the act of going viral, Churchill's play created a decentralized, anti-hierarchical artistic network—a new kind of production that existed not just in local, embodied performances, but as an expanding constellation of artists and activists, enlarging both the reach and the complexity of the original play by sending it across political and geographical boundaries, into theaters and public squares and into cyberspace.

New Networks: The *Gaza Monologues* and "Shinsai"

Kathryn Blume remembers the Lysistrata Project as a performance piece that, in going viral, allowed even those who did not take part in it to think about live performance in a new way. "Anybody who was deeply involved in professional theater in 2003 knew about the Lysistrata Project," she says.[134] "It influenced the way that people thought about what theater could do and what theater could be, in terms of using the Internet and in terms of the power of simultaneity."[135]

Such projects have proliferated since then. In 2010 the Ashtar Theatre—a Ramallah-based Palestinian theater company—responded to the 2008–9 Israeli war in Gaza (the same war that had inspired *Seven Jewish Children*) with a networked performance project. The company trained a group of young Palestinians living in Gaza by using techniques from the Theater of the Oppressed, teaching the young writer-performers to shape their experiences into monologues. Ultimately, Ashtar artistic director Iman Aoun says, a text comprising thirty-three monologues, some of them composite works created from multiple originals, took shape. Meanwhile, the company was constructing a complex international network for production.

Like the Lysistrata Project and *365 Days/365 Plays*, the *Gaza Monologues* was a networked performance from the start. In an interview, Aoun recalled that she conceived the project as a coordinated international effort, inspired, like Blume and Bower, by *The Vagina Monologues*. She believed that only a networked show of support would make the performances visible to international audiences. "I wanted the performances to create a massive impact, all at the same time," she explained. "Otherwise it would be just another piece of theater, just another story, that might find its way to some people and not others. But the impact of performing at the same time, in different places, would create a different kind of turning point in audiences' consciousness."[136] She hoped to create solidarity between young Palestinians and young leaders in other nations, building a network that would endure, and that could produce greater international solidarity for Palestinians in the long term. She also envisioned creating deeper theatrical meaning through geographical simultaneity.

Aoun drew on Ashtar's extensive network of existing international contacts to solicit participants for the project. Collaborators responded with enthusiasm, and the text was translated from Arabic into English, French, and German, disseminated internationally, and rehearsed locally. On October 17, 2010, approximately 1,500 participants from 50 theater companies or organizations representing 36 countries took part in the performances. The series of premieres began at 11:00 A.M. in Gaza, when the young creators of the monologues launched small wooden boats, bearing their theatrical texts, into the ocean—a gesture toward their international network as well as an act of protest against Israel's deadly suppression of the Gaza Freedom Flotilla that May. Following the morning event, Aoun notes, each participating organization began their performance at 7:00 in the evening, local time, creating a series of rolling, overlapping international premieres.

In recalling the event, Aoun implicitly gestured, as well, to the ways that networked performances counter networks of war—to the significance, for both, of numbers and numerical scale. Describing her motivation for the project, she explained, "after the Israeli occupation attacked Gaza in 2009, my people became numbers—of casualties and of injured people—and only numbers. The stories, the personal faces, of the people disappeared. This is what happens in every war and in every atrocity."[137] As in *365 Days/365 Plays*, networks here represented both inclusion and destruction, both individual solidarity and the effacement of individuality. Since the 2010 event, the project has grown. In 2016 Ashtar worked with a group of Syrian refugees living in Jordan to create the "Syrian Monologues." Meanwhile, Aoun reports, "There is hardly any month that passes without someone, somewhere around the world, presenting the *Gaza Monologues*. A school, a university, a theater company, a community group."[138]

New networks continue to emerge. In March 2012, a group of major theaters and theatrical organizations—the New York Theatre Workshop, the Public Theater, TCG, Playwrights Horizons, and others—joined together to organize a day of simultaneous, geographically dispersed benefit performances to be staged on the one-year anniversary of the earthquake and nuclear disaster that struck Japan in March 2011. The proceeds were intended to provide continuing disaster relief, and the organizers commissioned new ten-minute plays from well-known American and Japanese theater artists (Tony Kushner, Edward Albee, Toshiki Okada) to be compiled into a theatrical "menu" from which individual participating theaters could select and curate their own program. Entitled "Shinsai: Theaters for Japan," the benefit performances, held on March 11, 2012, took place in seventy-six theaters around the country, from New York to Florida to Pennsylvania to California.[139]

"Shinsai" was explicitly modeled on the structure and concept of *365 Days/365 Plays* (Suzan-Lori Parks was also one of the playwrights commissioned to provide a text for the occasion).[140] In a panel discussion held on March 12, 2012, the day following the readings, numerous participating artists commented on the project's emotional significance for them. Central, for many, was the potency of dispersed simultaneity. Describing the impetus driving the project's networked structure, the Lincoln Center dramaturge Anne Cattaneo proposed that one of the essential aspects of the project was "that it all happened on this one day, March 11 . . . it's something new that's happening in America, where there have now been a few events where everybody does something on the same day . . . everybody around the country was doing the same thing at the same time."[141] "Everybody around the country," to use Cattaneo's words, was actively embodying a network: not simply participating in one that already existed, but forging a new, expanding, shifting, viral network in theatrical action, "becoming-number" as they did.

Conclusion

Virus in the Theater

We are living in a viral moment now. Over the first two decades of the twenty-first century, technological and affective contagions have emerged as structuring principles in performance and media, and have deeply inflected the cultural imagination. Our collective modes of envisioning digital networks, the circulation of emotion, and the dissemination of image, gesture, and information are profoundly viral. Viruses course through computer networks, and videos go viral. Communicable diseases inspire international epidemiologies of fear. Financial markets infect each other, or are shored up through sequester and quarantine. Viruses, today, are disruptions. They are replicable (but frequently mutating) information. And they are agitations that make systems less seamless, or that call attention to unseen systems operating in everyday life. The viral is a mode of dissemination—linked to the virus, but not the same as it—implying widespread and rapid circulation following horizontal rather than hierarchical paths, and often describing phenomena that attract popularity swiftly, then abruptly fade from view. The viral belongs both to countercultural intervention and to the corporate marketing manual, to mainstream entertainment and to underground art. Indeed, its availability as a figure for both resistance and control is one of its primary sources of power in the contemporary world.

But, this book has argued, we are not alone. Ours is not the only age of universal contagion. As I have described in the preceding chapters, performance has always held the possibility of being viral. Theater was contagious from the start. The viral has captured the imagination of performance makers during particular kinds of fraught historical moments: during times of technological upheaval and reinvention, and at moments when artists most needed to intervene in systems of government and corporate control. New performance technologies have provoked anxiety and euphoria by presenting new modes of circulation; and when artists have sought new strategies for political intervention and for the mobilization of spectators, viral structures and dramaturgies have frequently emerged. Art-making will continue to hold the possibility of being viral—and artists will continue to imagine politically radical art-making in viral terms—whether or not viral culture continues to develop in close proximity to the digital world. Viral performance has not always been digital, or digitally inflected, and it may not always be in its future forms. This conclusion, looking both forward and back, draws on the examples explored in previous chapters to imagine the continued significance of the viral in performance, as the viral's larger cultural connotations continue to evolve.

In "Virus, Viral," Zach Blas points out the necessity of such a project, the importance of imagining forms of virus and of the viral that are no longer necessarily linked to rapid digital dissemination. After surveying the array of meanings that concepts of viral culture hold in the twenty-first century, Blas diagnoses the limits bounding our current viral imaginations. From pop culture disseminated through social media to contagious financial panics, he affirms, the viral has become a defining concept for our own era; but such models have also circumscribed understandings of what both virus and viral can be. "In this axis of the virus|viral relation," Blas writes,

> that mysterious, allusive thing called a virus, evolving over time in biological matter and silicon, existing in ever complexifying, generational forms, somewhere between life and death, instigating excessive panic, hype, and thrill, is reduced to its properties of action.[1]

Such reduction, Blas suggests—our impulse, in other words, to understand a virus only or primarily in terms of its dissemination—will ultimately limit our ability to perceive the full spectrum of viral culture, to probe the many meanings the viral holds. To be viral today is to spread infectiously, to evolve rapidly and in multiple directions at once, to evoke simultaneity and uncontrolled proliferation. "Perhaps this particular viral is rightly dominant," Blas continues, "because its focus on speedy replication and mutation is at the heart of contemporary capitalism, neoliberalism, and globalization, and even though there are uses of this viral form that proffer and fight for an anticapitalism, can the viral go *elsewhere*? To another viral that might drastically depart from replication, mutation, speed, and capitalism?"[2]

Several of the artists described in this book already demonstrate the possibility for such "another viral"—and demonstrate, moreover, that "other" models of viral culture and artistic virus long predated the age of rapid digital dissemination. The Living Theatre understood contagion in emotional terms, viewing theatrical plague as an element spread not globally but locally, from body to body, through the act of participating in performance. Augusto Boal envisioned the spread of socially transformative gesture and idea through difference, rather than replication, and through an extended series of individual encounters, rather than widespread spontaneous proliferation. Critical Art Ensemble, though deeply engaged with the viral elements of "replication, mutation, speed, and capitalism," chooses other formats for its own performances, staging detailed, careful pieces seen by small audiences in site-specific locations.

Yet nearly every artist and artistic work examined in the preceding chapters is concerned with the relationship between a virus and its viral spread. Indeed, a deep engagement with the terms of dissemination is frequently what makes these performances viral. And so, in my conclusion, I describe a new example, reexamining the principles of viral performance through the lens of a twenty-first-century project that conceived of theatrical virus in local, singular terms, as an entity bounded in time and space, and as a force inherently tied to the elements of live theater. In 2006, six years before Blas's call for a departure from the most recognizable forms of twenty-first-century viral contagion, the Polish artist and curator Joanna Warsza staged a performance that pointed both back in time, to the viral dramaturgies of early modernism, and forward, toward a mode of viral performance that does indeed depart from the media-fueled panics and the bio-art incitements of twentieth and early twenty-first-century viral performances. "Virus in the Theater," staged at Warsaw's TR Warszawa, was performed only once, with no aspirations toward replication, viral or otherwise, no attempt to spread (or counter) contagious panic among its spectators, no live bacteria, and no proliferating computer code. The project reenvisioned the virus as a model for the deliberate opening of perceptual space: a tear in the fabric of performance that insisted upon an audience's ability—and its right—to think, feel, and voice its desires during the otherwise conventional performance of an otherwise conventional play. As I will argue in this conclusion, the structure of "Virus in the Theater" offers one way that viral performance will endure: as a break, a rupture, a point of difference in a sea of sameness, one that does not necessarily spread through replication, one that may not need to spread at all.

"Virus in the Theater" was conceived as part of an ongoing project series Warsza organized with a group she'd founded called the Laura Palmer Foundation. Warsza, whose curatorial practice ranges across the fields of theater, performance, and visual art, with an emphasis on public and socially engaged art, had created the Laura Palmer Foundation as an umbrella for a collection of provocative theatrical ventures examining the terms of public art, performance, and curation. The "Laura Palmer Foundation," explains the organization's mission statement, "was operating on the verge of fiction and reality . . . Incorporating real life, political reality and fictious or staged events, confronting experience and its representation, Laura Palmer Foundation examined the formats of curating, art and activist practice."[3] (The name refers to the absent character at the center of David Lynch's *Twin Peaks* television series, deliberately invoking a figure who represents the blurring of rumor, mirage, and truth.)

"Virus in the Theater" was a performance inside a performance, a small theatrical coup that erupted during a run of the Polish repertory standard *Maiden's Vows, or Magnetism of Hearts*, a comedy of manners by the nineteenth-century Polish playwright Aleksandr Fredro. In selecting

Magnetism of Hearts as their target for disruption, Warsza and her collaborators did not intend, precisely, to mock the conventional theater, or to display scorn for the performance of a dog-eared romantic comedy. To the contrary, they wrote in a statement:

> This play was one of the most beloved and intelligent stagings of a romantic comedy in Warsaw in recent years. Considered a classic even in this very contemporary form, the production seemed a perfect post-bourgeois convention potentially open to being questioned and virused.[4]

This operation—the "virusing" of the play—began about twenty minutes into the performance. Warsza had called upon a pair of performance artists, Karolina Wiktor and Aleksandra Kubiak, who created performance art together under the name Chief Judge (Sędzia Główny), to interrupt the play. Kubiak and Wiktor, notably, emerged from the world of visual arts (they had studied arts education and painting) rather than theater, and their works to date had taken the form of body-centered performance: a piece in which they poked fun at consumption by lying inside a giant hamburger, for instance, or a piece in which they immersed themselves in ice water for an hour.[5] With Chief Judge's entrance, in other words, the body invaded the space of the dramatic text, and performance art invaded the theater.

Kubiak and Wiktor strode onstage, insisting that their purpose was to serve as advocates for the will of the public and that they would do whatever the audience wanted done. The actors in *Magnetism of Hearts* had been notified in advance that such an action would take place, and Warsza had spent substantial time discussing plans for the "virus," both with the performance artists and with the play's director. They debated how the two members of Chief Judge should take over the performance and what they should ask the audience to do, ultimately deciding that they would simply ask the spectators what they most wanted. The project, as Warsza has explained it, was overtly an homage to the Italian Futurists, whose performance events routinely included audience provocations and in which a heated exchange between spectators and performers was an essential part of the success of any given evening.

On the night of Warsza's action, the members of Chief Judge give the audience the following command: "Ladies and gentleman," they announce, "We don't want to stay passive during our action. The Chief Judge group is asking you for some suggestions." The stage set, with a prim pink sofa at its center, is suddenly flooded with smoke, and the performance artists, wearing long black dresses and trailed by a highly groomed white poodle, arrive onstage and demand the spotlight be turned around and fixed on the audience. There follows a long, awkward silence, as performance artists and spectators confront each other, each waiting for the other to take action.

Sędzia Główny performing "Virus in the Theater," TR Warszawa, 2006, curated by Joanna Warsza, part of Akcje TR. Used with permission of Joanna Warsza.

Eventually, a man toward the rear of the auditorium stands up and demands that one of the actors from *Magnetism of Hearts* exit the stage, and that the performance continue without her. She goes, but not without a fight, flinging herself on the sofa and kicking up her heels to demonstrate that she's still in a nineteenth-century drawing room comedy. A woman in the audience turns the tables on the Chief Judge artists, demanding that they take on the roles of the actors and "try to repeat what [the actors] do," which the pair of performance artists gamely attempts. Finally, one member of the audience demands the inevitable: that all of the artists should leave the stage, and that the public should replace them there. Some eagerly and some reluctantly, the spectators stagger onstage, only to be told (by Chief Judge, by fellow audience members, or by performers from the original play; in the confusion, it's difficult to tell), to much laughter, that they should return to their seats.[6] Warsza's interruption comes to a close when the spectators, ultimately deciding to resist Chief Judge's rebellious interruption, demand that the performance artists welcome the original cast back to the stage, that the performance of *Magnetism of Hearts* continue—so that, as one audience member says, "they have something to infect."

"Virus in the Theater" thus practiced a dramaturgy of interruption and surprise, but in the service of a far more open-ended agenda than the artists' modernist predecessors did. The proposition that a theatrical virus could be, simply, a means of creating perceptual space within the real time of a performance represents both a radical departure from the artistic works described in the earlier chapters of this book—and, at once, the distillation of many of the viral dramaturgies I have analyzed into their most concise and concentrated form. The differences reveal themselves immediately: Warsza's was, among the many viral dramaturgies explored in this book, perhaps the only one that did not place emphasis on the terms of its dissemination and circulation. It did not aspire to recruit audience members in the service of proliferation and revision, and it did not invite replication, the expansion of networks, or the tracing of communications routes. It was, perhaps uniquely, a virus that did not aim to go viral.

Different, too, was the emotional pitch, the affective tenor and the thematic preoccupation, from many of the viral works explored in this book, which engaged with viral proliferation in terms of extreme and saturated emotional states. Artaud envisioned the plague as a source of bloodshed, breakdown, and emergency, setting the terms for viruses in many theaters to come. The Living Theatre translated his vision into utopian optimism, but proposed equally all-consuming affective contagion in the key of ecstasy and rage—ecstatically angry participation, in the case of *Mysteries*; and the gulf between confused affect and revolutionary emotion, in the case of *Paradise Now*. Eva and Franco Mattes's computer virus, though modest in its real implications for computer systems, was violent in conceptual orientation, proposing to tear through the digital bodies of the computers in its path, and investigating, like many of the works explored in my third chapter, the affective relationship between contagion and fear. Critical Art Ensemble's *Radiation Burn* proposed to explode a dirty bomb in a park, to test the real-time spread of public anxiety, while *Plan C* exposed audience-participants to radiation from a real-world catastrophe whose effects have continued to circulate in the air, water, and bloodstream decades after the fact. Anicka Yi's installation was contained in a single gallery space, but it evoked a vast biological network, linking unseen bodies with the bodies of spectators, and suggesting the terror of quarantine. Caryl Churchill's *Seven Jewish Children* spread digitally, wafted along by anger, fear, and conviction, by histories of violence and premonitions about future acts of war. The networked performances of the Lysistrata Project and *365 Days/365 Plays* traded on emotional contagion too: not the infectiousness of fear, but the joy of perceived simultaneity and solidarity, buoyed along by the optimistic ethos of radical inclusion. "Virus in the Theater," by eschewing concerns with rapid dissemination and proliferation, with technology and media, and with the emotional extremities of ecstasy, joy, or fear, thus departed from many of the patterns shaping other instances of viral performance. It suggested another emotional and affective model for viral performance altogether.

Yet, though Warsza's project models "another viral," it does so in dialogue with the many modes of viral performance I have explored in this book, and it is equally revealing to parse its relationship to them, its concentration of many viral dramaturgies into a single, eloquent gesture, a return to the bones of viral performance. Warsza's project stages virus as an interruption to conventional dramatic structure—and in doing so, gestures to the ways all "viruses in the theater," all forms of viral performance, constitute challenges to deeply embedded assumptions about dramatic form. They stretch, interrupt, and expand performance time. They upend relationships between performers and spectators and test lines of artistic influence. They shift the terms of performance's reception, sometimes into the digital world, through secondary representation or acts of individual replication and revision. They challenge assumptions about liveness and recording. They find theatrical significance in the simultaneous staging of plays and performances in theaters across the country or around the world.

Perhaps most fundamentally, viral performance pressurizes and upends conventional ideas about spectatorship and participation. In constructing her performance around the open-ended desires of the audience, Warsza invoked the deep legacy of viral performances that investigate the politics of spectatorship and insist that their spectators act, in every sense of the word—even one as apparently distant as *Paradise Now*. After all, Rufus Collins had insisted, to his Living Theatre collaborators in 1968, that their goal with the piece that would become *Paradise Now* was "to do something . . . in which the cooperation of the Audience is essential to the completion of the act."[7] Like "Virus in the Theater," *Mysteries* and *Paradise Now* provide a reminder that viral performance, whatever its technological aspirations, is always also anchored in the relationships among bodies. Reshaping Artaud's violent vision to their radical utopian ends, the Living Theatre imagined contagion as physical and affective, reliant on shared choreographies of emotion. Theatrical contagion, for them, was inherently political and historically specific—drawing on an emotional tenor in the company's audiences that was particular to their times—and spread through the transformation of spectators into actors, of audience members into participants, in an acting exercise. The Living Theatre's use of Artaudian contagion offers a reminder that the theatrical "plague" need not consist of vast, immediate proliferation, but can be located, rather, in the lines of artistic influence, from Artaud to the Living Theatre and from the Living Theatre to their followers and those who took up their artistic legacy.

In clearing the stage of performers so that spectators could replace them, "Virus in the Theater" also bore affinities with the Miss General Idea pageant series: works in which audience members rehearsed the recognizable gestures of spectatorship, with the constantly deferred 1984 Miss General Idea pageant on the horizon. Warsza's project, in a modest way, also—like General Idea's extended pageant series—stretched the horizons of performance time, staging an open-ended interruption to conventional dramatic structure and planned duration. Such challenges to the expected boundaries of performance time likewise belong to viral performance as a whole, emerging across multiple eras and artistic orientations. Think of Schlingensief's performance installation, occupying public space in a Viennese square for days; or of Suzan-Lori Parks's yearlong festival, at once a celebration of brief, simultaneous performances and vastly expanded theatrical time.

In more oblique ways, Warsza's project bears affinities with the works of Estrin, Eva and Franco Mattes, and Critical Art Ensemble, and with the networked dramaturgy of *365 Days/365 Plays*. Chief Judge's appearance onstage employed the strategy of infiltration and surprise, theatrical ambush leading to the sudden rupture of everyday events, as did Estrin's "infiltrative" strategies of the 1970s. The project inserted a wedge between stage fiction and audience reality, as have many of the Matteses' and Critical Art Ensemble's projects. And, although in most respects presenting nothing like the aesthetics of scale evinced by Parks's yearlong, worldwide festival of work, it is difficult not to see Chief Judge's insistence on open-ended advocacy for audience members' wishes as a form of radical inclusion.

Of course, the viral predecessors that Warsza had in mind were none of these, but rather, the early modernist aesthetics of violent disruption practiced by the Italian Futurists. "At the beginning of the twentieth century the Futurists used to take over the stage during evenings at the variétés. Interrupting a performance to read out manifestos during these famous seratas was for Marinetti or Soffici a performative means of forcing the audience to take note of their ideas," states the Laura Palmer Foundation's description of the event.[8] Though Kubiak and Wiktor did not overtly "force" the audience into any particular action, "Virus in the Theater" is striking in its resurrection of the Futurists' paradigmatic performance model of rupture and confrontation, in its insistence that an unscripted encounter between performers and spectators is a radical act. In his manifesto for radio performance, quoted in the introduction to this book, Marinetti described his desire to eradicate the bourgeois theatergoing audience in its incarnation as a "judgmental mass," and to remove the "self-electing" elements of spectatorship.[9] Simply by confronting the spectators at TR Warszawa and announcing their intention of realizing audience members' desires, the artists of Chief Judge forced an opening between spectators—whose desires may have been quite different from one another—and addressed them precisely as self-electing members of an audience. Indeed, perhaps most radically, "Virus in the Theater" insisted that spectators *had* desires, emerging independently and not imposed upon them by the affective force of the play.

The Laura Palmer Foundation described this unscripted encounter in terms that testify to such a belief in its radicalism and possibility, and that gesture toward the larger artistic politics at play in the project:

> Once the audience got on stage, the action was suspended for 15 minutes. The play has been killed. An extraordinary clash was produced, somewhere between theater and performance art, echoing those Futurist evenings. They also somehow made clear that in the dominant form of mimetic theatre, the invasion of reality is still a nightmare of which legends are recounted.[10]

The distinction between theater and performance art, between "mimetic theatre" and "the invasion of reality," is not incidental. The actions of Chief Judge—including but not limited to "Virus in the Theater"—deliberately mixed the terms of the visual art world with those of the theater. The Futurists, in their *serate* and in their dissemination of self-mythologizing radical manifestos, challenged the terms of the many art forms with which they engaged: theater, vaudeville, visual art, radio, poetry. "Virus in the Theater," likewise, pressed against such disciplinary boundaries. The host body, in Warsza's model, was conventional theater, and the infecting virus was performance art.

In invoking this relationship, "Virus in the Theater" also obliquely gestured to the long history of theater itself as a form of contagion. In many theoretical models, such infection runs the other way: theater has long been seen as an infectious force, from Plato's injunction that theater could not be allowed into his ideal city to Michael Fried's famous anxiety about the theatrical qualities of Minimalist visual art.[11] Warsza's actions deliberately "infected" the theater—not with another form of theater, but with performance art. This is, Wiktor and Kubiak have suggested, an entirely different form of live art, reliant on spontaneity rather than rehearsal. In contrast with the "extremely trained actor," they have written, "a performance artist . . . doesn't define her gesture (as a medium) until the moment of creation."[12] By inserting performance art into a conventional theater space, Warsza, Kubiak, and Wiktor reciprocated the moves, over the last decade or so, on the part of visual artists and curators to bring theater and dance into gallery spaces and museums. Sibyl Kempson has taken up residence in the Whitney Museum, staging rituals for the changing seasons, while My Barbarian performs at the New Museum. These curatorial moves alter the terms of audience engagement; and Warsza's action, disrupting the middle of the play, asked to be understood not like conventional theater but like visual art—where audience members move when they want to, watch what they please, and leave when they get bored. The virus interrupts our experience of an art form, its aesthetic ambush altering our mode of attention.

This nondigital, noncontagious model for viral performance does not always exist in opposition to viral models that rely on swift, virulent proliferation. Such concepts merge, for instance, in the computer virus, which is both rupture and transmission. But "Virus in the Theater" is provocative because it is a virus without digital dissemination, because it reconceives the virus as a form of live encounter in direct dialogue with the terms of the theater itself. As I see it, the most significant moment in the piece is also the simplest: the moment right after the members of Chief Judge appear onstage and inform the audience that they will do whatever the collective will desires. What follows this announcement is a charged pause, an instance of collective uncertainty. For just a moment, before suggestions and commands begin emerging from the audience, the spectators—collectively, or individually—have no desire. They weren't expecting to be called upon, and they wait silently, still half-believing that someone else will step in and take control. "Virus in the Theater" thus constructs and centers on an instant of silence, hesitance, and uncertainty.

This kind of rupture was the variety of virus that theater invited long before there were viral videos, before capitalism was contagious, before globalization was viewed in terms of epidemiology. Thierry Bardini's "Hypervirus: A Clinical Note," written the same year "Virus in the Theater" was performed, reminds us that as early as the 1960s, William S. Burroughs and Jacques Derrida were using the image of the virus—in addition to its technological and epidemiological implications—as a way of understanding the relationship between identity and difference. "The word BE in the English language contains, as a virus contains, its precoded message of damage, the categorical imperative of permanent condition," wrote Burroughs.[13] For Derrida, by contrast, virus was not fixed identity but otherness. "The virus is in part a parasite that destroys, that introduces disorder into communication," he wrote.[14] Both of these viral visions can be linked to technological contagion, but neither depends on it. They are, instead, visions of the virus as a central metaphor for understanding language and identity.

My argument, in this conclusion, is that—as suggested by Warsza's "Virus in the Theater" and the array of theatrical legacies it invokes—the concept of the viral is fundamentally linked to communication, and new modes of communication; to shared presence, and the pressures artists put on that shared presence; and to the aesthetics of rupture in all of its forms. Most importantly, "Virus in the Theater" offers a reminder of the fundamentally theatrical qualities of the virus, and the ways that viral performance always puts pressure on foundational ideas about theater itself. Warsza's project suggests that viral structures and viral concepts will continue to shape radical performance long beyond the viral's present-day association with digital culture, and that viral concepts hold power in the public imagination beyond immediate or surface relationships to marketing, quick and easy politics, and shallow and short-lived fads. Warsza's action, in its narrative setting, its disruption, and its open-endedness, began to shape new theatrical relationships in the moment of its creation. It created an opening in which emotions were not scripted, as they are in nineteenth-century romantic comedy, but in fact were unknowable because they were unrehearsed and offered open-ended space to emerge. The two performance artists claim they will represent the audience's will—as if the audience, collectively, had one. Such openness about what spectators and performers might think or desire opens up a long, uncertain pause. It's a brief silence, but it's an eternity of stage time. That pause is the virus in the theater.

NOTES

Introduction

1. Caryl Churchill, *Seven Jewish Children* (London: Nick Hern Books, 2009), 8.

2. For instance: David Román's *Acts of Intervention: Performance, Gay Culture, and AIDS*; Petra Kuppers's *The Scar of Visibility: Medical Performances and Contemporary Art*; Stanton B. Garner's essay "Artaud, Germ Theory, and the Theatre of Contagion"; and Alex Mermikides and Gianna Bouchard's *Performance and the Medical Body*.

3. Zach Blas, "Virus, Viral," *WSQ: Women's Studies Quarterly* 40, no. 1 and 2 (spring/summer 2012): 29.

4. Gilles Deleuze and Félix Guattari, *A Thousand Plateaus: Capitalism and Schizophrenia* (New York: Continuum, 2004), 266.

5. Jean Baudrillard, *Cool Memories II*, trans. Chris Turner (Cambridge: Polity, 1996), 52.

6. Michael Hardt and Antonio Negri, *Empire* (Cambridge, Mass.: Harvard University Press, 2000), 136.

7. Thierry Bardini, "Hypervirus: A Clinical Report," *CTHEORY*, February 2, 2006, http://ctheory.net/articles.aspx?id=504.

8. Ibid.

9. Jussi Parikka, *Digital Contagions: A Media Archaeology of Computer Viruses* (New York: Peter Lang, 2007), 96.

10. *Women's Studies Quarterly* 40, no. 1 and 2 (spring/summer 2012).

11. Tony D. Sampson, *Virality: Contagion Theory in the Age of Networks* (Minneapolis: University of Minnesota Press, 2012), 3.

12. Plato, *The Republic*, trans. Desmond Lee (New York: Penguin, 1987), 84.

13. Ibid., 85.

14. Ibid., 94.

15. Ibid., 94–95.

16. Aristotle, *On Poetry and Style*, trans. G. M. A. Grube (Indianapolis, Ind.: Hackett, 1989), 12.

17. This debate is summarized, for instance, in George Whalley's introduction to his translation of *The Poetics* (Montreal: McGill-Queen's University Press, 1997), 27–28; and in the appendix to Dana LaCourse Munteanu's *Tragic Pathos: Pity and Fear in Greek Philosophy and Tragedy* (New York: Cambridge University Press, 2012).

18. Qtd in G. M. A. Grube, "Aristotle as a Literary Critic," in *On Poetry and Style*, trans. G. M. A. Grube (Indianapolis, Ind.: Hackett, 1989), xv–xvi.

19. Daniel Gerould, *Theatre, Theory, Theatre: The Major Critical Texts from Aristotle and Zeami to Soyinka and Havel* (New York: Applause Theatre & Cinema Books, 2000), 21.

20. Philip Sidney, "A Defense of Poesy," in *Theatre, Theory Theatre*, ed. Daniel Gerould (New York: Applause Theatre & Cinema Books, 2000), 119–27.

21. William Prynne, *Histrio-mastix* (London: Printed by E.A. and W.I. for Michael Sparke, 1633), available through Early English Books Online.

22. Jeremy Collier, "A Short View of the Immorality and Profaneness of the English Stage" (London: printed for S. Keble at the Turk's-Head, 1698), available through Google Books.

23. Eric Bentley, *The Playwright as Thinker* (Minneapolis: University of Minnesota Press, 1987), 27.

24. Gustave Le Bon, *The Crowd: A Study of the Popular Mind*, 2nd ed. (New York: Macmillan, 1897), xv.

25. Gabriel de Tarde, *The Laws of Imitation*, trans. Elsie Clews Parsons (New York: Henry Holt, 1903), 50.

26. "And so, the epithet *natural* is generally and not improperly bestowed upon the spontaneous and non-suggested resemblances which arise between different societies in every order of social facts," Tarde wrote (*Laws of Imitation*, 50).

27. Ibid., 76.

28. Le Bon, 12.

29. Simonetta Falasca-Zamponi, *Fascist Spectacle: The Aesthetics of Power in Mussolini's Italy* (Berkeley: University of California Press, 1997), 21.

30. Teresa Brennan, in her 2004 *The Transmission of Affect*, notes the continuing significance that Le Bon held, even through the late twentieth century, observing that studies of group psychology beginning in the 1960s often constituted efforts to disprove Le Bon, "whose class-based and race-imbued assumptions led to a politically reactionary view of crowds. In the more recent studies," she writes, "crowd behavior in demonstrations, rallies and so forth is seen as rational attempts to achieve goals." Teresa Brennan, *The Transmission of Affect* (Ithaca, N.Y.: Cornell University Press, 2004), 61.

31. Erika Fischer-Lichte, *Theatre, Sacrifice, Ritual: Exploring Forms of Political Theatre* (New York: Routledge, 2005), 30.

32. Elias Canetti, *Crowds and Power*, trans. Carol Stewart (New York: Farrar, Straus and Giroux, 1962), 77.

33. Ibid., 17.

34. Kimberly Jannarone, *Artaud and His Doubles* (Ann Arbor: University of Michigan Press, 2010), 116–17.

35. Antonin Artaud, *The Theater and Its Double*, trans. Mary Caroline Richards (New York: Grove, 1958), 27.

36. Ibid., 17.

37. Ibid., 30.

38. Ibid., 21.

39. Jannarone, *Artaud and His Doubles*, 53.

40. Stanton B. Garner, "Artaud, Germ Theory, and the Theatre of Contagion," *Theatre Journal* 58, no. 1 (2006): 11.

41. Jane Goodall, "Cruelty and Cure," in *Antonin Artaud and the Modern Theater*, ed. Gene A. Plunka (Cranbury, N.J.: Fairleigh Dickinson University Press, 1994), 57.

42. Artaud, *The Theater and Its Double*, 23.

43. Ibid., 31.

44. Ibid., 31.
45. Ibid., 25.
46. Antonin Artaud, *Selected Writings*, ed. Susan Sontag (New York: Farrar, Straus and Giroux, 1976), 578.
47. Ibid., 581.
48. Qtd. in "Antonin Artaud: French Dramatist, Actor, and Theatre Director, 1896–1948," by Tony Gardner, in *Censorship: A World Encyclopedia*, ed. Derek Jones (New York: Routledge, 2015): 414.
49. Denis Hollier, "The Death of Paper, Part Two: Artaud's Sound System," *October*, vol. 80 (spring 1997): 28.
50. Mario Dessy, *Madness (La Pazzia)*, in *Futurist Performance*, ed. Michael Kirby (New York: PAJ Publications, 2001), 282.
51. Hadley Cantril, *The Invasion from Mars: A Study in the Psychology of Panic* (Princeton, N.J.: Princeton University Press, 1940), 23.
52. Ibid., 47.
53. Ibid., 140 (emphasis in original).
54. Ibid., 47.
55. Richard Butsch, *The Citizen Audience* (New York: Routledge, 2008), 118.
56. Cantril, *Invasion from Mars*, xii.
57. Hadley Cantril and Gordon Allport, *The Psychology of Radio* (New York: Harper and Brothers, 1935), 3.
58. Ibid., 3.
59. F. T. Marinetti, *Critical Writings*, ed. Günter Berghaus (New York: Farrar, Straus and Giroux, 2006), 411.
60. Ibid., 413.
61. Stephen Kern, *The Culture of Time and Space, 1880–1918* (Cambridge, Mass.: Harvard University Press, 1983), 113–19.
62. Marinetti, *Critical Writings*, 412.
63. Michael Warner, *Publics and Counterpublics* (New York: Zone Books, 2002), 77–78.
64. Walter Benjamin, *Understanding Brecht*, trans. Anna Bostock (New York: Verso, 1998), 19.
65. Marc Silberman, "Introduction," in Bertolt Brecht, *Brecht on Film and Radio,* ed. Marc Silberman (London: Methuen, 2000), xi.
66. Marc Silberman, in Bertolt Brecht, *Brecht on Film and Radio*, ed. Marc Silberman (London: Methuen, 2000), 32.
67. Bertolt Brecht, "The Radio as a Communications Apparatus," in *Brecht on Film and Radio*, ed. Marc Silberman (London: Methuen, 2000), 41.
68. Ibid., 41.
69. Ibid., 43.
70. Silberman, in *Brecht on Film and Radio*, 41.
71. Bertolt Brecht, "Explanations [about *The Flight of the Lindberghs*] in *Brecht on Film and Radio*, ed. Marc Silberman (London: Methuen, 2000), 39 (emphasis in original).
72. Ibid., 42.
73. Ibid., 45.
74. Richard Dawkins, *The Selfish Gene* (Oxford: Oxford University Press, 1989), 192.

75. Ibid.

76. Kate Distin, *The Selfish Meme: A Critical Reassessment* (New York: Cambridge University Press, 2005), 16.

77. Ibid., 2.

78. Sampson, *Virality*, 37.

79. Ibid., 78.

80. Bill Wasik, *And Then There's This: How Stories Live and Die in Viral Culture* (New York: Viking, 2009), 7.

81. "Movements of Mass Pointlessness," *Sunday Times* (South Africa), August 10, 2003, 3.

82. James Cowan, "Toronto's First Flash Mob Has Its Ups and Downs," *National Post* (Canada), August 8, 2003, A2.

83. Megan Merrill, "Flash Mob: Art, Smart or Just Absurd," *The Moscow Times*, September 22, 2003.

84. Deleuze and Guattari, *A Thousand Plateaus*, 266–67.

85. Anna Gibbs, "Contagious Feelings: Pauline Hanson and the Epidemiology of Affect," *Australian Humanities Review*, no. 24 (December 2001), http://australianhumanitiesreview.org/2001/12/01/contagious-feelings-pauline-hanson-and-the-epidemiology-of-affect/.

86. Brennan, *Transmission of Affect*, 1.

87. Sara Ahmed, *The Cultural Politics of Emotion* (New York: Routledge, 2004), 10–11.

88. Warner, 65–66.

89. Jacques Rancière, *The Emancipated Spectator* (New York: Verso, 2009), 7.

90. Ibid., 17.

91. Claire Bishop, *Artificial Hells: Participatory Art and the Politics of Spectatorship* (London: Verso, 2012), 2.

Chapter 1

1. Dilexi Series program note, Pacific Film Archive.

2. Julian Beck, *The Life of the Theatre* (New York: Limelight Editions, 1972), 66.

3. Judith Malina, diary entry, May 15, 1968, Beinecke Library, UNCAT MSS 1006, March 2008 Acquisition, box 14. I am grateful to Kate Bredeson for calling my attention to this event. For further information on the Living Theatre in May 1968, see her forthcoming book, *Occupying the Stage: The Theater of May '68*.

4. Rita Felski, "Introduction," *New Literary History* 33, no. 4 (autumn 2002): 609. I am indebted to Jacob Gallagher-Ross for directing me to this essay. For further information about performance and the theory of the everyday, see his forthcoming book, *Theaters of the Everyday: Aesthetic Democracy on the American Stage* (Evanston, Ill.: Northwestern University Press, 2018).

5. Judith Malina and Julian Beck, "Messages," box 31, Living Theatre Records, 13 (emphasis in original).

6. Philip Fisher, *The Vehement Passions* (Princeton, N.J.: Princeton University Press, 2002), 41.

7. Henry Lesnick, "Introduction," in *Guerrilla Street Theater* (New York: Bard Books, 1973), 16.

8. Jannarone, *Artaud and His Doubles*, 13.
9. Such concepts emerge in several of the critiques I cite later in this chapter; for instance, Gilman; Munk; DeKoven; and Brecht.
10. Jannarone, *Artaud and His Doubles*, 195.
11. Judith Malina, "Notebook 8.31.68–3.10.69," box 14, Living Theatre Records, Yale Collection of American Literature, Beinecke Rare Book and Manuscript Library, Yale University, 175.
12. Judith Malina, "European Diary" folder, box 2, Living Theatre Records, 37.
13. Judith Malina, interview with author, April 17, 2011.
14. Julian Beck, *Theandric: Julian Beck's Last Notebooks*, ed. Erica Bilder (Philadelphia: Harwood Academic, 1992), 122.
15. The Living Theatre, *Mysteries and Smaller Pieces*, in *The Great American Life Show: 9 Plays from the Avant-Garde Theater*, John Lahr and Jonathan Price, eds. (New York: Bantam Books, 1974), 347.
16. Ibid., 348.
17. Ibid., 349.
18. Ibid.
19. Saul Gottlieb, "The Living Theatre in Exile: 'Mysteries, Frankenstein,'" *Tulane Drama Review* 10, no. 4 (1966): 145.
20. Judith Malina, notes from "European Diary, April 1969–July 23, 1970" folder, Living Theatre Records, 16.
21. Judith Malina, Julian Beck, and Richard Schechner, "Containment Is the Enemy," *TDR: The Drama Review* 13, no. 3 (spring 1969): 35.
22. Richard Gilman, "The Living Theatre on Tour," in *The Drama Is Coming Now: The Theater Criticism of Richard Gilman, 1961–1991* (New Haven: Yale University Press, 2005), 123.
23. Fisher, *Vehement Passions*, 43.
24. Ibid., 44.
25. Qtd. ibid., 53–54.
26. Ibid., 54.
27. John Tytell, *The Living Theatre: Art, Exile, and Outrage* (New York: Grove, 1995), 30.
28. Malina, Beck, and Schechner, "Containment," 35–36.
29. Ibid., 36.
30. Ibid., 35.
31. Judith Malina, journal folder, January 27–May 12, 1972, Living Theatre Records, box 2, 169.
32. Ibid., 168.
33. Living Theatre, "Six Public Acts" binder, box 183, Living Theatre Records, 5.
34. Ibid., 3.
35. Ibid., 6.
36. This note is unsigned and may have been written by Beck or Malina.
37. Living Theatre, "Six Public Acts—Diverse Notes," box 150, Living Theatre Records.
38. Living Theatre, "Six Public Acts" binder, box 183, Living Theatre Records, 52.
39. Living Theatre, "Six Public Acts," Italy binder, box 183, Living Theatre Records. These files document the company's 1976 tour of the piece across Italy.

40. Bradford Martin, *The Theater Is in the Street* (Amherst, Mass.: University of Massachusetts Press, 2004), 82.
41. Ibid., 83.
42. Beck, *Life of the Theatre*, 86.
43. Ibid.
44. Living Theatre, *Paradise Now,* Notebook #2, 67, Yale Collection of American Literature, Beinecke Rare Book Room and Manuscript Library.
45. Ibid., 108.
46. Living Theatre, *Paradise Now,* Notebook #1, 74, Yale Collection of American Literature, Beinecke Rare Book and Manuscript Library.
47. Living Theatre, *Paradise Now,* Notebook #2, 58, Yale Collection of American Literature, Beinecke Rare Book and Manuscript Library.
48. Ibid., 58.
49. Ibid., 62.
50. Identified as RC in rehearsal notes, most likely Rufus Collins.
51. Julian Beck, Notebook #1, box 3, Living Theatre Records, 5–6.
52. Ibid., 20.
53. Ibid., 113.
54. Antonin Artaud, "The Theater and the Plague," in *The Theater and Its Double*, trans. Mary-Caroline Richards (New York: Grove, 1958), 27.
55. Ibid., 30.
56. Ibid., 17.
57. Ibid., 26.
58. Living Theatre, *Paradise Now: Collective Creation of the Living Theatre* (New York: Vintage Books, 1971), 16.
59. Howard Stein, Review of *Antigone* and *Paradise Now* at Yale University Theatre, September 1968, *Educational Theatre Journal* 21, no. 1 (March 1969): 108.
60. Erika Munk, "Only Connect: The Living Theatre and Its Audiences," in *Restaging the Sixties: Radical Theaters and Their Legacies*, ed. James Harding and Cindy Rosenthal (Ann Arbor: University of Michigan Press, 2006), 46–47.
61. Gilman, "The Living Theatre on Tour," 122.
62. Marianne DeKoven, *Utopia Limited: The Sixties and the Emergence of the Postmodern* (Durham, N.C.: Duke University Press, 2004), 152–53.
63. Stefan Brecht, "Revolution at the Brooklyn Academy of Music," *TDR: The Drama Review* 13, no. 3 (spring 1969): 64 (emphasis in original).
64. Living Theatre, *Paradise Now*, 15.
65. Ibid., 6.
66. Judith Malina and Julian Beck, "Messages," box 31, Living Theatre Records, 16.
67. Julian Beck, Notebook #1, box 3, Living Theatre Records, 92–93.
68. Judith Malina and Julian Beck, "Messages," box 31, Living Theatre Records, 2.
69. Michael Kirby, "On Acting and Not-Acting," *TDR: The Drama Review* 16, no. 1 (March 1972): 6–7.
70. Lawrence Grossberg, *we gotta get out of this place*, 81, qtd. in *Ugly Feelings,* by Sianne Ngai (Cambridge, Mass.: Harvard University Press, 2005), 25.
71. Raymond Williams, "Structures of Feeling," in *Marxism and Literature* (Oxford: Oxford University Press, 1977), 130.

72. Charles Brover, “Some Notes in Defense of Combative Theatre,” in *Guerrilla Street Theater*, 35.

73. Judith Malina and Julian Beck, “Messages,” box 31, Living Theatre Records, 3–4.

74. Living Theatre, “Paradise Now Notebook #1,” box 31, Living Theatre Records, I-83–83.

75. Living Theatre, “Paradise Now Draft II,” box 31, Living Theatre Records, 2.

76. Ibid., 2. What is possibly the first typewritten version of the Rite, written in French and giving the time and place of the play’s premiere in Avignon, includes a bare-bones Rite with very little in the way of stage directions.

77. Box 31, Living Theatre Records.

78. Judith Malina, Notebook 8.31.6–83.10.69, box 14, Living Theatre Records, 170.

79. Dilexi Series program note, provided courtesy of the Pacific Film Archive.

80. Ibid.

81. Malina, Notebook 8.31.68–3.10.69, box 14, Living Theatre Records, 175.

82. Tytell, *Living Theatre*, 256.

83. Judith Malina, Notebook 8.31.68–3.10.69, box 14, Living Theatre Records, 175. (Malina writes, “It was to make some money because of the financial crisis that we allowed such a mad-paced day as Saturday March 8—on which we did three performances in one day.”)

84. All quotations and descriptions of the Dilexi broadcast are taken from the Living Theatre video (John Coney, author), *Rites of Guerrilla Theatre*, filmed March 8, 1969, Pacific Film Archive Film and Video Collection, available on archive.org, https://archive.org/details/cbpf_000051_p1.

85. Martin, *Theater Is in the Street*, 84.

86. DeKoven, *Utopia Limited*, 153.

87. Malina, Notebook 8.31.68–3.10.69, box 14, Living Theatre Records, 175.

88. Ibid.

Chapter 2

1. General Idea, “Target Audience,” General Idea Archives, National Gallery of Canada, Ottawa, Ontario (pages not numbered).

2. Ibid.

3. To amplify the discussion of the differences in scholarly approaches to these artists: Boal’s work is widely studied, and his direct approach to interventionist performance has been influential to artists and activists around the world for decades; his own pieces were staged mainly in Argentina, Brazil, Peru, and various European countries during his exile from South America. Estrin, on the other hand, worked in the United States, has not been written about in a scholarly context, and realized many of his most ambitious theatrical visions only in the form of theoretical texts. And General Idea, whose Canadian work I prioritize here (the trio moved to New York City in the mid-1980s), took a more oblique approach to politically motivated art and performance—but a more direct approach to media circulation—and has been studied most extensively as a group of visual and conceptual artists, their theater and performance pieces frequently sidelined in favor of painting, sculpture, and written work.

4. Marshall McLuhan, *Understanding Media: The Extensions of Man* (Cambridge, Mass.: Massachusetts Institute of Technology Press, 1964), 118.
5. Ibid., v. I am indebted to Lance Strate and Edward Wachtel (*The Legacy of McLuhan*) for this observation.
6. Ibid., 107.
7. Ibid., 117.
8. Blas, "Virus, Viral," 31.
9. Jan Cohen-Cruz, ed., *Playing Boal: Theatre of the Oppressed Anthology* (New York: Routledge, 1994), 232.
10. McLuhan, *Understanding Media*, 71.
11. Augusto Boal, *Theatre of the Oppressed*, trans. Charles A. McBride and Maria-Odilia Leal McBride (New York: Theatre Communications Group, 1985), 141.
12. Qtd. in Munk, "Only Connect," 42.
13. Marc Estrin, phone interview with author, October 15, 2010.
14. Ibid.
15. Dick Higgins, "Fluxus: Theory and Reception," in *The Fluxus Reader*, ed. Ken Friedman (New York: Academy Editions, 1998), 234.
16. Allan Kaprow, "Self-Service: A Happening," *TDR: The Drama Review* 12, no. 3 (spring 1968): 161.
17. Estrin, *ReCreation: Some Notes on What's What and What You Might Be Able to Do about What's What* (New York: Dell, 1971), pages not numbered.
18. R. G. Davis, "Guerrilla Theatre," *Tulane Drama Review* 10, no. 4 (summer 1966): 130.
19. Ibid., 133–35.
20. Richard Schechner, "Guerrilla Theatre: May 1970," *TDR: The Drama Review* 14, no. 3 (1970): 163.
21. Marc Estrin, *ReCreation*, pages not numbered. (A shortened version appeared in *TDR*.)
22. Estrin, *ReCreation*; Melvin Laird was Nixon's secretary of defense from 1969 to 1973.
23. Estrin, phone interview.
24. Estrin, "Four Guerrilla Theater Pieces," 73.
25. Marc Estrin, "City Lights Piece," unpublished.
26. Estrin, "Four Guerrilla Theater Pieces," 74.
27. Ibid.
28. Ibid.
29. Martin Trueblood and Marc Estrin, "Letter," *TDR: The Drama Review* 14, no. 1 (1969): 189.
30. Ibid., 189 (emphasis in original).
31. Estrin, phone interview with author.
32. Estrin, *ReCreation*, pages not numbered.
33. Ibid.
34. Ibid.
35. Laura Levin, *Performing Ground: Space, Camouflage, and the Art of Blending In* (New York: Palgrave Macmillan, 2014), 170.
36. Ibid., 141.
37. Ibid.

38. Augusto Boal, *Hamlet and the Baker's Son: My Life in Theatre and Politics*, trans. Adrian Jackson and Candida Blaker (New York: Routledge, 2001), 194–95.

39. Arnold Aronson, *American Avant-Garde Theatre: A History* (New York: Routledge, 2000), 74.

40. Boal, *Hamlet and the Baker's Son*, 191.

41. Ibid., 194.

42. Ibid.

43. Ibid., 304.

44. Ibid., 303–4.

45. Ibid., 304.

46. Joanne Pottlitzer, "Symbols of Resistance: The Legacy of Artists under Pinochet (1973–1990)," forthcoming.

47. Boal, *Theater of the Oppressed*, 154–55.

48. Augusto Boal and Susana Epstein, "Invisible Theatre: Liège, Belgium 1978," *TDR: The Drama Review* 34, no. 3 (1990): 25.

49. Ibid.

50. Ibid., 28.

51. Ibid., 25.

52. McLuhan, *Understanding Media*, 136.

53. Levin, *Performing Ground*, 161–62.

54. Boal and Epstein, "Invisible Theatre," 31–32.

55. Ibid., 32.

56. Ibid.

57. Ibid., 33.

58. See the "Introduction" for a full discussion of Rancière's "Emancipated Spectator" and its implications for viral performance.

59. Boal and Epstein, "Invisible Theatre," 34.

60. Ibid., 33.

61. Ibid.

62. Ibid.

63. Ibid.

64. Augusto Boal, "Poetics of the Oppressed," in *The Community Performance Reader*, ed. Petra Kuppers and Gwen Robertson (New York: Routledge, 2007), 17.

65. Ibid., 23.

66. General Idea, "Pablum for the Pablum Eaters: A Method of Invasion," *FILE Megazine* 2, nos. 1 and 2 (May 1973): 26.

67. Burroughs's fiction—and particularly his use of viral imagery—also provided inspiration to several visual and performance artists, who pursued his contagious visions farther. One of these is the musician and performance artist Laurie Anderson, who collaborated with Burroughs, and who in 1984 wrote a song called "Language Is a Virus from Outer Space," recorded on her album *Home of the Brave* (which is, in turn, part of a larger performance project entitled *United States*), a multipart work that comments on human relationships to media, technology, and language in a mass media age.

68. AA Bronson, "Myth as Parasite/Image as Virus: General Idea's Bookshelf 1967–1975," in *The Search for the Spirit: General Idea 1968–1975*, curated by Fern Bayer (Toronto: Art Gallery of Ontario, 1997), 18.

69. Philip Monk writes, in his book *Glamour Is Theft: A User's Guide to General Idea* (Toronto: Art Gallery of York University, 2012), that "while for correspondence artists viral images were liberating, in Burroughs's science fiction mythological system, language was an alien virus used to control humans—hence the need to cut word lines, shift lingual, and storm the Reality Studio" (53).

70. General Idea, "Glamour," *FILE Megazine* 3, no. 1 (Fall 1975): 22.

71. Monk, *Glamour Is Theft*, 45.

72. AA Bronson et al., *From Sea to Shining Sea: Artist-Initiated Activity in Canada, 1939–1987* (Toronto: Power Plant, 1987), 48. Also quoted in and brought to my attention by Fern Bayer, "Uncovering the Roots of General Idea: A Documentation and Description of Early Projects 1968–1975," in *The Search for the Spirit: General Idea 1968–1975* (Toronto: Art Gallery of Ontario, 1997), 28.

73. This is according to a history of the company delivered in a speech by Mimi Paige, collaborator and Miss General Idea 1968, during a performance entitled *Hot Property* (filmed September 1977, Kingston, Ontario, General Idea Fonds, National Gallery of Canada Archive).

74. From the finding aid, General Idea Fonds, National Gallery of Canada Archive.

75. All above information is taken from unpublished documentation found in General Idea Fonds, box 1A, Projects Series 1968–1971, National Gallery of Canada Archive.

76. Michael Tims, "What Happened," General Idea Fonds, box 1A, Projects Series 1968–1971, National Gallery of Canada Archive.

77. Gertrude Stein, "Plays," in *Last Operas and Plays*, ed. Carl van Vechten (Baltimore: Johns Hopkins University Press, 1977), xxx.

78. Ibid., xlii.

79. Ibid., xliv.

80. General Idea, telex printout, August 19, 1970, General Idea Fonds, box 1A, Projects Series 1968–1971, National Gallery of Canada Archive.

81. McLuhan, *Understanding Media*, 23–24.

82. Ibid., 217.

83. General Idea, untitled document, General Idea Fonds, box 1A, Projects Series, 1968–1971, National Gallery of Canada Archive.

84. Peggy Phelan, *Unmarked: The Politics of Performance* (New York: Routledge, 1993), 146.

85. Untitled Photo, General Idea Fonds, box 1A, Projects Series, 1968–1971, National Gallery of Canada Archive.

86. General Idea, "Miss General Idea Pageant 1971" pamphlet, General Idea Fonds, box 1B, Projects Series 1968–1971, National Gallery of Canada Archive (pages not numbered).

87. These documents can be found in the folder labeled "Miss General Idea Pageant 1971," General Idea Fonds, box 1B, Projects Series 1968–1971, National Gallery of Canada Archive.

88. José Esteban Muñoz, *Cruising Utopia: The Then and There of Queer Futurity* (New York: New York University Press, 2009), 116.

89. Ibid., 117.

90. For instance, *FILE* Special Double Issue, vol. 2, no. 1 and 2 (May 1973): 52.

91. General Idea, "Pablum for the Pablum Eaters," *FILE* Special Double Issue, vol. 2, no. 1 and 2 (May 1983): 26.

92. Quoted in Monk, *Glamour Is Theft*, 54.
93. Bronson, "Myth as Parasite/Image as Virus," 18.
94. Monk, *Glamour Is Theft*, 76.
95. General Idea, "Target Audience."
96. Ibid.
97. General Idea, *Going Thru the Motions* script, box 45, Manuscript Series A, Manuscripts for Performances and Video Tapes, National Gallery of Canada Archive, 10.
98. Ibid., 10.
99. Although *Hot Property* was performed in 1977, the most thorough documentation of the piece comes from the video that was edited and produced in 1978 with some additional footage, and therefore, much of my discussion is drawn from the video.
100. General Idea, *Hot Property*, General Idea Fonds, box 4A, Projects Series 1977–1979, National Gallery of Canada Archive.
101. From the General Idea Finding Aid, General Idea Papers, National Gallery of Canada Archive.
102. Finding Aid, General Idea papers, National Gallery of Canada, pages not numbered.
103. Gregg Bordowitz, *Imagevirus* (London: Afterall Books, 2010), 75.
104. Ibid., 64.

Chapter 3

A previous version of portions of this chapter was published as "Viral Performance" in *Theater* 42:2, "Digital Dramaturgies."

1. Douglas Rushkoff, *Media Virus! Hidden Agendas in Popular Culture* (New York: Random House, 1996), 9–10.
2. Ibid., 272.
3. Ibid., 298–99.
4. Kalle Lasn, *Culture Jam: How to Reverse America's Suicidal Consumer Binge—And Why We Must* (New York: HarperCollins, 1999), 123–24.
5. Sampson, *Virality*, 2.
6. Christoph Schlingensief and Hans Ulrich Obrist: "My Work Always Has Something to Do with a Change of Perspective," in *AC: Christoph Schlingensief: Church of Fear*, ed. Alice Koegel (Germany: Museum Ludwig, Cologne, and Verlag der Buchhandlung Walther König, Cologne, 2005), 21.
7. Jean Baudrillard, *The Transparency of Evil: Essays on Extreme Phenomena*, trans. James Benedict (New York: Verso, 1990), 67. I am indebted to Thierry Bardini's 2006 essay "Hypervirus: A Clinical Report" (http://ctheory.net/articles.aspx?id=504) for directing me to this quotation.
8. Jean Baudrillard, *Cool Memories II*, trans. Chris Turner (Cambridge: Polity, 1996), 52.
9. Douglas Rushkoff, *Coercion: Why We Listen To What "They" Say* (New York: Riverhead Books, 1999), 235.
10. Dennis W. Allen, "Viral Activism and the Meaning of Post-Identity," *Journal of the Midwest Modern Language Association* 36, no. 1, "Thinking Post-Identity" (Spring 2003): 9.
11. Steve Kurtz, phone interview with author, April 3, 2011.

12. Tilman Baumgärtel, "Interview with Eva and Franco Mattes," in *Eva and Franco Mattes: 0100101110101101.org*, ed. Maurizio Cattelan, Domenico Quaranta, and Roselee Goldberg (Milan: Charta, 2009), 74.

13. Steve Lambert, Mike Bonnano, and Andy Bichlbaum, "The Yes Men," *BOMB* no. 107 (spring 2009): 82.

14. Guy Debord, *Society of the Spectacle* (London: Bread and Circuses Publishing, 2012), pages not numbered. (Debord is quoting the French writer Isodore Ducasse.)

15. Carrie Lambert-Beatty, "Make-Believe: Parafiction and Plausibility," *October*, vol. 129 (summer 2009): 54.

16. Ibid., 79.

17. Critical Art Ensemble, "Selected Short Films, 1987–1994," http://critical-art.net/Videos.html.

18. Steve Kurtz, phone interview with author.

19. Ibid.

20. Kurtz acknowledged that he and the other members of CAE are too young to have seen *Paradise Now* or the Living Theatre's other groundbreaking 1960s-era performance works; rather, they are influenced by the Living Theatre's legacy of theatrical texts and theoretical writings.

21. Ibid.

22. The Yes Men's success testifies to their strategic use of media's newly viral properties, and to their alignment with Rushkoff's original vision for the "media virus." Yet their significance to viral dramaturgy runs deeper than this: in describing their work, the Yes Men frequently evince artistic and ethical philosophies that align them closely with earlier practitioners of invisible and infiltrative theater, particularly Estrin and Boal. In a book and web project entitled *Beautiful Trouble: A Toolbox for Revolution* (its online presence is heralded with the slogan "The most contagious solutions for building a just and resilient world"), Bonnano and Bichlbaum's contributions include entries on the subversive tactics of "hoax" and "infiltration." Bonnano's discussion of "hoax" as a strategy for subversion advocates the following ethical and dramaturgical philosophy—distinctly echoing Estrin's 1969 defense of his theatrical strategies in the pages of *TDR*: "It is generally best to reveal a hoax promptly. The ultimate goal here is more truth for more people. At the Yes Lab, we have an ethos: Never leave a lie on the table. This ethos is the opposite MO of those in power. The grand hoaxes they perpetrate on the people—everything from simple greenwashing campaigns to complex conspiracies to subvert democracy—are never meant to be debunked." In his discussion of "infiltration," Bichlbaum counsels artist-activists to explicitly pitch their performances toward viral media, prioritizing virtual audiences above live ones: "Remember: it's not the audience there in the room that you're most concerned with, but the audience who will see your footage, read the press release, or benefit from the secrets you've liberated from behind closed doors," he writes. The Yes Men's work thus engages the contemporary viral media landscape. Laura Levin argues that their projects, by employing not only performers but also web programmers, filmmakers, and graphic designers, partake in what Henry Jenkins has called "convergence culture," revealing the significance of performative networks over individual artists. Simultaneously, they reveal the deep dramaturgical and philosophical connections

between contemporary viral performances and radically contagious works of earlier eras.

23. Blas, "Virus, Viral," 31.

24. Critical Art Ensemble, *The Electronic Disturbance* (New York: Autonomedia, 1994), 27, http://critical-art.net/books/ted/.

25. Ibid., 30.

26. Ibid., 62.

27. Ibid.

28. Priscilla Wald, *Contagious: Cultures, Carriers, and the Outbreak Narrative* (Durham, N.C.: Duke University Press, 2008), 159.

29. Critical Art Ensemble, "Marching Plague" video, 2006, http://critical-art.net/Videos.html.

30. Ibid.

31. Ibid.

32. Steve Kurtz, phone interview with author, April 3, 2011.

33. Critical Art Ensemble, *Marching Plague* (New York: Autonomedia, 2006), 59, http://critical-art.net/books/mp/.

34. In one article CAE, citing their affinities with earlier generations of avant-gardes, lists "plagiarism" and "detournement" along with such familiar notions as "readymades" and "appropriation" as central methods for accomplishing revolutionary art. Critical Art Ensemble, "Recombinant Theatre and Digital Resistance," *TDR: The Drama Review* 44, no. 4 (2000): 152.

35. Critical Art Ensemble, "Target Deception, 2007," http://critical-art.net/Videos.html.

36. Kurtz, phone interview with author.

37. According to Kurtz, CAE made prior arrangements with the local police and the fire departments, and members of both departments agreed to feign surprise at the explosion and to behave as if a possible radioactive device had really detonated. Ibid.

38. Ulrich Wolf, speech for CAE's *Radiation Burn*, presented at performance of *Radiation Burn*, Halle, Germany, 2010.

39. Critical Art Ensemble, "Radiation Burn, 2010," http://critical-art.net/Tactical Media.html.

40. Kurtz, phone interview with author.

41. Ibid.

42. Franco Mattes, interview with author.

43. Ibid.

44. Reena Jana, "Wanna See Some Really Sick Art?" *Wired*, June 27, 2001, http://www.wired.com/culture/lifestyle/news/2001/06/44728.

45. Cattelan, Quaranta, and Goldberg, eds., *Eva and Franco Mattes* (Milan: Charta, 2009), 82.

46. Ibid., 82–83.

47. Ibid.

48. Mattes, interview with author.

49. Ibid.

50. Nicholas Abercrombie and Brian J. Longhurst, *Audiences: A Sociological Theory of Performance and Imagination* (London: SAGE, 1998), 76.

51. Mattes, interview with author.

52. Jana, "Wanna See Some Really Sick Art?"

53. Quaranta, "Traveling by Telephone," in *Eva and Franco Mattes*, eds. Cattelan, Quaranta, and Goldberg (Milan: Charta, 2009), 34–35.

54. Wald, *Contagious*, 182.

55. Jacques Derrida with Peter Brunette and David Wills, "The Spatial Arts: An Interview with Jacques Derrida," in *Deconstruction and the Visual Arts: Art, Media Architecture*, ed. Peter Brunette and David Wills (Cambridge: Cambridge University Press, 1994), 12. I am grateful to Thierry Bardini's essay "Hypervirus: A Clinical Report" for directing me to this quotation.

56. Cattelan, Quaranta, and Goldberg, eds., *Eva and Franco Mattes*, 85.

57. Jason Farman, "The Virtual Artaud," in *TechKnowledgies: New Imaginaries in the Humanities, Arts, and TechnoSciences*, ed. Mary Valentis (Newcastle, Eng.: Cambridge Scholars, 2007), 158.

58. Artaud, "The Theater and the Plague," 23.

59. Ibid., 25–26.

60. Mattes, interview with author.

61. "A-Z List of All Threats and Risks," Symantec, http://www.symantec.com/security_response/threatexplorer/azlisting.jsp?azid=P.

62. "Virus Profile: Python/Bien," McAfee, http://home.mcafee.com/VirusInfo/VirusProfile.aspx?key=102561.

63. "Virus: Python/Biennale," Microsoft Malware Protection Center, http://www.microsoft.com/security/portal/Threat/Encyclopedia/Entry.aspx?Name=Virus%3APython%2FBiennale&ThreatID=-2147424951.

64. Franco Mattes, email to author, September 16, 2011.

65. Kurtz, phone interview with author.

66. Eva and Franco Mattes, "Nike Ground," http://0100101110101101.org/nike-ground/.

67. Ibid.

68. Ibid.

69. Ibid.

70. "Why Doesn't Nike Want to Play with Me?" 0100101110101101.org, October 17, 2003, http://www.0100101110101101.org/texts/nike_prelease2-en.html (link no longer active).

71. "The Hardly Believable Nike Ground Trick," 0100101110101101.org, http://0100101110101101.org/home/nikeground/story.html (link no longer active).

72. Cattelan, Quaranta, and Goldberg, eds., *Eva and Franco Mattes*, 92.

73. Tom McDonough, "Introduction," in *Guy Debord and the Situationist International: Texts and Documents* (Cambridge, Mass.: MIT Press, 2002), xiii.

74. Ibid., xiii–xiv.

75. "Nike Ground," 0100101110101101.org, http://0100101110101101.org/home/nikeground/index.html.

76. Maurya Wickstrom, *Performing Consumers: Global Capital and Its Theatrical Seductions* (New York: Routledge, 2006), 14. Otto Riewoldt's book *Brandscapes*, published in 2002, describes a trend toward the creation of retail-store "environments" and includes two Nike megastores, NikePark in Paris and NikeTown in London, in its analysis.

77. Wickstrom, *Performing Consumers*, 18.

78. Ibid., 20.

79. Cattelan, Quaranta, and Goldberg, eds., *Eva and Franco Mattes*, 92.

80. "Nike Ground," 0100101110101101.org, http://0100101110101101.org/home/nikeground/index.html.

81. Mattes, interview with author.

82. Ibid.

83. Ibid.

84. "Let Them Believe," created by Jeff Stark, Todd Chandler, and Todd Seelie, online video, http://letthembelievemovie.com/video.html.

85. Mattes, interview with author.

86. Ibid.

87. Ibid.

88. Ibid.

89. Marina Galperina, "Chernobyl Plan C Revealed: The Radioactive Ride," Animal New York blog, October 12, 2010, http://www.animalnewyork.com/2010/chernobyl-plan-c-revealed-the-radioactive-ride/.

90. Artaud, "The Theater and the Plague," 32.

91. Introduction to Schlingensief, *AC: Christoph Schlingensief: Church of Fear*, 7.

92. Stephen E. Atkins, *Encyclopedia of Modern Worldwide Extremists and Extremist Groups* (Westport, Conn.: Greenwood, 2004), 120.

93. Ibid.

94. Denise Varney, "'Right Now Austria Looks Ridiculous': *Please Love Austria!* Reforging the Interaction between Art and Politics," in *Christoph Schlingensief: Art without Borders*, ed. Tara Forrest and Anna Teresa Scheer (Chicago: University of Chicago Press, 2010), 105.

95. Atkins, *Encyclopedia*, 120.

96. Christopher Balme, *The Theatrical Public Sphere* (Cambridge: Cambridge University Press, 2014), 181.

97. Varney, "Right Now," 114–18.

98. Balme, *Theatrical Public Sphere*, 183.

99. Michael Shane Boyle, "Container Aesthetics: The Infrastructural Politics of Shunt's *The Boy Who Climbed Out of His Face*," *Theatre Journal* 68, no. 1 (March 2016): 64.

100. Bishop, *Artificial Hells*, 283.

101. Ibid., 283.

102. Paul Poet, *Ausläunder Raus! Schlingensief's Container*, Videorecording (Wien: Hoanzl, 2006).

103. Schlingensief, *AC: Christoph Schlingensief: Church of Fear*, 22.

104. Silvija Jestrovic, "Performing like an Asylum Seeker: Paradoxes of Hyper-Authenticity," *Research in Drama Education* 13, no. 2 (2008): 166.

105. My thanks to Matthew Cornish and Ryan Davis for these translations.

106. Sandra Umathum, email to author, May 18, 2011.

107. Varney, "Right Now," 107.

108. Lothar Mikos, "Big Brother as Television Text," in *Big Brother International: Formats, Critics and Publics*, ed. Ernest Mathijs and Janet Jones (London: Wallflower, 2004), 93.

109. Ibid., 99.

110. Ibid., 96.

111. Jean Baudrillard, "Requiem for the Media," in *For a Critique of the Political Economy of the Sign* (St. Louis, Mo.: Telos, 1981), 171.

112. Qtd. on http://www.nowyteatr.org/en/event/Schlingensief_Przegl%C4%85d.

113. For instance, Varney, "Right Now" (117); Jestrovic, "Performing like an Asylum Seeker," 164.

114. Jennifer Kapczynski, *The German Patient: Crisis and Recovery in Postwar Culture* (Ann Arbor: University of Michigan Press, 2010), 3. I am indebted to Jack Davis's article "Pathogenic Polemics: Heldenplatz and the 'Bernhard Virus,'" cited in full below, for this citation and the one that follows.

115. Robert Esposito, *Bios: Biopolitics and Philosophy* (Minneapolis: University of Minnesota Press, 2008), 137.

116. Jack Davis, "Pathogenic Polemics: Heldenplatz and the 'Bernhard Virus,'" *Journal of Austrian Studies* 46, no. 1 (Spring 2013): 57.

117. Qtd. in Randall Halle and Reinhild Steingröver, eds., *After the Avant-Garde: Contemporary German and Austrian Experimental Film* (New York: Camden House, 2008), 212–13.

118. Shu Lea Cheang, "U.K.I. Concept," http://www.u-k-i.co/performance/html/concept.html.

119. Ibid.

120. Shu Lea Cheang, "Enter the BioNet," https://vimeo.com/112516427. This video was filmed at the 2014 Piksel Festival in Norway.

121. Michelle Kuo, "Portfolio: Anicka Yi," *Artforum International* 53, no. 7 (March 2015): 234.

122. The Kitchen, http://thekitchen.org/event/anicka-yi-you-can-call-me-f.

123. "Anicka Yi: You Can Call Me F," The Kitchen, http://thekitchen.org/event/anicka-yi-you-can-call-me-f.

124. Kuo, "Portfolio," 234.

125. Brennan, *Transmission of Affect*, 1.

126. The Kitchen, http://thekitchen.org/event/anicka-yi-you-can-call-me-f.

Chapter 4

1. Kathryn Blume, phone interview with author, September 6, 2012.

2. Ibid.

3. Robert Neblett, email message to author, September 11, 2012.

4. Jussi Parikka, "Contagion and Repetition: On the Viral Logic of Network Culture," *Ephemera* 7, no. 2 (2007): 288.

5. Ibid., 291.

6. Rebecca Rugg, "Radical Inclusion 'Til It Hurts: Suzan-Lori Parks's *365 Days/365 Plays*," *Theater* 38, no. 1 (2008): 61.

7. Campbell Robertson, "What Do You Get If You Write a Play a Day? A Lot of Premieres," *New York Times*, November 10, 2006, http://query.nytimes.com/gst/fullpage.html?res=9905EFDF1F3FF933A25752C1A9609C8B63&pagewanted=all.

8. Bruno Latour, "On Recalling ANT," in *Actor-Network Theory and After* (Oxford: Blackwell, 1999), 15.

9. Ibid., 15.

10. Benjamin Piekut, *Experimentalism Otherwise* (Berkeley: University of California Press, 2011), 8.

11. Alexander Galloway and Eugene Thacker, *The Exploit* (Minneapolis: University of Minnesota Press), 4.

12. Alan Liu, *The Laws of Cool* (Chicago: University of Chicago Press, 2004), 144.

13. Qtd. ibid., 145.

14. Rugg, "Radical Inclusion," 58.

15. Galloway and Thacker, 62.

16. H. D. Westlake, "The *Lysistrata* and the War," *Phoenix* 34, no. 1 (1980): 38–41.

17. Matthew Dillon, "The Lysistrata as a Post-Decelian Peace Play," *Transactions of the American Philological Association* 117 (1987): 100.

18. Westlake, 41.

19. Ibid.

20. Simone Beta, "The Metamorphosis of a Greek Comedy and Its Protagonist," in *Ancient Drama in Music for the Modern Stage* (New York: Oxford University Press, 2010), xcii.

21. Ibid., xcviii–xcix.

22. Ibid., ci.

23. Kathryn Blume, "My Big Long Essay for Which I Have No Title," unpublished, 2.

24. Ibid., 5.

25. Kathryn Blume, phone interview with author, September 6, 2012.

26. Ibid.

27. Ibid.

28. "Why V-Day Started," http://www.vday.org/about/why-vday-started.html#.

29. "How Do I Register to Organize a V-Day Event?" http://www.vday.org/organize-event.html#when.

30. V-Day Organization, *V-Day Annual Report*, 2016, 56, https://www.joomag.com/magazine/v-day-annual-report-2016-one-billion-rising-rise-for-revolution-1/0312547001480096618?short.

31. Christine M. Cooper, "Worrying about Vaginas: Feminism and Eve Ensler's *The Vagina Monologues*," *Signs* 32, no. 3 (Spring 2007): 729.

32. Ibid., 738.

33. Sealing Cheng, "Questioning Global Vaginahood: Reflections from Adapting *The Vagina Monologues* in Hong Kong," *Feminist Review*, no. 92 (2009): 20.

34. "What Is Lysistrata Project?" Lysistrata Project, http://lysistrataproject archive.com/lys/about.html

35. Ibid.

36. Blume, phone interview.

37. "What Is Lysistrata Project?"

38. Ibid.

39. Jesusa Rodríguez and Liliana Felipe, "Lysistrata," Plaza Coyoacán, Mexico City, Mexico, filmed March 3, 2003, http://hidvl.nyu.edu/video/000066021.html.

40. Emily Davis, "Puppets for Peace: The Remake of Aristophanes' *Lysistrata*," *Voices: The Journal of New York Folklore* 30 (2004), http://www.nyfolklore.org/pubs/voic30–3–4/fldnt.html.

41. *Operation Lysistrata*, directed by Michael Patrick Kelly (New York: Aquapio Films, 2006), DVD.
42. Donovan King, "Optative Theatre: A Critical Theory for Challenging Oppression and Spectacle" (M.F.A. thesis, University of Calgary, 2004), 228.
43. Ibid., 228–29.
44. Ibid., 229.
45. Ibid.
46. Ibid., 230.
47. Aristophanes, *Lysistrata*, trans. Douglass Parker, in *Four Plays by Aristophanes* (New York: Penguin Books, 1994), 426–33.
48. Ibid., 382.
49. Ibid., 399–400.
50. Ibid., 403.
51. Blume, phone interview.
52. Neblett, email message to author, September 11, 2012.
53. Sheila Cohen Tissot, phone interview with author, September 23, 2012.
54. Blume, phone interview.
55. Randall Stuart, phone interview with author, September 20, 2012.
56. "National New Play Network," www.nnpn.org.
57. Philip Kolin, "Redefining the Way Theatre Is Created and Performed: The Radical Inclusion of Suzan-Lori Parks's *365 Days/365 Plays*," *Journal of Dramatic Theory and Criticism* 22, no. 1 (2007): 65.
58. Robertson, "What Do You Get?" http://query.nytimes.com/gst/fullpage.html?res=9905EFDF1F3FF933A25752C1A9609C8B63&pagewanted=all.
59. Ibid.
60. Kolin, "Redefining," 67.
61. Ibid., 81.
62. Suzan-Lori Parks, *365 Days/365 Plays* (New York: Theatre Communications Group, 2006), 61.
63. Ibid., 119.
64. Ibid., 330.
65. Ibid., 210.
66. Deborah Geis, *Suzan-Lori Parks* (Ann Arbor: University of Michigan Press, 2008), 161.
67. Parks, *365 Days/365 Plays*, 54–55.
68. Ibid., 45–46, 80, 43–44, 100–101; 133–35, 137.
69. Ibid., 334.
70. Ibid., 335.
71. Out of the Black Box Theatre Company's Facebook page, https://www.facebook.com/OutOftheBlackBox.
72. Geis, *Suzan Lori-Parks*, 158.
73. Terry Morgan, "*365 Days/365 Plays* (Week 1: Nov. 13–19)," *Variety*, November 16, 2006, http://www.variety.com/review/VE1117932141.
74. Rugg, "Radical Inclusion," 61.
75. Everett Evans, "Much Ado about Almost Nothing," *Houston Chronicle*, January 17, 2007, 2.
76. Jocelyn Brown, phone interview with author, September 29, 2012.
77. Parks, *365 Days/365 Plays*, 64.

78. Ibid., 65.
79. Ibid.
80. Ibid.
81. Ibid.
82. Brown, phone interview.
83. Parks, *365 Days/365 Plays,* 103, 119.
84. Ibid., 6.
85. Ibid., 172.
86. Ibid., 173.
87. Geis, *Suzan-Lori Parks*, 162.
88. Walter Benjamin, *Understanding Brecht*, trans. Anna Bostock (New York: Verso, 1998), 19.
89. Parks, *365 Days/365 Plays,* 368.
90. Ibid.
91. Kolin, "Redefining," 80.
92. Ibid., 80.
93. Geis, *Suzan Lori-Parks*, 158.
94. Bonnie Metzgar and Suzan-Lori Parks, "The 365 National Festival," in *365 Days/365 Plays* (New York: Theatre Communications Group, 2006), 401–2.
95. "365 National Festival Participant Letter of Agreement," unpublished, provided to author by producer Bonnie Metzgar on March 23, 2017.
96. A previous version of my discussion of *Seven Jewish Children* was published as "Clamorous Voices: *Seven Jewish Children* and Its Proliferating Publics." *TDR* T211 (Fall 2011): 156–64.
97. "Seven Jewish Children: A Play for Gaza," YouTube video, Rooms Productions, posted April 2, 2009, www.youtube.com.
98. Ibid.
99. Caryl Churchill, *Seven Jewish Children* (London: Nick Hern Books, 2009), 1.
100. Ibid., 6.
101. Ibid.
102. Ibid., 7.
103. The play deliberately moves from depicting a dispersed European Jewish community to an aggressively coordinated Israeli public. This tactic has drawn substantial criticism from spectators and reviewers who believe that Churchill is intentionally, or at least irresponsibly, conflating the actions of the Israeli government and military with the behavior and beliefs of Jews the world over. Here, to be accurate to the play, I use both words to refer to Churchill's subjects.
104. Qtd. in Michael Warner, "Public and Private," in *Publics and Counterpublics* (New York: Zone Books, 2002), 61.
105. Ibid., 72–75.
106. Churchill, *Seven Jewish Children*, 5.
107. Ibid., 5.
108. Ibid., 4.
109. Ibid.
110. Ibid.
111. Robert Fisk, "CNN Caves in to Israel over Its References to Illegal Settlements," *London Independent*, September 3, 2001, http://www.independent.co

.uk/news/world/middle-east/cnn-caves-in-to-israel-over-its-references-to-illegal-settlements-667860.html.

112. Uri Ayalon, "New IBA Chief Bans Use of Term 'Settlements,'" *Ha'Aretz*, May 30, 2002, http://www.haaretz.com/news/new-iba-chief-bans-use-of-term-settlements-1.43700.

113. Churchill, *Seven Jewish Children*, 7.

114. Caryl Churchill, *Far Away* (London: Nick Hern Books, 2000).

115. Melanie Phillips, "The Royal Court's Mystery Play" *The Spectator*, February 8, 2009, http://www.spectator.co.uk/melaniephillips/3334851/the-royal-courts-mystery-play.thtml. (Article no longer online.)

116. Ben Dowell, "BBC Rejects Play on Israel's History for Impartiality Reasons," *The Guardian*, March 16, 2009, http://www.guardian.co.uk/media/2009/mar/16/bbc-rejects-caryl-churchill-israel.

117. Phillips, "Royal Court's Mystery Play."

118. Jeffrey Goldberg, "The Royal Court Theatre's Blood Libel," *Theatlantic.com*, February 9, 2009, http://www.theatlantic.com/international/archive/2009/02/the-royal-court-theatre-apos-s-blood-libel/9521/.

119. Robert Mackey, "Is a Play about Gaza Anti-Semitic? Read the Script," *New York Times*, February 18, 2009, http://thelede.blogs.nytimes.com/2009/02/18/is-a-play-about-gaza-anti-semitic-read-the-script/.

120. Deborah Margolin, *Seven Palestinian Children*, Reb Barry's Blog, http://www.neshamah.net/reb_barrys_blog_neshamahn/seven-palestinian-children.html.

121. Robbie Gringas, *The Eighth Child*, http://washingtondcjcc.org/center-for-arts/theater-j/on-stage/middle-east-festival/tj-sevenjewishchildren.htm. (No longer online.)

122. Richard Stirling, *Seven Other Children*, Harry's Place blog, http://hurryupharry.org/2009/05/16/seven-other-children-a-theatrical-response-to-seven-jewish-children/.

123. Ibid.

124. Dowell, "BBC Rejects Play," http://www.guardian.co.uk/media/2009/mar/16/bbc-rejects-caryl-churchill-israel.

125. *Seven Arab Children*, Elder of Ziyon blog, http://elderofziyon.blogspot.com/2009/03/seven-arab-children.html.

126. Ibid.

127. *7 Muslim Children*, BlueTruth blog, http://www.bluetruth.net/2009/04/seven-muslim-children.html.

128. Edward Einhorn, "The More Things Change," Theater of Ideas blog, April 1, 2009, http://theaterofideas.blogspot.com/2009/04/several-responses-to-seven-jewish.html.

129. Margolin, *Seven Palestinian Children*.

130. Described on Pulse Media's blog at https://pulsemedia.org/2009/06/11/the-israel-democracy-fraud/#more-12414.

131. "Seven Jewish Children—A Play for Gaza," YouTube video, posted by "7jewishchildren," June 14, 2009, http://www.youtube.com.

132. And controversy was nearly guaranteed, with (among other events) the New York Theatre Workshop's 2006 "postponement" of *My Name Is Rachel Corrie* fresh in audiences' minds.

133. "Seven Jewish Children: A Play for Gaza . . . Read to AIPAC delegates," YouTube video, posted by "7pillarsOwisdom," May 7, 2009, http://www.youtube.com.

134. Kathryn Blume, phone interview with author.

135. Ibid.

136. Iman Aoun, phone interview with author, March 2, 2017.

137. Ibid.

138. Ibid.

139. "Shinsai: Theaters for Japan," Theatre Communications Group website, http://www.tcg.org/shinsai/archive.cfm.

140. Ibid.

141. Transcript of "Shinsai: The Conversation," March 12, 2012, Japan Society, New York, http://www.tcg.org/shinsai/archive.cfm.

Conclusion

1. Blas, "Virus, Viral," 32.

2. Ibid., 32–33 (emphasis in original).

3. Laura Palmer Foundation, http://www.laura-palmer.pl/en/info/.

4. "Virus in the Theater Performance," Laura Palmer Foundation, http://www.laura-palmer.pl/en/projects/10/actions-tr/18/virus-in-the-theater-performance/.

5. These pieces are described in the artists' biographies at http://culture.pl/en/artist/sedzia-glowny.

6. Joanna Warsza and Laura Palmer Foundation, "Virus in the Theater," filmed February 2006, online video, http://artmuseum.pl/pl/filmoteka/praca/sedzia-glowny-part-lxiii-virus-action-in-and-quotmagnetism. All quotations and observations about the performance are drawn from this video, and I am grateful to Lauren Dubowski for the translation of dialogue from Polish to English.

7. Living Theatre, *Paradise Now* Notebook #1, Living Theatre Records, 81.

8. "Virus in the Theater Performance," Laura Palmer Foundation.

9. Marinetti, *Critical Writings*, 412.

10. "Virus in the Theater Performance," Laura Palmer Foundation.

11. See Michael Fried, "Art and Objecthood," in *Art and Objecthood: Essays and Reviews* (Chicago: University of Chicago Press, 1998), 148–72.

12. Wiktor and Kubiak, http://culture.pl/en/artist/sedzia-glowny.

13. William S. Burroughs, *The Electronic Revolution* (Expanded Media Editions, published by Bresche Publikationen Germany, 1970), qtd. in Thierry Bardini, "Hypervirus: A Clinical Report," *CTHEORY*, February 2, 2006, http://ctheory.net/articles.aspx?id=504#_ednref7.

14. Derrida with Brunette and Wills, "The Spatial Arts," 12, qtd. in Bardini, "Hypervirus: A Critical Report."

BIBLIOGRAPHY

Ackerman, Alan, and Martin Puchner, eds. *Against Theatre: Creative Destructions on the Modernist Stage*. New York: Palgrave Macmillan, 2006.

Ahmed, Sara. *The Cultural Politics of Emotion*. New York: Routledge, 2004.

Aitken, Hugh J. *Syntony and Spark—The Origins of Radio*. New York: John Wiley and Sons, 1976.

Aristophanes. *Lysistrata*. Translated by Douglass Parker. In *Four Plays by Aristophanes*. New York: Penguin Books, 1994.

Aristotle. *Aristotle's Poetics*. Translated by George Whalley. Montreal: McGill-Queen's University Press, 1997.

———. *On Poetry and Style*. Translated by G. M. A. Grube. Indianapolis, Ind.: Hackett, 1989.

Aronson, Arnold. *American Avant-Garde Theatre: A History*. New York: Routledge, 2000.

Artaud, Antonin. *Selected Writings*. Edited by Susan Sontag. New York: Farrar, Straus and Giroux, 1976.

———. *The Theater and Its Double*. Translated by Mary Caroline Richards. New York: Grove, 1958.

Atkins, Stephen E. *Encyclopedia of Modern Worldwide Extremists and Extremist Groups*. Westport, Conn.: Greenwood, 2004.

Balme, Christopher. *The Theatrical Public Sphere*. Cambridge: Cambridge University Press, 2014.

Barish, Jonas. *The Antitheatrical Prejudice*. Berkeley: University of California Press, 1985.

Baudrillard, Jean. *Cool Memories II*. Translated by Chris Turner. Cambridge: Polity, 1996.

———. *The Mirror of Production*. St. Louis, Mo.: Telos, 1975.

———. "Requiem for the Media." In *For a Critique of the Political Economy of the Sign*, 164–84. St. Louis, Mo.: Telos, 1981.

———. *The Transparency of Evil: Essays on Extreme Phenomena*. Translated by James Benedict. New York: Verso, 1990.

Bayer, Fern, ed. *The Search for the Spirit: General Idea 1968–1975*. Toronto: Art Gallery of Ontario, 1997.

Beck, Julian. *The Life of the Theatre*. San Francisco: City Lights, 1972.

———. *Theandric: Julian Beck's Last Notebooks*. Edited by Erica Bilder. Philadelphia: Harwood Academic, 1992.

Benjamin, Walter. "One-Way Street." In *Reflections*, edited by Peter Demetz, 61–94. New York: Schocken Books, 1978.

———. *Understanding Brecht*. Translated by Anna Bostock. New York: Verso, 1998.

Bentley, Eric. *The Playwright as Thinker*. Minneapolis: University of Minnesota Press, 1987.

Beta, Simone. "The Metamorphosis of a Greek Comedy and Its Protagonist." In *Ancient Drama in Music for the Modern Stage*, lxxxix–ciii. New York: Oxford University Press, 2010.

Bishop, Claire, ed. *Artificial Hells: Participatory Art and the Politics of Spectatorship*. London: Verso, 2012.

———. *Participation*. Cambridge, Mass.: MIT Press, 2006.

Blas, Zach. "Virus, Viral." *WSQ: Women's Studies Quarterly* 40, no. 1 and 2 (2012): 29–39.

BlueTruth blog. *7 Muslim Children*. http://www.bluetruth.net/2009/04/seven-muslim-children.html.

Blume, Kathryn. "My Big Long Essay for Which I Have No Title." Unpublished.

———. Phone interview with author. September 6, 2012.

Boal, Augusto. *Hamlet and the Baker's Son: My Life in Theatre and Politics*. Translated by Adrian Jackson and Candida Blaker. New York: Routledge, 2001.

———. "Poetics of the Oppressed." In *The Community Performance Reader*, edited by Petra Kuppers and Gwen Robertson, 13–23. New York: Routledge, 2007.

———. *Theater of the Oppressed*. New York: TCG, 1985.

Boal, Augusto, and Susana Epstein. "Invisible Theatre: Liège, Belgium 1978." *TDR: The Drama Review* 34, no. 3 (1990): 24–34.

Bordowitz, Gregg. *Imagevirus*. London: Afterall Books, 2010.

Boyle, Michael Shane. "Container Aesthetics: The Infrastructural Politics of Shunt's *The Boy Who Climbed Out of His Face*." *Theatre Journal* 68, no. 1 (March 2016): 57–77.

Brecht, Bertolt. *Brecht on Film and Radio*. Edited by Marc Silberman. London: Methuen, 2000.

———. *Brecht on Theatre: The Development of an Aesthetic*. Edited and translated by John Willett. New York: Hill and Wang, 1992.

———. *Collected Plays: Three*. London: Methuen, 1997.

Brecht, Stefan. "Revolution at the Brooklyn Academy of Music." *TDR: The Drama Review* 13, no. 3 (1969): 46–73.

Brennan, Teresa. *The Transmission of Affect*. Ithaca, N.Y.: Cornell University Press, 2004.

Bronson, AA, et al. *From Sea to Shining Sea: Artist-Initiated Activity in Canada, 1939–1987*. Toronto: Power Plant, 1987.

Brown, Jocelyn A. Phone interview with author. September 29, 2012.

Butsch, Richard. *The Citizen Audience*. New York: Routledge, 2008.

Campbell, Timothy. *Wireless Writing in the Age of Marconi*. Minneapolis: University of Minnesota Press, 2006.

Canetti, Elias. *Crowds and Power*. New York: Viking, 1963.

Cantril, Hadley. *The Invasion from Mars: A Study in the Psychology of Panic*. Princeton, N.J.: Princeton University Press, 1940.

Cantril, Hadley, and Gordon Allport. *The Psychology of Radio*. New York: Harper and Brothers, 1935.

Cattelan, Maurizio, Domenico Quaranta, and Roselee Goldberg. *Eva and Franco Mattes: 0100101110101101.org*. Milan: Charta, 2009.
Churchill, Caryl. *Seven Jewish Children*. London: Nick Hern Books, 2009.
———. *Far Away*. London: Nick Hern Books, 2000.
Cohen-Cruz, Jan, ed. *Playing Boal: Theatre of the Oppressed Anthology*. New York: Routledge, 1994.
Cohen Tissot, Sheila. Phone interview with author. September 23, 2012.
Coney, John. "Rites of Guerrilla Theater." Filmed March 8, 1969. Pacific Film Archive Film and Video Collection. Available on archive.org, https://archive.org/details/cbpf_000051_p1.
Critical Art Ensemble. http://critical-art.net/.
———. *The Electronic Disturbance*. New York: Autonomedia, 1993. http://critical-art.net/books/ted/.
———. *Marching Plague*. New York: Autonomedia, 2006. http://critical-art.net/books/mp/.
———. "Recombinant Theatre and Digital Resistance." *TDR: The Drama Review* 44, no. 4 (2000): 151–66.
Dark Star, ed. *Beneath the Paving Stones: Situationists and the Beach, May 1968*. San Francisco: AK Press USA, 2001.
Davis, Emily. "Puppets for Peace: The Remake of Aristophanes' *Lysistrata*." *Voices: The Journal of New York Folklore* 30 (2004). http://www.nyfolklore.org/pubs/voic30–3–4/fldnt.html.
Davis, R. G. "Guerrilla Theater." *Tulane Drama Review* 10, no. 4 (Summer 1966): 130–36.
Davis, Tracy. *Stages of Emergency: Cold War Nuclear Civil Defense*. Durham, N.C.: Duke University Press, 2007.
Dawkins, Richard. *The Selfish Gene*. Oxford: Oxford University Press, 1989.
Debord, Guy. "The Decline & Fall of the 'Spectacular' Commodity-Economy." In *The Situationists and the Beach, May 1968*. San Francisco: AK Press USA, 2001.
———. *The Society of the Spectacle*. Translated by Donald Nicholson-Smith. New York: Zone Books, 1995.
DeKoven, Marianne. *Utopia Limited: The Sixties and the Emergence of the Postmodern*. Durham, N.C.: Duke University Press, 2004.
Deleuze, Gilles, and Félix Guattari. *Anti-Oedipus*. London: Continuum, 2004.
———. *A Thousand Plateaus: Capitalism and Schizophrenia*. New York: Continuum, 2004.
Dilexi Series program note. 1991. Pacific Film Archive.
Dillon, Matthew. "The Lysistrata as a Post-Decelian Peace Play." *Transactions of the American Philological Association* 117 (1987): 97–104.
Distin, Kate. *The Selfish Meme: A Critical Reassessment*. New York: Cambridge University Press, 2005.
Einhorn, Edward. "The More Things Change." Theater of Ideas blog. April 1, 2009. http://theaterofideas.blogspot.com/2009/04/several-responses-to-seven-jewish.html.
Elder of Ziyon blog. *Seven Arab Children*. http://elderofziyon.blogspot.com/2009/03/seven-arab-children.html.
Elsom, John. *Cold War Theatre*. New York: Taylor and Francis Group, 1992.

Enzensberger, Hans Magnus. "Constituents of a Theory of the Media." In *Critical Essays*, edited by Reinhold Grimm and Bruce Armstrong, 46–76. New York: Continuum, 1982.

Estrin, Marc. "Four Guerrilla Theater Pieces: From the American Playground." *TDR: The Drama Review* 13, no. 4 (1969): 72–79.

———. Phone interview with author, October 15, 2010.

———. *ReCreation: Some Notes on What's What and What You Might Be Able to Do about What's What*. New York: Dell, 1971.

Estrin, Marc, and Martin Trueblood. "Letter." *TDR: The Drama Review* 14, no. 1 (1969): 189.

Evans, Everett. "Much Ado about Almost Nothing." *Houston Chronicle*, January 17, 2007, 2.

Falasca-Zamponi, Simonetta. *Fascist Spectacle: The Aesthetics of Power in Mussolini's Italy*. Berkeley: University of California Press, 1997.

Farman, Jason. "The Virtual Artaud." In *TechKnowledgies: New Imaginaries in the Humanities, Arts, and TechnoSciences*, edited by Mary Valentis, 157–67. Newcastle, Eng.: Cambridge Scholars, 2007.

Felski, Rita. "Introduction." *New Literary History* 33, no. 4 (Autumn 2002): 607–22.

Fischer-Lichte, Erika. *Theatre, Sacrifice, Ritual: Exploring Forms of Political Theatre*. New York: Routledge, 2005.

Fisher, Philip. *The Vehement Passions*. Princeton, N.J.: Princeton University Press, 2002.

Galloway, Alexander R., and Eugene Thacker. *The Exploit*. Minneapolis: University of Minnesota Press, 2007.

Garner, Stanton B. "Artaud, Germ Theory, and the Theatre of Contagion." *Theatre Journal* 58, no. 1 (2006): 1–14.

Geis, Deborah. *Suzan-Lori Parks*. Ann Arbor: University of Michigan Press, 2008.

Gelber, Jack. *The Apple*. New York: Grove, 1960.

General Idea. *FILE Megazine* 2, no. 1 and 2 (May 1973).

———. *FILE Megazine* 3, no. 1 (Fall 1975).

———. *FILE,* Special Double Issue, vol. 2, no. 1 and 2 (May 1983).

———. General Idea Archives. National Gallery of Canada. Ottawa, Ontario, Canada.

Gibbs, Anna. "Contagious Feelings: Pauline Hanson and the Epidemiology of Affect." *Australian Humanities Review* 24 (December 2001).

Gilman, Richard. "The Living Theatre on Tour." In *The Drama Is Coming Now: The Theater Criticism of Richard Gilman, 1961–1991*, 119–24. New Haven, Conn.: Yale University Press, 2005.

Ginsburg, Steve, and Annah Feinberg. Conversation with author. February 16, 2012.

Gladwell, Malcolm. *The Tipping Point: How Little Things Can Make a Big Difference*. New York: Back Bay Books, 2002.

Goodall, Jane. "Cruelty and Cure." In *Antonin Artaud and the Modern Theater*, edited by Gene A. Plunka. Cranbury, N.J.: Fairleigh Dickinson University Press, 1994.

Gottlieb, Saul. "The Living Theatre in Exile: 'Mysteries, Frankenstein.'" *Tulane Drama Review* 10, no. 4 (1966): 137–52.

Gringas, Robbie. "The Eighth Child." http://washingtondcjcc.org/center-for-arts/theater-j/on-stage/middle-east-festival/tj-sevenjewishchildren.htm. (No longer online.)

Habermas, Jürgen. *The Structural Transformation of the Public Sphere: An Inquiry into a Category of Bourgeois Society*. Translated by Thomas Burger and Frederick Lawrence. Cambridge, Mass.: MIT Press, 1989.

Hardt, Michael, and Antonio Negri. *Empire*. Cambridge, Mass.: Harvard University Press, 2000.

Hoover, J. Edgar. *Masters of Deceit: The Story of Communism in America and How to Fight It*. New York: Holt, 1958.

Jana, Reena. "Wanna See Some Really Sick Art?" *Wired*, June 27, 2001. http://www.wired.com/culture/lifestyle/news/2001/06/44728.

Jannarone, Kimberly. *Artaud and His Doubles*. Ann Arbor: University of Michigan Press, 2010.

Jestrovic, Silvija. "Performing like an Asylum Seeker: Paradoxes of Hyper-Authenticity." *Research in Drama Education* 13, no. 2 (2008): 159–70.

Kalb, Jonathan. *The Theater of Heiner Müller*. New York: Limelight Editions, 2001.

Kelly, Michael Patrick. *Operation Lysistrata*. DVD. New York: Aquapio Films, 2006.

Kennan, George Frost. "The Sources of Soviet Conduct." In *The Geopolitics Reader*, edited by Simon Dalby, Paul Routledge, and Gearóid Ó Tuathail, 61–65. New York: Routledge, 1998.

Kennedy, Dennis. *The Spectator and the Spectacle: Audiences in Modernity and Postmodernity*. New York: Cambridge University Press, 2009.

Kern, Stephen. *The Culture of Time and Space, 1880–1918*. Cambridge, Mass.: Harvard University Press, 1983.

King, Donovan. "Optative Theater: A Critical Theory for Challenging Oppression and Spectacle." M.F.A. thesis, University of Calgary, 2004.

Kirby, Michael. "On Acting and Not-Acting." *TDR: The Drama Review* 16, no. 1 (March 1972): 3–15.

Kittler, Friedrich. *Gramophone, Film, Typewriter*. Stanford, Calif.: Stanford University Press, 1999.

———. "Gramophone, Film, Typewriter." In *Literature, Media, Information Systems*, edited by John Johnston, 31–49. Amsterdam: Overseas Publishers Association, 1997.

Kolin, Philip C. "Redefining the Way Theatre Is Created and Performed: The Radical Inclusion of Suzan-Lori Parks's *365 Days/365 Plays*." *Journal of Dramatic Theory and Criticism* 1 (2007): 65–86.

Kurtz, Steve. Phone interview with author, April 3, 2011.

Kurtz, Steve, Lucia Sommer, and Brian Holmes. *Critical Art Ensemble: Disturbances*. London: Four Corners Books, 2012.

LaCourse Munteanu, Dana. *Tragic Pathos: Pity and Fear in Greek Philosophy and Tragedy*. New York: Cambridge University Press, 2012.

Lambert-Beatty, Carrie. "Make-Believe: Parafiction and Plausibility." *October*, vol. 129 (Summer 2009): 51–84.

Lasn, Kalle. *Culture Jam: How to Reverse America's Suicidal Consumer Binge—And Why We Must*. New York: HarperCollins, 1999.

Latour, Bruno. "On Recalling ANT." In *Actor-Network Theory and After*, 15–25. Oxford: Blackwell, 1999.

Le Bon, Gustave. *The Crowd: A Study of the Popular Mind*. New York: Viking, 1960.

Lehmann, Hans-Thies. *Postdramatic Theatre*. Translated by Karen Jürs-Munby. New York: Routledge, 2006.

Lesnick, Henry, ed. *Guerrilla Street Theater*. New York: Bard Books, 1973.

Levin, Laura. *Performing Ground: Space, Camouflage, and the Art of Blending In*. New York: Palgrave Macmillan, 2014.

Lilienthal, Matthias. *Schlingensiefs Ausländer raus: bitte liebt Österreich: Dokumentation*. Frankfurt Am Main: Suhrkamp, 2000.

Living Theatre, Company of the. "Avignon Statement." *TDR: The Drama Review* 13, no. 3 (1969): 45.

———. Living Theatre Records. Yale Collection of American Literature, Beinecke Rare Book and Manuscript Library.

———. *Mysteries and Smaller Pieces*. In *The Great American Life Show: 9 Plays from the Avant-Garde Theater*, edited by John Lahr and Jonathan Price, 319–50. New York: Bantam Books, 1974.

———. *Paradise Now: Collective Creation of the Living Theatre*. New York: Random House, 1971.

Liu, Alan. *The Laws of Cool*. Chicago: University of Chicago Press, 2004.

Lysistrata Project. http://lysistrataprojectarchive.com.

Malina, Judith. Interview with author, April 17, 2011.

Malina, Judith, Julian Beck, and Richard Schechner. "Containment Is the Enemy." *TDR: The Drama Review* 13, no. 3 (1969): 24–44.

Manovich, Lev. *The Language of New Media*. Cambridge, Mass.: MIT Press, 2001.

Margolin, Deborah. *Seven Palestinian Children*. Reb Barry's Blog. http://www.neshamah.net/reb_barrys_blog_neshamahn/seven-palestinian-children.html.

Marinetti, F. T. *Critical Writings*. Edited by Günter Berghaus. New York: Farrar, Straus and Giroux, 2006.

Martin, Bradford. *The Theater Is in the Street*. Amherst: University of Massachusetts Press, 2004.

Mattes, Franco. Interview with author, September 20, 2011.

Mattes, Eva, and Franco Mattes. http://0100101110101101.org/.

McConachie, Bruce. *American Theater in the Culture of the Cold War: Producing and Contesting Containment*. Iowa City: University of Iowa Press, 2003.

McKenzie, Jon, and Rebecca Schneider. "Critical Art Ensemble, Tactical Media Practitioners." *TDR: The Drama Review* 44, no. 4 (2000): 136–50.

McLuhan, Marshall. *Understanding Media: The Extensions of Man*. New York: Signet Books, 1964.

Mikos, Lothar. "Big Brother as Television Text." In *Big Brother International: Formats, Critics and Publics*, edited by Ernest Mathijs and Janet Jones, 93–104. London: Wallflower, 2004.

Monk, Philip. *Glamour Is Theft: A User's Guide to General Idea*. Toronto: Art Gallery of York University, 2012.

Morgan, Terry. "*365 Days/365 Plays* (Week 1: Nov 13–19)." *Variety*. November 16, 2006. http://www.variety.com/review/VE1117932141.

Moscovici, Serge. *The Age of the Crowd: A Historical Treatise on Mass Psychology*. Translated by J. C. Whitehouse. New York: Cambridge University Press, 1985.

Munk, Erika. "Only Connect: The Living Theatre and Its Audiences." In *Restaging the Sixties: Radical Theaters and Their Legacies*, edited by James Harding and Cindy Rosenthal. Ann Arbor: University of Michigan Press, 2006.

Muñoz, José Esteban. *Cruising Utopia: The Then and There of Queer Futurity*. New York: New York University Press, 2009.

Muse, John. "Flash Mobs and the Diffusion of Audience." *Theater* 40, no. 3 (2010): 8–23.

Nadel, Alan. *Containment Culture: American Narratives, Postmodernism, and the Atomic Age*. Durham, N.C.: Duke University Press, 1995.

National New Play Network. www.nnpn.org.

Neblett, Robert. Email message to author. September 11, 2012.

Ngai, Sianne. *Ugly Feelings*. Cambridge, Mass.: Harvard University Press, 2005.

Oddey, Alison, and Christine White, eds. *Modes of Spectating*. Chicago: University of Chicago Press, 2009.

Out of the Black Box Theatre Company's Facebook page. https://www.facebook.com/OutOftheBlackBox.

Parikka, Jussi. "Contagion and Repetition: On the Viral Logic of Network Culture." *Ephemera* 7, no. 2 (2007): 287–308.

———. *Digital Contagions: A Media Archaeology of Computer Viruses*. New York: Peter Lang, 2007.

Parks, Suzan-Lori. *365 Days/365 Plays*. New York: Theatre Communications Group, 2006.

———. *The America Play and Other Works*. New York: Theatre Communications Group, 1995.

Perucci, Tony. "The Red Mask of Sanity: Paul Robeson, HUAC, and the Sound of Cold War Performance." *TDR: The Drama Review* 53, no. 4 (2009): 18–48.

Phelan, Peggy. *Unmarked: The Politics of Performance*. New York: Routledge, 1993.

Piekut, Benjamin. *Experimentalism Otherwise*. Berkeley: University of California Press, 2011.

Plato. *The Republic*. Translated by Benjamin Jowett. New York: Barnes and Noble Classics, 2004.

———. *The Republic*. Translated by Desmond Lee. New York: Penguin, 1987.

Poet, Paul. *Ausländer Raus! Schlingensief's Container*. Videorecording. Wien: Hoanzl, 2006.

Pottlitzer, Joanne. "Symbols of Resistance," forthcoming.

Rancière, Jacques. *The Emancipated Spectator*. New York: Verso, 2009.

Robertson, Campbell. "What Do You Get If You Write A Play a Day? A Lot of Premieres," *New York Times*, November 10, 2006. http://query.nytimes.com/gst/fullpage.html?res=9905EFDF1F3FF933A25752C1A9609C8B63.

Rodríguez, Jesusa, and Liliana Felipe. "Lysistrata." Plaza Coyoacán, Mexico City, Mexico. Filmed March 3, 2003. http://hidvl.nyu.edu/video/000066021.html.

Roggencamp, Karen. *Narrating the News: New Journalism and Literary Genre in Late Nineteenth-Century American Newspapers and Fiction*. Kent, Ohio: Kent State University Press, 2005.

Román, David. *Acts of Intervention: Performance, Gay Culture, and AIDS.* Bloomington: Indiana University Press, 1998.

Rooms Productions. "Seven Jewish Children: A Play for Gaza." YouTube video, posted April 2, 2009. www.youtube.com/watch?v=1OBA30Ax51s.

Rugg, Rebecca. "Radical Inclusion 'Til It Hurts: Suzan-Lori Parks's *365 Days/365 Plays*." *Theater* 38, no. 1 (2008): 52–75.

Rushkoff, Douglas. *Coercion: Why We Listen to What "They" Say.* New York: Riverhead Books, 1999.

———. *Media Virus! Hidden Agendas in Popular Culture.* New York: Random House, 1996.

Sampson, Tony D. *Virality: Contagion Theory in the Age of Networks.* Minneapolis: University of Minnesota Press, 2012.

Schechner, Richard. "Guerrilla Theatre: May 1970." *TDR: The Drama Review* 14, no. 3 (1970): 163–68.

Shifman, Limor. "An Anatomy of a YouTube Meme." *New Media & Society* 14, no. 2 (2012): 187–203.

Silberman, Marc, ed. *Brecht on Film and Radio.* London: Methuen, 2000.

Sontag, Susan. *Illness as Metaphor and AIDS and Its Metaphors.* New York: Picador, 1990.

Sperber, Dan. *Explaining Culture: A Naturalistic Approach.* Cambridge, Mass.: Blackwell, 1996.

Stark, Jeff, Todd Chandler, and Todd Seelie. *Let Them Believe.* Online video. http://letthembelievemovie.com/.

Stein, Gertrude. *Last Operas and Plays.* Edited by Carl van Vechten. Baltimore: Johns Hopkins University Press, 1977.

Stein, Howard. Review of *Antigone* and *Paradise Now* at Yale University Theatre, September 1968. *Educational Theatre Journal* 21, no. 1 (March 1969): 107–8.

Stirling, Richard. *Seven Other Children.* Harry's Place blog. http://hurryupharry.org/2009/05/16/seven-other-children-a-theatrical-response-to-seven-jewish-children/.

Stuart, Randall. Phone interview with author. September 20, 2012.

Tarde, Gabriel. *The Laws of Imitation.* Translated by Elsie Clews Parsons. New York: Henry Holt, 1903.

Tertullian. *Apology, De Spectaculis.* Translated by T. R. Glover and W. C. A. Kerr. Cambridge, Mass.: Harvard University Press, 1960.

Theatre Communications Group website. "Shinsai: Theaters for Japan." http://www.tcg.org/shinsai/archive.cfm?type=theatres.

Thorley, Chantelle. "Feel the Power of Mass Engagement." *Marketing Event*, July 7, 2009, 20.

Trueblood, Martin, and Marc Estrin. "Letter." *TDR: The Drama Review* 14, no. 1 (1969): 189.

Tytell, John. *The Living Theatre: Art, Exile, and Outrage.* New York: Grove, 1995.

Umathum, Sandra. Email message to author. May 18, 2011.

Varney, Denise. "'Right Now Austria Looks Ridiculous': *Please Love Austria!* Reforging the Interaction between Art and Politics." In *Christoph Schlingensief: Art without Borders*, edited by Tara Forrest and Anna Teresa Scheer, 105–18. Chicago: University of Chicago Press, 2010.

Virilio, Paul. *The Paul Virilio Reader*. Edited by Steve Redhead. New York: Columbia University Press, 2004.

Wald, Priscilla. *Contagious: Cultures, Carriers, and the Outbreak Narrative*. Durham, N.C.: Duke University Press, 2008.

Warner, Michael. *Publics and Counterpublics*. New York: Zone Books, 2002.

Warsza, Joanna, and Laura Palmer Foundation. "Virus in the Theater." Filmed February 2006. Online video. http://artmuseum.pl/pl/filmoteka/praca/sedzia-glowny-part-lxiii-virus-action-in-and-quotmagnetism.

———. "Virus in the Theater Performance." http://www.laura-palmer.pl/en/projects/10/actions-tr/18/virus-in-the-theater-performance/.

Wasik, Bill. *And Then There's This*. New York: Viking, 2009.

Westlake, H. D. "The *Lysistrata* and the War." *Phoenix* 34, no. 1 (1980): 38–54.

Wickstrom, Maurya. *Performing Consumers: Global Capital and Its Theatrical Seductions*. New York: Routledge, 2006.

Williams, Raymond. *Marxism and Literature*. Oxford: Oxford University Press, 1977.

Winthrop-Young, Geoffrey, and Michael Wutz. Translators' introduction to *Gramophone, Film, Typewriter*, by Friedrich Kittler, xi–xxxviii. Stanford, Calif.: Stanford University Press, 1999.

Wolf, Ulrich. Speech for CAE's *Radiation Burn*, presented at performance of *Radiation Burn*, Halle, Germany, 2010.

Yi, Anicka. "Anicka Yi: You Can Call Me F." Exhibition at The Kitchen, New York, March 5–April 11, 2015. Materials on The Kitchen website, http://thekitchen.org/event/anicka-yi-you-can-call-me-f.

INDEX